D0982829

The Stem of Jesse

❏

The Costs of Community
at a
1960s Southern School

❏

■

*And there shall come forth a rod out of the stem of Jesse, and a
Branch shall grow out of his roots; and the Spirit of the Lord
shall rest upon him, the spirit of wisdom and understanding, the
spirit of counsel and might, the spirit of knowledge and the fear
of the Lord.*

—Isaiah 11:1-2 KJV

■

The Stem of Jesse

❏

The Costs of Community
at a
1960s Southern School

❏

by
Will D. Campbell

Mercer University Press

ISBN 0-86554-449-2

LD
3241
.M302
C36
1995

MUP/H356

The paper used in this publication meets the minimum requirements
of American National Standard for Information Sciences—
Permanence of Paper for Printed Library Materials,
ANSI Z39.48-1984.

Library of Congress Cataloging-in-Publication Data

Campbell, Will D.
The stem of Jesse :
the costs of community at a 1960s Southern school /
by Will D. Campbell.
x+212+(16 [insert]) pp. 6x9" (15x23cm.).
ISBN 0-86554-449-2 (alk. paper)
1. Mercer University—History.
2. School integration—Georgia—Macon—History.
I. Title.
LD3241.M302C36   1994
378.758'513—dc20   94-25708

<u>CIP</u>

Contents

List of illustrations

(*A photo album* appears between pages 86 and 87.
Illustrations are listed by plate number.)

The photographs and newspaper articles are by courtesy of the WSB-TV Newsfilm Archives of Instructional Resources Center of the University of Georgia; the Mercer *Cauldron* (yearbook); the *Mercer Cluster* (student newspaper); and the *Macon Telegraph*.

Preface

Today, Powelton, Georgia is a small village nine miles south of Interstate 20 which runs from Atlanta to Augusta. In 1815 Powelton was larger than either city.

In May 1815 the Powelton Baptist Society for Foreign Missions was formed with Jesse Mercer as its president. The stated purpose of the Society was "to evangelize the heathen in other lands." At the conclusion of the meeting establishing the Society, Jesse Mercer, William Rabun, and others, all slaveholders, prayed earnestly for its success.

This story has to do with an oblique answer to their prayer—long time passing, like an echo that ricochets through groves and mountain peaks and returns an octave higher than what was uttered.

In May 1845 another meeting also having to do with missions was held in Georgia, this time in Augusta. John L. Dagg, Mercer's third president, met with 325 other delegates and organized the Southern Baptist Convention. Although it is well known that the real issue was slavery, the stated reason was a difference in methods of missions. The existing national Baptist body, called the Triennial Convention, had refused to approve James E. Reeve, a slaveholder, as a missionary.

One hundred eighteen years later Sam Oni, an African convert, was admitted to Mercer University, the first black issue of the Southern Baptist missionary enterprise to be enrolled.

Jesse Mercer and John L. Dagg did not live to see this bewildering answer to their unspecified petitions. Perhaps they did not consider that it is not good to be too specific with God. Perhaps they did not consider that inherent in conversion is equality. If the "heathen" has a soul to save, then once saved there is a body to be cared for, a mind to be trained. And answers to prayers come in strange and circuitous ways.

Jesse Mercer died and sleeps with his fathers, buried at his beloved Penfield, the original site of the modest institute that became Mercer University.

John L. Dagg is buried at Hayneville, Lowndes County, Alabama, a place he never saw for he was blind, a place where Jonathan Daniel, a missionary not from, but to, the South—preaching the good news of freedom to the sons and daughters of slavery—was gunned down by Thomas Coleman when the first African student Sam Oni was in his junior year at Mercer University.

This story has many beginnings. It begins in 1833 at Penfield, Georgia, when Jesse Mercer and his little band of visionaries had a dream.

It begins in an African village when Mrs. Elizabeth Oni and her husband Daniel brought forth a son and named him Sam.

It begins in a courtroom on May 17, 1954 when Chief Justice Earl Warren read a decision to an audience part hostile and part enraptured, summed up with the historic and world-shaping words:

> We conclude that in the field of public education the doctrine of "separate but equal" has no place. Separate educational facilities are inherently unequal.

From that day forth Mercer University was compelled either to continue to defy its Lord or obey both Him and Caesar. Or let the academies of Caesar go on ahead.

The story should have no beginning at all. It should never have happened, because another little baby was born in Bethlehem nineteen hundred and fifty years earlier. *All* of the players in the story call that child the Son of God. And one of His earliest followers said that in Him there was neither male nor female, bond nor free.

But it did happen. The story has few heroes, many casualties, and has left many scars. Some of the scars have healed so smoothly that the blemishes are virtually undetectable. Others are so hideous as to be constant reminders of gross misconduct and unfaithfulness. Under still others remain seething cauldrons of infection that might erupt on another day.

The story has not ended. The dream of Penfield has survived. And it not only survived, but—as the world measures things—flourished in the time of testing, though derelictions along the path are legion.

And truly there were heroes. If not heroes certainly stalwarts, scions of Jesse Mercer, but also of Roger Williams, Thomas Helwys, and John Leland, reaching all the way back to the prophets and apostles. Men and women of abiding faith and inbred integrity who loved the academy but who had an even higher loyalty. White and black men and women who, risking the scorn of kith and kin, the jeers of peers, and dangers unpredictable, ran the gauntlet of meanness and age-old bigotry, reaping a harvest from seeds they did not plant but whose ingathering was imposed upon them.

Although in the most literal and direct way this is a story about Mercer University and its racial crucible in the 1960s, it is, even more, a chronicling of the agonizing social conflict that enveloped the South and the nation in those years. It is a story of bravery and frailty, of denial and affirmation, as America struggled to be one people.

No writer can claim to be free of slant and bias. Where such leanings and misappropriations appear on these pages, they reflect the bent of the writer. What appears is what I have found—with no interference or direction from the cast of characters. The manner in which the findings are presented is mine alone.

—Will D. Campbell

Chapter 1

Where cross the crowded ways . . .

In the fall of 1963 Sam Oni was admitted to Mercer University in Macon, Georgia. He was the first black student in Mercer's 130-year history.

Mr. Oni was a native of Nigeria and had been converted to the Baptist faith in Ghana by Southern Baptist missionaries. Three years after being admitted to Mercer, on September 25, 1966, he decided to attend a church located on the edge of the campus, the Tattnall Square Baptist Church.

"You can't go in there," a deacon, standing on the churchhouse doorstep, said as Oni approached.

"You know our position," said another deacon standing beside him. "We're with the majority of the church."

In 1961 Sir Francis Ibiam, a medical doctor and governor of Eastern Nigeria, asked an American house guest what would happen if a black person walked into a congregation of white worshipers in the American South. When told that many would probably walk out, he replied, "I hope that God will spare me to get to the United States. I would like to go into some of those white congregations and see whether people walked out. If they did I would tell them the meaning in God's sight of what had happened!"

Sir Francis, who later renounced his British title, did not live to put his American brothers and sisters to the test.

Sam Oni had been born not far from where Sir Ibiam spoke those words. Mr. Oni would be Dr. Ibiam's surrogate. After three years in the United States, Sam decided it was time for him to put the members of the Tattnall Square Baptist Church of Macon to the test.

While in California for the summer of 1966, Oni was reading the Oakland *Tribune* one day and was startled to see his Macon campus mentioned in Ralph McGill's syndicated column. McGill wrote that Pastor

Thomas Holmes was in trouble with his congregation for advocating racial integration in church. It was more than Oni could tolerate. He resolved that when he returned to Mercer in September he would do what Sir Francis Ibiam had said he would do: go, and if rejected tell them what they were doing. The world would see as well.

Five months earlier an army coup had deposed Dr. Kwame Nkrumah, the first president of Ghana. Oni could do nothing about the troubles in the country he had left. There was something he could do to unmask the churchiness that sauntered defiantly under the banner of Christ in the land to which he had come. And he would do it.

In the early 1960s, Tattnall Square Baptist Church had a membership approaching 2,000. Located on the university campus and named for Tattnall Square Park, the area that claimed the antebellum homes of some of Macon's oldest and most affluent residents, it had been the spiritual edifice of the carriage trade as well as church home to much of the Mercer compound.

It seems obscene to use the term "deteriorating neighborhood" when discussing the alleged mission and message of a church. Or a "democratic society." Nevertheless, "deteriorating neighborhood" was the term applied to the Tattnall Square surroundings in the mid-1960s. Old families were dwindling, dying, or moving elsewhere. Heirs, who earlier would have taken over the family business and built an elegant home nearby or inherited and occupied the parents' mansion, sought their fortunes in other cities. Church pews that had carried the same name for generations were vacant.

Many of the fading Victorian houses were divided into apartments and rented to blue-collar workers. A single residence that had once been home for the family of a lawyer, doctor, banker, or industrialist might house several families: mechanics, truck drivers, construction workers, single-parent waitresses. And each year Negro residents edged a little closer. While in the 1920s Chinese immigrants were at least grudgingly welcomed as converts and new members of the church, native-born Americans, if they were black, were not. Chinese were seen as quaint but accepted; sixth-generation American blacks were scorned as aliens to be avoided.

But that was not the whole story. Thomas Holmes, the minister, and a sizeable number of his communicants saw the changing neighborhood as a lump to be leavened, not a clamoring horde to be rejected. They had a vision of renewal. They labored hard to establish a multiracial and cross-cultural ministry in the community. That effort got them fired. It remained for Sam Oni to bear witness to the truth.

Sam Oni left his room in Sherwood Hall that Sunday morning alone. He walked the short block to the Tattnall Square Baptist Church. Although a few students had offered to go with him, he felt that as an African and a product of the Southern Baptist missionary enterprise, it was he who must test the faith of this assemblage of God's people. They had been a party to those sent as missionaries to his people. For 113 years his people had heard, and many had believed. If the Baptists of Tattnall Square would not allow him to worship in their midst, the African Christian would know it was because they had turned away.

What Mr. Oni had read in California had to do with a business meeting of the Tattnall Square congregation. That day, July 24, 1966, by a vote of 289 to 109, they had closed their doors to blacks. It was all done in the Baptist, democratic way. Numbered ballots were signed by each person voting and a careful check made to verify that each one was in fact on the membership rolls. But not even the tellers counting the ballots had any way of knowing how another had voted.

When the count was verified the ballots were burned. The cremains were placed in the sewer at the corner of the church lot, which, within minutes, would further dilute the conscience-ridden ashes with the Sunday morning bathwater and body-waste flushes of Tattnall Square's inhabitants, that mixture presently finding its way to the treatment plant and finally into the Ocmulgee River.

Three hundred ninety-eight guardians of the tattered coat of Christ would sit at Sunday dinner with only them, and their God or gods, knowing for sure what they had done on a morning they called "the Lord's Day."

On this day, two months later, Sam Oni would extend to the congregation a bid for repentance and reconciliation. With network television as his magnifying lens, he would put the drop of water on the microscopic slide so that all the world could see precisely what was there.

Neatly dressed and walking with the air of one with abounding authority for his mission, he made his way toward the red-brick edifice. Mr. Oni spoke impeccable English, and French as well. In addition, he was fluent in German and three African languages.

Seeing two hefty deacons standing at the top of the wide and steep steps he greeted them politely, starting up the steps. "Good morning, Gentlemen," he said, with a slight bow. The men stood with their hands clasped tightly in the middle of their backs, thus extending the elbows, filling in the space between them.

"You can't go in there," one of the men replied.

When Mr. Oni veered to go around them, they did a quick dance-step to the side, blocking the way. When he angled to the other side, they did the same fleet shuffle. By then he was within one step of them. The men, in perfect rhythm, stood bumping the pelvic area forward and back, suggestive of a burlesque chorus line.

"I wish to join you in worshiping the living God," Oni said. "The God of us all."

"Then go to your own church," one of the men said.

"God can hear you there," said someone else standing nearby.

"We have voted," the second deacon said. "You can't go in there."

"Then may I have the privilege of speaking with your deacon board? Grant me that and I shall no longer tarry."

Even when the student advanced no farther, the men still moved their hips in the same striptease fashion, doing the two-step from side to side, as if rehearsed. A six-year-old child, son of one of the deacons, stood to one side of the steps, paralyzed with fear, not understanding why someone was being barred from the church. Today he says no one ever explained it, and the experience has haunted him all those years.

The deacons were not accustomed to this crisp and lyrical British enunciation by a black man. Nor had they ever been so forthrightly challenged by one of his color.

Mr. Oni advanced no farther. Back on the flat sidewalk he tried again to reason with them.

"Do you realize what you are doing? Why do you treat me in this fashion? I am your brother. My people have heard the gospel from the lips of your people. Did they deceive?"

"We told you we have voted. You can't go in there."

"We have voted!"

"Go to the church where you are a member!"

"Or some other church!"

"You're not going in there!"

"Not in our church! Go! Go away!"

The two deacons and most of those standing near were speaking at once.

"But it is my desire, my call of God, to worship here," Oni, still composed, responded.

By then the service inside had begun. Three men from the university, sympathetic to Mr. Oni's effort to attend the Tattnall Square Church, stood across the street watching. A small campus dog, apparently belonging to no one in particular, made its way in and out of the guarded door. Then in and out again.

The robed choir moved down the aisle, the congregation joining them in the processional hymn:

> *Where cross the crowded ways of life,*
> *Where sound the cries of race and clan,*
> *Above the noise of selfish strife,*
> *We hear Thy voice, O Son of man!*

Some in the congregation saw the selection of the hymn itself as further violation of Southern mores by Reverend Holmes and his associates.

Outside, another procession was in progress, without the accompaniment of organ pipes or trained choir. The chairman of the deacon board had summoned the police, stationed nearby with a patrol car. Two officers in summer gray, pistols holstered with Sam Browne belts, arrived and led Mr. Oni to their car.

Sitting alone in the back seat of the police car Sam Oni could hear the plaintive strains of Frank Mason North's song of brotherhood:

> *In haunts of wretchedness and need,*
> *On shadow'd thresholds dark with fears,*
> *From paths where hide the lures of greed,*
> *We catch the vision of thy tears.*
>
> *Sing on, my brothers and sisters. Sing on.*
> *Sing of our own sweet Jesus.*

From the sanctuary, streaming through a life-sized stained-glass figure of a barefoot Jesus cuddling a snow-white lamb, the stained-glass colors reflecting and distorting the whirling red patrol car lights, the sounds continued:

> *O Master, from the mountain side,*
> *Make haste to heal the hearts of pain;*

Among these restless throngs abide,
   O tread the city's streets again.

The police were not harsh to Oni. They were doing their job.

Then, seeing that his accusers were not there and there were none left to condemn him, they released him and let him go.

The black man said that he would come again.

Following the evening service, Thomas Holmes and his associates Douglas Johnson and Jack Jones were relieved of their duties by a vote of 250 to 189.

❏

Chapter 2

A judge named Gus . . .

When Sam Oni reached Atlanta in the fall of 1963, on his way to become
the first black student at Mercer University, the country he knew only
from books and missionaries was nursing early disillusionment from a
presidential administration that had begun with exhilaration and promise.
"The New Frontier" it was called. The young, handsome, and energetic
John Fitzgerald Kennedy had chosen a cadre of the brightest minds ever
assembled by a national administration. But the promised renaissance was
beginning to deteriorate from successive blunders, bad luck, and miscal-
culations.

Even so, the nation had seldom known such energizing euphoria as
it enjoyed in those early months of 1961. From the blinding snow and
sun of inauguration day Kennedy and his team of Phi Beta Kappas,
Rhodes Scholars, and college professors had plunged into a whirlwind of
activity—executive orders, directives, official messages, and legislative
initiatives. "With vigor!" the young president intoned. Not since Franklin
D. Roosevelt was elected to lead the nation out of the Great Depression
had there been such winged and radical social legislation and change as
was seen during the first one hundred days of Kennedy.

The Brahmin president would soon falter. Only with the hindsight of
history can it be understood how flawed some of the decisions had been.
It began with the farcical Bay of Pigs, an attempt to overthrow Cuba's
Fidel Castro with a few poorly trained and ill-equipped exiles and refu-
gees from Castro's Communist government. The attempt ended in igno-
minious defeat.

For a while the president's star shone anew with the Peace Corps, a
program that would send thousands of American men and women volunteers around the globe to assist underdeveloped countries, Sam Oni's
African homeland among them.

Likewise, Kennedy's prestige in international affairs was briefly
regenerated and approval ratings climbed when, in October 1962, the
Soviet Union placed long-range missiles with nuclear warheads in Cuba,

aimed at the United States. There followed thirteen of the most hazardous and nerve-wracking days the world had ever seen. It was an exacting and grim test of whether sanity would prevail or civilization as it then existed would be annulled in a moment of nationalistic madness by one side or the other. The survival of the globe was at stake. In the end Kennedy and his counsel backed Khrushchev down. The missiles were dismantled.

On one of those harrowing days, while the two nations stood eyeball to eyeball, perched on the brink of apocalyptic mischief, the Mercer University board of trustees met in Macon, Georgia. On that day, October 18, 1962, oblivious to the precariousness of their own longevity, their most pressing problem was whether one lone black man, known to them as Sam Jerry Oni, a product of the Baptist missionary venture, would be afforded access to their halls of learning. "But the instruction of fools is folly. . . ."

The day itself had been long in coming. It had been eight years since the Supreme Court ruling of May 17, 1954 on public school segregation, a decision that grabbed and held fast to the emotions of the South and the nation as nothing had done since the Civil War. There had been no doubt in the minds of most political leaders and educators that the Court would rule as it did. Yet when the ruling came it seemed as if a hurricane had roared in, out of season and without warning, sure to lay waste the South without mercy. Those who thought the region would make the change from a rigidly segregated system to an evenhanded adjustment to honor were not acquainted with the human capacity for baneful deeds. A resistive white citizenry, infected by centuries of racial pride, privilege, and prejudice, with passions fanned by political blindness and ambition, would fabricate the most outlandish roadblocks to peaceful compliance. States' rights, interposition, nullification, and massive resistance became code words for lawlessness and sometimes mob rule. Dire predictions of miscegenation and amalgamation were fuel poured on the flames of unrelenting wrath.

It was an unparalleled constitutional crisis. But the circuit and district courts endured. Although some Southern judges, themselves victims of the same atmosphere of partiality as their constituency, aided and abetted the dissenters, most honored their profession when cases reached their chambers, sometimes paying a heavy price of rejection, hostility, and family harassment.

One such stalwart was Judge William Augustus Bootle, who had presided over the U.S. Middle District of Georgia since 1954. When I asked,

"Who knows the Macon and Mercer University picture from the white side?" the name of Judge Bootle kept appearing. He would have to be visited.

"Will he talk freely?"

"O yes. He is ninety-one years old, but he knows the story and will talk freely."

When called, Judge Bootle replied that he could not grant an interview that afternoon for it was Thursday and he had a standing engagement to shoot skeet on Thursday afternoons. He quickly added, "Why don't you come on out now?"

Prior to becoming a judge, Attorney Bootle was a conservative practitioner known to oppose progressive proposals at Mercer and liberal politics in general. Few would have nominated Mr. Bootle for even a minor role in the cast of characters for the approaching drama that would desegregate higher education in Georgia, let alone one who would be a hero to the cause of racial change and an archenemy of the status quo.

Twice a graduate of Mercer, at the time Sam Oni applied for admission Judge Bootle was a prominent member of the board of trustees.

The nonagenarian judge and skeet shooter meets his visitor at the bottom of a steep driveway. Instead of riding the hundred yards or so with his guest he says, "Follow me," and proceeds up the drive to his elegant home on the brow of one of Macon's highest hills. Cordially seating his visitor in a sunroom overlooking a spread of thick woods, refreshing in the summer heat, he glances at his watch and announces that it is time for a Coca-Cola. When a maid in her middle years brings the drinks in crystal glasses and on a silver serving tray, he politely stands until she leaves the room. Saying that his friends know him as Gus—a bid at the moment unthinkable—he says he has plenty of time and indicates a willingness to discuss any matter the interviewer has on the agenda.

The subject, of course, is Mercer University. As those with a good story are apt to do, he begins much earlier.

> I was born near Round Oak, South Carolina in 1902. It was a place where Revolutionary War soldiers camped. Not certain which side. Our side I suppose. I think the Indians named the place Round Oak. My father moved to Reidsville, Georgia where he rented land and had a little mill and made roofing shingles by hand. When I was just a boy I snaked logs out of the swamps.

"I haven't heard anyone say 'snaked logs' for a long time," I interrupted. "I used to snake crossties for the Illinois Central Railroad when I was a boy. Penny a piece."

"What did you use?" the judge asks.

"Mules. We used mules. Sometimes horses."

"I used oxen. Only oxen. A mule or horse would bog down with their pointed hoofs. Oxen have cloven hoofs. They spread out and won't sink in the mire."

The judge is a gentleman and doesn't mind the interruption. He talks at length about the temper and personality of oxen, about why ox teamsters don't use lines. Oxen, he says, will respond to the human voice better than if constrained with halters, bridles, and lines. Said he could turn his team around with two words.

"Is that how you put yourself through college?" The judge sips his Coca-Cola, then picks up his story without responding to the question:

> I was too young for World War I so I worked in a shipyard as a reamer. I was fifteen years old. We didn't have child labor laws in those days. I stayed there until the end of the war. A citizen of Reidsville by the name of Josh Beasley said to me, "Why don't you go to college?" I told him I didn't have the money. The truth was I had never given it much thought. Well, I had dreamed of it but a dream was all it was. This fellow was known as sort of a tightwad and what he said then surprised me. He said he was administrator of an estate and there was a little money he could lend me. We rented from E. C. Collins, a judge there in Toombs County. He endorsed the loan, along with my father, for 300 dollars.

"So you went to college on borrowed money."

Again the judge continues to chronicle his life without answering directly:

> I waited on tables for three years. Got my A.B. in 1924 and my law degree in '25. I knew you weren't supposed to solicit clients as an attorney and I assumed you weren't supposed to try to join a law firm on your own. So I simply planned to hang up my shingle and wait for clients to come in. Before doing that though I had debts I had to pay so I asked Guy Wells for a teaching job. You might have run across Guy in your civil rights work. He was superintendent of schools over in Eastville, Georgia, over near where Rufus Harris originated. Monroe, that was. Guy Wells was a graduate of Mercer, quite a liberal for his

day. I believe he also studied at Columbia and at George Peabody College for Teachers. Well-educated fellow. Later on he was president of Georgia State College for Women in Milledgeville. Went there in thirty-four, I believe.

I am impressed that a ninety-one-year-old man so clearly remembers such bygone names and dates, and say so. The judge modestly acknowledges the flattery, savors his Coca-Cola with brandy-like swirls, and moves along:

I was about to tell you about taking my last exam in law school. Baxter Jones was a practicing attorney in Macon and taught part-time. For some reason I neglected to answer one of the questions. The minute I got back to my room I realized my mistake. I ran all the way downtown to Baxter Jones's law office. Got there just as he was entering the elevator. I timidly explained that I knew the answer to the question, had consulted no book in the interim, and asked if it might be possible to finish the exam in his office. He readily agreed, then asked what I was going to do after graduation. I told him I hoped to teach school for Guy Wells. I remember it so well. He put his hand on my shoulder and asked if I would consider working for his law firm. Consider, mind you. There I was with a sizable debt to pay off, a law degree, and no job. That was in '25.

In '28 I took a job as assistant district attorney in a new federal court. About all I did was prosecute moonshiners. In a few months Al Smith was running as a wet against Herbert Hoover, who was a prohibitionist. I was twenty-six by then and had never voted. When I went to the polls it seemed a serious breach of honor to cast a vote against a prohibitionist when I was making my living prosecuting moonshiners. So I voted for Hoover. I was a Republican without even thinking about it—a matter of principle.

"I had always wondered how you got appointed by President Eisenhower," I put in. The judge is not through with his story:

Carl Vinson—Did you know Carl? Another Mercer man, you know—was defending a young lawyer for charging too much. In those days a congressman could work as a lawyer during off-season. Carl was a fine lawyer and got his client off. So I lost. After the trial he said to me, "Well, Gus, I suppose you want to be district attorney."

We had a Republican administration and the man who had been D.A. was out. I was twenty-six years old. Not much experience. "Yes," I said.

"You are a Republican, aren't you?"

"Yes," I replied.

It was the answer Carl wanted from me, though he, of course, was a Democrat. He told me to come to Washington and he would introduce me to the attorney general. I did go to Washington soon, on my wedding trip. I met John Marshall, then deputy attorney general. About all he asked was if there were many old clocks in Georgia—he collected old clocks—and if I voted Republican. I could answer yes to both questions and got the job.

The judge looks at his watch. Except for Guy Wells, Carl Vinson, and William Augustus Bootle's early days as a student, little has been said about Mercer. And nothing having to do with the 1960s. "Ah, but you wish to speak of the truculent sixties, do you not? And of Mercer in those days. Please forgive my excursions."

I am enthralled by the words of the courtly judge and have almost forgotten my mission. No apology is necessary. Since entering the room I have felt I was in the presence of a remarkable man.

Still I haven't told you how I chose Mercer in the first place. But that is a short story. There were three boys in my class. The other two were going to the University of Georgia. Georgia began two weeks earlier than Mercer. I chose Mercer so I could be at home for two extra weeks to help my father make shingles.

The venerable jurist pauses and gazes in the distance, then stands and strolls about the room. Together he and I watch midsummer humming-birds flitting, flirting, sometimes fighting to establish and defend their territory in the full-blossomed garden. The judge's carriage is that of a man half his age, his countenance that of a yearling boy. There is not the girth of aging males and his shoulders are broad and handsome. His eyes seem to darken when he is amused; his hair is full and well groomed. Though I had been surprised when I heard a ninety-one-year-old man say he shot skeet, I can now imagine this man erect and well positioned on the shooting range, quick with every pull, with the aim of a marksman. As my host returns to his chair, his mind moves back to what I had asked: "Tell me about yourself and Mercer."

"Mercer," he intones, "has been for me a long and glorious romance."

His words are lyrical as he launches into a lengthy soliloquy on the long and enchanting pilgrimage with his beloved alma mater. I am a mere eavesdropper. He talks of his lengthy friendship with President Rufus Harris and the high esteem in which he held him. They had grown up in the same era, and both had attended Mercer University, graduating seven years apart. Both were deans of the Mercer Law School, six years separating their tenure. Although he humbly says he was only acting dean, it was a position he held for four years. He was thirty-one years old when he began. He speaks of having been on the board of trustees since 1933, with one year rotation between terms. For more than an hour a man who has seen Mercer in sickness and in health, who stood by her as chariots of storm-clouds armed with thunderbolts boomed "Heresy! Heresy!" and threatened to surely destroy her, and then exulted as boulevards of blue led back to steady pace, pours forth an accounting of that love affair that would merit applause from the most militant civil rights activist or the finest historian of the judiciary. For more than seven decades Judge Bootle has lived never far from Mercer's side. And when at last he reaches the 1960s it seems an unburdening.

It is a mighty thing destiny throws from its chariot when it throws us morning. Judge Bootle echoes that as he begins:

> The sixties were an awakening for us all. We should have known but we didn't. For too long we had done those things we ought not to have done and left undone the things we should have done. Those of us who were judges in the trenches, at the district and circuit level, were in a sense blessed, though some saw it as a curse. The Supreme Court in the Brown decision [*Brown* v. *Board of Education of Topeka*, May 17, 1954] was but the catafalque of segregation. It was left to us to bury the dead.
>
> When Rufus Harris became president of Mercer in sixty, determined to integrate Mercer, I had already integrated the University of Georgia. I say "I" though I was a minor persona in the cast. Donald Hollowell— You perhaps knew him. Black lawyer from Atlanta—was in my court on another matter. When he finished he said, "Your honor, I have another matter." I asked if it could be presented in chambers and he said it could. There was a faint crowing of the cock as he told me he had a petition to admit two Negroes to the University of Georgia. I said, "Why don't you file it in the Northern District? You have jurisdiction there." He said, "No, the registrar lives in Athens and that is in your district."
>
> I was a judge of the United States. Solemnly sworn not to flinch from any duty that came my way. There were never two sides to the issue. Absolutely! It was absolutely clear to me from the outset that the

two young people must be admitted. It was the law! Judges do not make law. It is their task, brooding though it may sometimes be, to say to the citizenry, "Here is what the law says. And there is a penalty if you are found in violation."

Constance Baker Motley tried the case. An attorney of outstanding ability. I recall an occasion when she asked Georgia's chancellor how it could be that Charlayne Hunter and Hamilton Holmes had been refused admission on the ground that there was no room when she had a list of students that had been admitted subsequent to the application of Miss Hunter and Mr. Holmes. When the Chancellor rode off in several directions, Miss Motley asked the court recorder to read the question she had asked. Then she said, "Chancellor, is that the question you are answering?" Funny things did happen.

The judge laughs lustily—something he does easily and often. When asked if Vernon Jordan, then Georgia field secretary for the NAACP, assisted Attorney Motley, the Judge recalled that he had. (Thirty-four years later Mr. Jordan would give the commencement address and be awarded an honorary LL.D. degree by Mercer University.)

You perhaps recall that I did grant the University a delay, only because I wanted the matter decided finally in open court and not on summary. Judge Tuttle immediately reversed me.

All that to say that by the time Mercer was considering the application of Mr. Oni, the state university was already integrated. Since I had been the judge in the case I told President Harris that I felt I should resign from Mercer's board. He felt that for me to do so would send the wrong signal: that I opposed integrating Mercer. So I remained but did not participate in the discussion.

Perhaps it is true that Judge Bootle as trustee remained quiet in the heat of ensuing contention. But there can be no doubt that his commanding presence blossomed brightly in the silence.

The judge began to speak again. "I don't know how some of my fellow judges could rule as they. . . . ''

He reconsidered. As the names of federal judges who were known to block implementation of the Supreme Court decision against segregation were mentioned he would not comment. No amount of prompting would gain harsh words about another of the bench.

"Yes, I knew Judge Cox of Mississippi. Yes, I knew Judge Mize. Knew Seymour Lynn, Frank Scarlett, Hobart Grooms, Daniel Thomas. Knew them all. None of them went to Mercer."

That was all. That they did not go to Mercer seemed judgement enough.

I did not deem it appropriate to seek an estimate of Walter Franklin George, for whom Mercer's law school is named. Walter George graduated from Mercer in 1900, followed by a law degree the next year. Remembered as one of the most famed orators of Mercer's history, he was awarded the honorary LL.D. in 1920 and the Doctor of Humane Letters the year after he died. For thirty-five years he represented Georgia and the nation in the United States Senate. He was a vehement racist, and at times anti-Semitic in his rhetoric. Franklin Roosevelt actively campaigned against the Georgia senator because he fiercely opposed many of Roosevelt's New Deal proposals for change. Senator George, an authentic starched-collar conservative, only avoided a place in infamy because he was honest in his conservatism, was not tainted by corruption. But almost certainly he would not have agreed with his fellow Mercerian when Bootle ruled as he did.

One who might have agreed was another Mercer alumnus, Judge Bootle's colleague and predecessor, Judge T. Hoyt Davis. Throughout most of his career Davis was in the same law firm as Walter George. One of the last acts of President Roosevelt, Senator George's arch adversary, was to appoint Hoyt Davis as judge of the Middle District of Georgia.

Davis served on Mercer's trustee board for many years and was on the special committee to investigate charges of heresy brought in 1939. A group of ministerial students, among them John Birch (for whom a right-wing organization would be named in the 1960s), some not even in a class taught by the professors charged, had a secret organization called "The Fellowship Club." Their objective was to monitor the orthodoxy of their teachers. They had gone to the local ministerial association with allegations of doctrinal deviance against five of their elders whose task was to prepare the students to be preachers and teachers. The committee, and later the entire board, absolved the accused of the heresy charges but their verdict was couched in language that would send a signal of caution:

> While we would not abridge the legitimate academic freedom of any professor, we know that there are certain foundation tenets, such as the full inspiration of the Old and New Testament, the deity of the Lord Jesus Christ, redemption alone through the atoning blood of Christ, the bodily resurrection of Christ, the necessity of the new birth, the fact of

no salvation of any man except through personal faith in Christ, and the existence of both a hell and heaven—commonly held by the Baptists of Georgia who founded and own Mercer University—as being essential to the full message of Christianity to the world.

That creedal formulation left little room for scholarly wandering on the part of Mercer's faculty.

In 1945, a case came before Judge Davis that would be more difficult than mediating an altercation amongst the zealous, one that would forever change the politics of Georgia and the South. In a sense it was more far-reaching than *Brown* v. *Board* would be nine years later, for it opened the door to Negro participation in state elections. The Democratic Party of Georgia was considered a private organization. Almost a club. Those who were not members of the club could not vote in the Democratic primary. Those who were not white were excluded from the club. Since the Democratic Party ruled Georgia politics, Negroes were politically sterile.

The Reverend Primus E. King, a Negro of Columbus, Georgia, restless with his gelded status, filed for relief in the Middle District Court. As a Mercer-educated jurist, W. A. Bootle would be assigned the difficult case of Hunter and Holmes against the University of Georgia in 1962; another Mercerian, T. Hoyt Davis, drew the case of *King* v. *Chapman* in 1945.

Large crowds gathered daily, often standing in long lines for admission. A blistering heat wave was stranded over central Georgia, heightening the tempers of those who made it inside. Rigidly segregated in this federal courtroom, with funeral home fans bearing pictures of Jesus knocking at a closed door their only source of comfort from the heat, the sons and daughters of slavery sat in anxious silence. Waiting. Preparing themselves for the answer of ages.

Across the room, ablaze with resentment for the impertinence of the plaintiff and feeling the injury a ruling in the plaintiff's favor would levy, sat the uneasy whites, some of colonial ancestry.

Defending the white primary for the Democratic Party of Georgia were A. Edward Smith, Charles J. Bloch, and Ellsworth J. Hall. Both Bloch and Hall had attended Mercer.

Sitting with Reverend Primus King were Harry Strozier and Oscar D. Smith. Strozier was a teacher in the Mercer Law School as well as being a Macon attorney known for his leftist bent. It was a table fraught with peril for both plaintiff and counsel, not a device for longevity. Any black man pursuing the franchise had long been in fell danger. For a white attorney to assist him in that venture approached sedition.

On a balmy October morning, Judge T. Hoyt Davis took a veronica stance, passing the cape of justice over the charging bull. In an unhurried voice, as if the case were no more than a minor trespass, the gentle son of Mercer ruled that the white primary of Georgia was in violation of the fourteenth and fifteenth amendments to the Constitution of the United States. Affirmed later by the Fifth Circuit Court of Appeals, the man who had found no fault with the alleged apostates of his alma mater had found his native state to be in grievous violation of America's most sacred document.

Judge Bootle remembered and spoke of all that as if it were yesterday. Now the hour for his skeet match was near at hand. There was one other question. Following his University ruling, an effigy of Judge Bootle was hanged from the archway to the Mercer campus.

"How did you feel when you knew Mercer students would defame you in that manner?"

The judge brushed the question aside with a quick tilt of his head, and gave no verbal answer. William Augustus Bootle, class of 1924, would say no more of himself and Mercer on this day.

Standing on the portico with me as I took my leave there was a firm handshake. "Good-bye, my friend," he says. "Please come again."

"Good-bye, Gus," I manage to say. One who had entered this house with a previously unbending stereotype of what a Georgia Republican judge would be like now stands fixed in the fellowship.

"I am mightily beholden to you. For many reasons."

Gus Bootle smiles in affirmation of hearing spoken the name he has worn for ninety-one years, shakes my hand more vigorously, and watches until the parting vehicle is out of sight.

⌐

Chapter 3

Aunt Coreen didn't stop . . .

"And who is most conversant with Macon and Mercer from the black side?" I asked. Again the replies were unanimous: "William Randall."

Back in the inner city, William Randall, also in his years of eventide, is waiting. This one does not stand with the athletic deftness of the judge. He does not stand at all. He sits on the passenger side of a late-model Buick automobile, waiting for his grandson-in-law Clarence Williams to help him into a wheelchair. When he is comfortably seated he motions for a cherubic and spirited three-year-old to join him for the ride. Jessica is his great-granddaughter. Neatly dressed and with tightly braided hair and scarlet ribbons, she playfully climbs on his lap and they are wheeled up a ramp and into a large, tastefully decorated room. It is the business office of the Randall Memorial Mortuary on Pio Nono Avenue, a major Macon thoroughfare named for Pope Pius IX. (It is an unlikely name for a street in this Georgia Baptist town.)

William P. Randall is a seventy-eight-year-old man who knows what it means to be black in Macon, what it means to be a successful business man, father of six children, church leader, civil rights activist, and Bibb County commissioner. He is all of those things. Owning the funeral home is one of his many ventures. Following World War II he had one of the largest black-owned construction companies in the Southeast.

He grumbles good-naturedly that his mail has not been arranged as he is rolled behind a sturdy oak desk. He thanks the attendant, gives the giggling little girl a tender pat and asks a secretary to hold his calls.

"I was about her age when I got my first lesson in race relations," he begins.

Sitting on a vegetable wagon beside his Aunt Coreen as she peddled turnips, collard greens, okra, and tomatos on Walnut Street, he heard a white woman calling for his aunt to stop. He thought she did not hear the woman who was shouting, "Auntie! Auntie! Auntie!" It was a term used often by whites when addressing elderly black women. And thought to be a courtesy.

"Aunt Coreen didn't stop," he remembers. "Get up, Bell. Get up, Bell." She gently reined the mare to move along.

Only when the woman called "Vegetable woman!" did his aunt stop.

"Didn't you hear me call you?" the outraged potential customer exclaimed.

"No. I heard you calling your auntie and I don't have any white nieces."

Mr. Randall tells the story in a deep, graveled voice, weakened by his paralyzing illness. He laughs lightly, and begins another story.

> When I was a boy most Negro mothers and fathers taught their children subservience. Mine taught us humility. But not subservience. "You're not a bit better than anyone else," they told us. But they taught us assurance. "You're just as good as anyone else." Most taught their sons to step off the sidewalk when they met a white person. Ours taught us to hold our space. "If there's just room enough for one person to walk, let the other person, white or colored, have it. If there's room for both of you, walk on."

He smiles proudly and adds, "I was always a big boy. I don't remember anyone trying to push me off."

Mr. Randall, or Bill as he insists on being called by his friends, talks as freely of his ancestry as Gus Bootle. He had a close bond with his grandmother, who was six years old when the Civil War ended. She told him of a black overseer, a slave himself, who was more harsh on the other slaves than the whites. She remembered the day Jefferson Davis was captured in nearby Abbeville. The troops passed through their plantation on their way to Macon with the disesteemed president of the defeated Confederacy. The Northern soldiers told the old black overseer to curse Jefferson Davis. Randall remembers his grandmother telling him, "That old man stood flatfoot and cussed that man for thirty minutes without repeating himself. Not one time."

He pauses for a long time, as if his memory has lapsed. Instead he is trying to decide if he should say in the present company what he is thinking.

Addressing me directly he asks, "Have you found where Mercer University gave Robert E. Lee an honorary degree? One year after the fighting stopped, I believe."

Mr. Randall pauses again, looking about the room at the others. "My gracious," he adds, tapping cadence on the heavy wood of the desk top.

It is his only judgment of a university that gave honor to General Lee ninety-seven years before it admitted the first black student.

William P. Randall is obviously proud of his grandmother. For the stories she told him and for linking him to the early days of his family's struggle for freedom. She died at ninety-six. Her picture occupies a prominent place on his office wall.

Though not highly educated by today's standard, Mr. Randall speaks with never a lapse into dialect. His grammar is good, his mind is clear, and his stories of the black struggle are innumerable.

"Things got rough back in the '60s," he says.

He was at times president of the NAACP and on other occasions its executive secretary. Even that was dangerous at the time.

> Kids today don't believe how rough it was. They'll tell you if they had been around they wouldn't have put up with it. I tell them if some of us hadn't been around then they wouldn't be where they are now. Voting freely, holding elected offices, attending Mercer and other fine schools, holding jobs not even the highest-educated black person could have held thirty years ago.

As an aside he says,

> Mercer University has graduated 500 Negro students. Five hundred. Young people today just don't know how rough it was. Nostalgia for them is what they had for breakfast.

After the Montgomery bus boycott in the mid-1950s, the NAACP of Macon decided to challenge their own segregated city buses. "Colored people had to pay their fare at the front of the bus, get off and enter from the back door of the bus."

A number of high school students were recruited and trained in non-violence to refuse to go to the back of the buses after they had paid their fare. When they were arrested, Mr. Randall paid their bail and began organizing a boycott in the adult community, talking wherever he could, spreading circulars asking everyone to stay off the buses.

> I remember we called a meeting of black preachers and I asked Dean Joseph Hendricks from Mercer—Joe I call him—to come speak to them. Joe, a very close friend of mine and always a man to do what was right. He talked about the necessity of taking a stand, that white people wouldn't give up segregation voluntarily.

Bill Randall laughs as he says,

I got Joe Hendricks in more trouble back in those days. His speech to us got on television, radio, and in the newspapers. Then his phone started ringing all night. Threats. Hate mail. Cross burned right in his front yard too. And him with a wife and little babies. But he never let us down. Kept right on.

(Joseph Millard Hendricks came to Mercer as a student in 1951. Since returning to the campus in 1959 from three years in theological school in Kentucky, he has worn many Mercer hats and fought many battles, both within the university and in the state of Georgia. Reared in a land-poor family in rural Talbot County, he masks his power and toughness with a country-bumpkin bearing and sylvan innocence.)

The surprising thing to Mr. Randall and the NAACP was the light support they were getting from the local black clergy. "Some of our greatest opposition was from within the race," he said. "Just like that black overseer I was telling you about."

Only five of the preachers Dean Hendricks and Mr. Randall addressed agreed to be arrested by defying the segregation laws. Others preached that God was not the creator of confusion and the protesters were creating confusion.

Mass meetings were held nightly, with attendance building each night. Police took the slightest provocation to make arrests or abuse those entering or leaving the Steward Chapel African Methodist Episcopal Church. Parking tickets were placed on the windshields of cars in the vicinity. Still most of the ministers of black congregations stayed away.

Growing impatient and discouraged, Bill Randall chose a night when the church was packed to overflowing and people standing outside to throw down the gauntlet. He is generally soft-spoken. On this occasion, standing on the dais, his massive frame dwarfing the lectern as he leaned into it, his voice was that of thunder, roaring into the microphone, echoing through the chancel, ricocheting on the flagging outside:

If I had a preacher who couldn't support the effort of his people for freedom, I wouldn't put anything in the collection plate but a button and a penny with a hole in it!

Bill Randall gleefully reports that the following Sunday there were many buttons and holed pennies found in the collection baskets; offerings were down as much as ninety percent. "After that, here they come. 'Let's

"The '60s began in the beginning," he laughs. "Morality isn't measured in decades. What happened in the '60s had its origin in the '50s, '40s, '30s, and nineteenth century."

There is a sculptured brilliancy about his silver, close-cropped mustache. I am no stranger to my host. We have traveled many roads together, toured in conveyances of approval and of rejection. We stand together here, each in the saffron and vermillion of sunset, no time for deception. Neither of us is anxious to offend the other. The splendors of our days have marched on, their procession ending, no torches left to set fire in the minds of the young.

For a moment I wish I were elsewhere, that I had not come here at all. I sense in the old warrior's countenance something of Elisha's vision: horses of fire and chariots of fire and banners, ships, cities, seas of fire—one last conflagration. Mac Bryan will answer your questions.

"Why do you say it is a failure?" I ask, then brace myself for the response, turning down the volume of the tape recorder as if to lessen what I will hear.

The seasoned pedagogue leans for a minute against the gray barn wall, then suggests we move inside before it rains. Clouds, black, milky, and purple, have blown in from the west and hang like embroidered canopies, bringing comforting shade. As we two move along, a galloping wind changes the mood, blowing the clouds like flying rivers, lakes and oceans. Professor Bryan refers to them as God-chariots and I, his friend, now scribe, imagine the linchpins of iron creaking in the distance and a volcano belching flames. I am strangely disquieted in the presence of one I have known as coach and brother.

Inside, both of us comfortably seated, what I had anticipated rolls forth with the authority of Michelangelo's *Last Judgment*.

> How will you explain Mercer's conspiracy of silence—no different from all other allegedly Christian institutions—with regard to Jim Crow? Why was there no faculty, trustee, or campus recognition of the Supreme Court decision of 1954? And why did Caesar's Court have to tell us something that was settled for us at Pentecost?

The voice is calm, as the eye of a hurricane is calm while the storm-clouds armed with thunderbolts splinter all in its wake like the cannonading at Gettysburg, yielding to nothing.

> Why were aggressive, freedom-loving Negro speakers shunned as one with the plague while Uncle Toms were waltzed to the tune of our

denials of brotherhood? What do you intend to say about the academicians' unfeigned hatred of affirmative action?

Ah, and what about the elitism of Mercer et al. toward accepting truly and obviously disadvantaged blacks, not even to mention rednecks like you and me? You know, and I know, that the basic nature of liberal arts institutions is to admit on a false standard, grade on a false education, to train the rulers and governors and warriors and one-minute managers as replacements in perpetuity. You know, and I know, that there is no, absolutely no reason why the academy of Christ should be dictated to by the ACT or SAT scores of Caesar. Why can't we admit, and educate, *educate* any son or daughter of workers of mine, factory, and farm who come our way, for it was on their backs that the vast fortunes that endowed and empowered us were made? Daddies, mamas, and sometimes little children going into the sweatshops, pits, and fields before daylight and dragging out after dark to make rich the overlords they never saw, overlords who then had buildings and entire campuses carrying their names, buying indulgences and simony with riches for which they had not toiled.

The professor had turned proclaimer, with the force of Micah, appearing consumed by prophetic ecstasy. The little cassette turned steadily, recording his message. There was no other sound until he drew a breath and started again.

Will you not be compelled to say that the initial desegregation program of Mercer was just another way of tapping into the grant money that came available? What about the disproportionate number of black athletes, in an obvious exploitation of blacks for alumni glory and fund raising? Is this Christian integration or is it Sambo dancin' fo de man?

And then his most troublesome question of all, one I had anticipated and dreaded.

Are you going to admit that integration is a failure? Not just at Mercer but throughout the land? I see it. As do you. Blacks gathering at one place on campus, whites at another. In the cafeteria, social events, concert hall, athletic events. Black fraternities and sororities, white fraternities and sororities. How many white students attend black history week functions? Or enroll in black studies programs?

We sat discussing the subject of integration's failure for a long time, sometimes agreeing, sometimes differing, sometimes struggling together for an explanation of Mr. Bryan's allegation that "We shall overcome" at the college level has not come to pass. When he was confronted with an exception he was ready with a preponderance of evidence to repulse the challenge.

We could agree that African-Americans didn't invent separatism, that it was instituted into the laws of the new nation at the beginning, prevailed for two centuries, and still lives. Even constitutionally, Africans were three-fifths of a human being. It was whites who devised segregation and it was whites who designed what was called—by whites—"integration."

The aging prophet gazes through the window and into the distance, as if addressing the universe, as he talks of the black students of today who choose to form their own fraternity, dally on the "black bench" on campus, or sit with other blacks in the cafeteria.

> They are fully aware that white America resisted their hopes for a share of the democratic dream as long as it could: passing laws to shut them out, using the highest and lowest methods to squelch their initial efforts peacefully and legally to enter the mainstream, resorting to violence that would be of discredit to the most barbaric civilization—all to parry the blacks from the facilities granted late and reluctantly by the nation's highest judges.

The rain had not come and we moved back outside, as if to be as close as possible to the pulpit of creation. Professor Bryan picks up where he left off inside.

> Why should whites expect a ready acceptance of so tarnished a prize? What effort have whites made to integrate into black culture? Is it integration the white academy has offered or is it *migration*? We will let you into our schools, our clubs, sometimes our churches, if you behave as we imagine we behave, bathe often, keep your voices down, adapt to our music and dance. We will make you titular Caucasian. We will measure you by questions on pheasant under glass, not the breeding habits of cockroaches. Even then, we will accept the top percentiles. Is it any wonder that the New African-American is suspicious of "black and white together?"

"Well, Friend Mac, is there nothing we can now do to stem the torrent of our pernicious past?"

"Are you asking the question for yourself or for Mercer?"

"I'll take either answer you offer."

The good teacher turns the student's words back on him and this teacher had not lost the professorial edge.

Well, what has become of your own life-statement, that unless Christians act from moral and spiritual motives obedience to legal mandates are suspect? And that without genuine repentance on the part of the offending party there can be no real reconciliation? Where are you finding the evidences of repentance at Mercer?

The interviewee turned interviewer waited for an answer. When the only response was to change the tape on the machine, the professor continued.

"Who will you credit for the 'radical turn-about' in Mercer policy—as if any real alteration has ever occurred?"

As the interview wound down, any effort of rebuttal would have been inappropriate. I was not there to refute but to gather information to report. We had known one another for more than forty years, too long to quibble.

No one questions that Professor Bryan had a profound influence on those Mercer students of the 1950s and 1960s who chose to trouble the waters in the footsteps of their mentor. Harris Mobley, who had studied under Professor Bryan at Mercer and who was the missionary who recruited Sam Oni to reverse Mercer's pattern of segregation says, "Dr. Bryan invented me." Numerous other former students are similarly inclined.

Even when he was encouraging the changes in racial patterns, he knew that as new policies were adopted they were wrapped in mixed motives and clouded agendas, ambiguities that even now are difficult to sort out and classify. As a Mercer professor, Bryan railed against what he perceived as its connection with the Georgia political machine and Georgia's senators and congressmen who undergirded the unreconstructed resistance of the South.

It was he who founded and nurtured an underground movement, interracial from the outset, called "Fellowship of Concern," that went on to provide leadership in some of the subversive activities that led eventually to breaking down the rigid walls of separatism. While at Mercer he was a member of the Tattnall Square Baptist Church that would prove the most resistant in the desegregation process to come. He probably influenced a sizeable number of those who pulled out in protest of the recalcitrance, though by then he had been gone for ten years. And it was he who kept Clarence Jordan and the nearby interracial, pacifist Koinonia

Farm on the conscience of the Mercer community as a constant reminder of the way things ought to be.

I was in no position to challenge him. "The wind bloweth where it listeth," was about the only thing I could think of to say before moving back onto more comfortable, if perhaps compromising, terrain.

It had been a painful and intimidating interview. But fundamental to the task. For it was becoming clear that the undertaking would not be an easy one: that garnering the story of Mercer in the 1960s would require more than a cursory audit of official documents. Throwaway lines of seemingly minor actors in the drama, residue from the scrap heaps of major ones, and tidbits of the most ordinary would be required.

❒

Chapter 5

Based on qualification, without regard . . .

History, Stephen said, is a nightmare from which I am trying to awake.
—James Joyce, *Ulysses*

Rufus Harris had experienced opposition even before 1960 when he arrived back at Mercer University as president. In 1917 he completed his B.A. degree there, earned his LL.B. and J.D. degrees at Yale, and became dean of Mercer's law school in 1926. The law school was small and struggling, yet was accredited under Harris's leadership. Amelia Barclay, Harris's assistant and friend of many years, remembers him saying, "I opened and closed the campus." One year later he was appointed dean of the Law School at Tulane University. In 1937 he became president of Tulane, where he remained until 1959. At sixty-two it was his intention to retire and live the life of a writer and elder statesman in the field of higher education. His alma mater thought not.

When he was being considered for the presidency of Mercer University, many long-memoried Georgians had not forgotten his role in 1941 when Governor Eugene Talmadge had summarily purged regents at the University of Georgia because they would not fire five professors the governor thought to be soft on racial segregation. The Southern Association of Colleges and Secondary Schools withdrew accreditation, virtually shutting down the school. Rufus Harris was president of the Southern Association and was criticized in many Georgia quarters. The crisis at the University of Georgia became a campaign issue the following year and led to the defeat of Eugene Talmadge by Ellis Arnall.

And many had not forgotten that it was Rufus C. Harris, president of Tulane University, who defied the powerful political rightists of the McCarthy era. When they demanded that the Tulane faculty be required to sign a loyalty oath, Harris's answer was, "Perhaps we shall consider such a proposal. But only when you have gathered every butcher, every baker, and every candlestick maker into Tulane stadium, and after all of them have signed, then we shall deliberate upon the matter."

Such lines in the sand were not viewed with favor by many at a time when everyone knew the day of reckoning in racial patterns at Mercer was at hand. And it was no secret that Harris had thought he had the trustees of Tulane ready to desegregate that institution. Although he made no statement of protest, it was when they voted against that plan that he resigned. It was no wonder that his coming from Tulane to Mercer was watched by some with grim scrutiny.

On the other hand, there were things those of the left might have held against Mr. Harris. In 1947, President Truman's Commission on Higher Education issued its report and a portion of it questioned the validity of the "separate but equal" doctrine. Four Southern members of the Commission dissented from the majority report. A month later Rufus Harris, president of Tulane, joined the presidents of Vanderbilt, Rollins College, the University of Mississippi, and the University of Texas in issuing a statement in support of the minority report. President Harris, while not vociferously defending segregation, was widely cited by the Negro press as being unfriendly to racial equality in higher education.

There were other instances when liberals had reason to be critical of Mr. Harris. The truth was, Tulane University had not been desegregated under Harris's leadership. The bequest of Paul Tulane establishing Tulane University had specified that it would be for the training of white males. Many felt that, as a scholarly attorney, Harris must have known the Tulane will could be broken in court. But when Harris was being considered as president of Mercer University, white Georgia liberals, still smarting under the anticommunist litany of Senator McCarthy, and now subdued by the steady beat of racist rhetoric, were few and fearful. So there was no opposition to the selection of Harris from that quarter.

Harris handily survived the assault from the right. But it had been mild compared to the balancing of the clouds that would be required of him now. Some of his old friends at Mercer, among them Judge Gus Bootle, a trustee, warned him of the impending crisis and reminded him that Mercer did not have the metropolitan cushion he had known at Tulane. Those who wanted to desegregate Mercer were a distinct minority whose enunciations were stifled by the clattering cries of "segregation forever!" Rufus Harris would not be dissuaded. Perhaps smarting under the criticism of colleagues in other parts of the country that he had not desegregated a university in largely Catholic and cosmopolitan New Orleans, he was determined there would be no repeat in largely Baptist and diehard Macon. Like the Greek general Antigonus who, when forewarned by his troops that they were no match for the enemy who had so many more, replied, "How many do you reckon me to be?" Harris accepted the challenge. Modesty was not among his virtues.

◻

While the major item on Mercer's agenda was soon to be the admission of a missions convert, in 1962 Mercer was still an untroubled environment. There had been a few begrudged advances for American Negroes of the South but little of it had affected Macon and Mercer. That was about to change.

In early spring of that year the Voter Education Project had been formed by the Southern Regional Council. Its money would come from the vast fortunes of Marshall Field and Andrew Mellon, and later from Cyrus McCormick and John D. Rockefeller, men who, in their day, probably would not have been kindly disposed toward spending money for so momentous a challenge to the status quo. Directed by Wiley Branton, the Arkansas attorney who had gained admission of the nine Negro students to Little Rock's Central High School in 1957, the Voter Education Project was designed to add millions to the registration rolls in a short time. Though called Voter Education Project for purposes of tax exemption, VEP was founded for the sole purpose of registering new black voters. (Later directors were Vernon Jordan, now friend and adviser to President Clinton, and John Lewis, now the congressman from Atlanta.)

Any politician who had eyes at all knew that such programs would lead to mass voting among black citizens, and changes of momentous proportions in Southern politics. It was enough to soften the hearts of some. But most, with stiffened resistance, saw it as a hurled gauntlet over which they must prevail at any cost.

At the time, a young Mercerian, Missionary Harris Mobley, was responding to a request from some other young Mercerians to assist them in breaking the color barrier at Mercer. He and his wife Vivian picked Sam Oni to blaze the trail.

Some other young people were meeting in Port Huron, Michigan. Something called the New Left was developing out of the sleepy and disengaged 1950s generation of students. The most politically minded organization of students at that point had been the U.S. National Student Association. Until then one of the most radical actions it had taken was to challenge in loco parentis rules on college and university campuses. Dormitory visitation across gender lines was a whispered goal; coed dormitories were not even dreamed of.

In loco parentis was not on the agenda of Tom Hayden and forty-four other young people who met at a summer camp of the AFL-CIO in June 1962. Race, the cold war, and The Bomb were. Sacred cows were being cut from the herd for slaughter. Ranchers would resist in a manner the young students did not foresee. Calling themselves Students for a Democratic Society, their words were tame compared to what they would inspire. At the time, rejecting violence as a catalyst for change, they talked of such modest goals as "replacing power rooted in possession, privilege, or circumstances by power rooted in love, reflectiveness, reason, and creativity."

Probably most founders of the SDS had never heard of Mercer University. Yet within five years their influence, by then radicalized by subsequent developments in a fashion beyond their most grotesque nightmares, would be a whirlwind on Mercer's campus, leaving efforts to admit a lone black student as a droll interlude, not even worthy of remembered embarrassment. A student invitation for Jane Fonda, later to be Tom Hayden's wife, to address the student assembly would rock Macon and Georgia in a way the advent of Sam Oni did not approach. "Burn, baby, burn!" was as common at what had once been a drowsy little Baptist college in Bibb County, Georgia as it was in Berkeley or Lansing. Tom Hayden, the frail, acne-scarred youth who had penned the SDS manifesto, was high on the list of public enemies.

It was the 1960s. The sleeping giant, the Academy, had been roused from its slumber. All was in motion.

But in 1962 and 1963 Mercer University was still trying as quietly as possible to bring one black African within its walls.

In the fall of 1962, at the very time Mercer trustees were forming a committee to make recommendations on racial policies, James Meredith was admitted to the University of Mississippi. Incited to riot by the fulminations of Governor Ross Barnett, a Mississippi mob assembled and sought to win the day. Although two people were killed and many injured, U.S. marshals and federal troops prevailed.

While the New Left was modest in its thinking and timid in proposals for radical change, the New Right was extreme in its proclamations. Its influence reached the highest level of government. Mercer was not a stranger to its excesses. After all, one of the most intemperate organizations of the Right, founded by Joseph Welch, was named for a Mercer alumnus, John Birch.

Birch was the quintessential fundamentalist Christian while at Mercer, being one of those who participated in the heresy charges against five teachers of religion in his senior year. He was a classmate of Thomas Holmes, later pastor of the Tattnall Square Baptist Church on the edge of the campus. Birch graduated from Mercer in 1939, attended the Bible Baptist Seminary in Fort Worth, a school operated by the Reverend J. Frank Norris. Norris is best remembered today for having killed a political opponent, and for being the fiery guardian of fundamentalist theology and foe of many mainline Baptist pastors and educators. John Birch went to China as a missionary for the World Fundamentalist Missionary Movement. During World War II he became an intelligence officer of the Office of Strategic Services and was credited with aiding General James Doolittle when the planes Doolittle commanded landed in China in 1942 after a raid over Tokyo. In an encounter with Chinese Communist soldiers ten days after the War ended, Birch was killed. Joseph Welch, calling John Birch the "first uniformed casualty of World War III," named his fanatical anticommunist organization the John Birch Society, giving the Mercer alumnus fame he never knew in life. Though he was never acclaimed as one of Mercer's favorite sons, the society that bore his name would exert considerable pressure against the admission of Sam Oni, a young man John Birch would have sought to convert had Oni been Chinese. The project to bring Oni to the school Birch attended was seen as a communist ploy by those who utilized Birch's name.

In a strange and ironic way John Birch brings to mind another name closely associated with Mercer University, and with warfare in China: Josiah Tattnall. There were three Tattnalls named Josiah, all of English aristocratic breeding, all important in the history of Georgia as a colony and state.

The first Josiah was a Loyalist and at the beginning of the Revolutionary War left the spacious estate of Bonaventure, the family home, and returned to England. The second Josiah, while only eighteen years old, joined the British Navy at his father's insistence. When the ship of his first voyage changed its destination from India to Port Royal, South Carolina the young sailor, loyal to his native Georgia, left the port and made it back to Georgia on foot. There he succeeded in war and politics, being both a Georgia governor and senator at a very young age. It was he who joined Colonel James Gunn, a man of egregious repute, in what amounted to mass slaughter of several hundred slaves at Abercorn Creek. Trained and armed by the British, the slaves had formed their own forti- fied community, living independently off the land. Still claiming to be soldiers of the king of England after the British evacuation of Savannah, they were said to be dangerous marauders and were seen as a grave threat to the area, as well as to the system of slavery. Gunn and Tattnall were dispatched to end the insurgency. When the Negroes saw the detachment of light infantrymen approaching, they made a hasty retreat into the swamps with the soldiers in firing pursuit. Most were killed, their makeshift houses burned, crops destroyed, and cattle confiscated.

Governor Tattnall's only son, Josiah III, was nine years old when his father died at thirty-eight. As an officer in both the Union and Con- federate navies, he saw action throughout the world. Although much of history has recorded him as having a distinguished military career, that appears unduly generous. While in the China area, despite America's alleged neutrality, he supported the French and British against China in the Second Opium War. On one occasion, when the French were facing certain defeat, Captain Tattnall, located above the French on the Yangtze River, opened fire, literally shooting the Chinese in the backs. Tattnall, while serving in the Confederate Navy as Captain of the Merrimac, destroyed his ship after the famed battle with the Monitor rather than let it fall into Union hands. Court-martialed but acquitted, he was assigned to command the defenses of the Savannah River. There he destroyed his entire fleet to prevent its capture.

Whether or not Tattnall's feats measure up to distinction, the once- elegant Tattnall Square in Macon, Georgia, as well as the Tattnall Square Baptist Church, carry on the Tattnall name. Fifty years after firing on the Chinese, their descendants, immigrants to Macon, Georgia, would be accepted in the Tattnall Square Church. Ninety-one years later an African Christian would be turned away.

Ninety-seven years after Tattnall's Chinese encounter, the Reverend Dr. Walter Moore, esteemed pastor of the Vineville Baptist Church in Macon, a graduate and trustee of Mercer, was appointed by the trustee board to head a special committee to study Mercer's racial policy and make recommendations as to whether they should be changed. As Moore turned to the task at hand, he soon met intractable foes. Organizations such as the John Birch Society, the White Citizens' Council, and others mounted a campaign of propaganda to hinder a favorable report. Moore soon realized that the assignment of his committee was not an effortless venture with a secure outcome. Yet he approached the task with resolve, rectitude, and obsession. His position was legible to all, but there is no evidence that he sought to impose his thinking upon the others.

Moore listed four items to be considered: the legal questions, accreditation, Christian ethics, and public relations. No one doubted that the chairman would have been pleased to discuss only the third item.

An advisory committee had been appointed by the Georgia Baptist Convention, ostensibly to assist Moore's committee. It was headed by the Reverend Dr. James W. Merritt, retired secretary-treasurer of the Georgia Baptist Convention. Although the committee included Lamar R. Plunkett, a man known for his sympathy for desegregaton at Mercer, his position did not prevail over the more cautious ministerial members and the committee proved to be a decided hindrance to Walter Moore's work. At a meeting of the Special Committee of the Board of Trustees on January 4, 1963, the Merritt committee said it was their consensus that no action be taken on the matter of changing admission policies at Mercer. They further advised that any future proposed plans be brought before the Georgia Baptist Convention in annual session.

The negative report of Dr. Merritt's committee was not the only reversal Walter Moore suffered that cold January day. Since they met in executive session and used coded initials for names, I find it impossible to say who said what. No effort is made to unscramble the code, and the initials here are not the same ones used in the official minutes. However, the minutes show that it was a meeting of caloric dimensions, at times resembling a political brawl.

> Mr. H. felt it was a matter for all Baptists of Georgia to decide. Mr. B. said it was the responsibility of the trustees as are all other matters affecting the university. Mr. A. injected the resolution of the Law School alumni. Mr. D. said they didn't speak for him and he was a lawyer. Mr. M. stated that the fourteenth amendment deals with the rights of individuals as citizens and not with social rights. Mr. E. feels they should do nothing to interfere with the unity of Georgia Baptists. Mr. J. was emphatically opposed to any kind of integration and cited the high criminal rate among Negroes. Mr. K. was impressed by Mr. J's feelings. Then Mr. F. addressed his brethren. Mr. F. stated that he is not worried over controversy so long as what we are doing is ethically and morally right. He does not feel that individuals should sacrifice their conscience for unity and he does feel that integration is the Christian thing to do. Mr. L. does not believe the climate is right and feels a

rising tide of resentment among Georgia Baptists. Mr. M. stated that he believes that judging a man by his color is wrong, and that should we decline to accept students solely because of race or color, Mercer University and the work of Baptists everywhere will be irrevocably harmed. Mr. L. stated simply that he does not think that now is the proper time to establish a policy admitting Negroes to the university.

There being no further business to come before the committee and following prayer by Mr. W., the meeting adjourned at 3:00 p.m.

So ended the minutes of the January 4, 1963 meeting of the special committee.

They had been there for three-and-a-half hours. Nine men, representing a kingdom founded almost 2,000 years earlier, deliberating nine years after nine other men, representing a domain younger than 200 years, with only its 1787 secular document to guide them, decided the matter for Caesar's realm.

Rufus Harris listened. Walter Moore presided. Neither man was through.

Back in his study after the joint meeting Walter Moore felt he had been drenched by a flood of indecency. In his personal notes he wrote:

The committee from the executive committee of the Georgia Baptist Convention came with a written statement they had prepared in a meeting prior to our meeting. It was a disappointment to me. They had asked for and received no information with reference to legal requirements, accreditation matters, or the experience of other Baptist schools.

They did not address themselves to the question of Christian ethics nor even nod toward the missionaries who with one voice are crying for Christian attitudes on the race question, many saying that if we do not change we may as well bring them home.

The one consideration was the effect on the Cooperative Program [the unified budget of Southern Baptists] and the fear of controversy in the convention.

They declared that the matter of the acceptance of Negro students at Mercer should not be considered at this time, and that at such time as it should be necessary it should be referred to the convention "for determination."

Their action seemed distressing to me. 1. They had not first heard our problem. 2. They had met [separately] to agree, so that none might speak in disagreement with others. 3. They had met without letting me know, indicating that I had nothing to contribute.

It seemed to me a cynical action, and hurt me deeply.

These were grievous words for so gentle a man as Walter Moore. But when he spoke of the minds of the missionaries, he knew whereof he spoke. He had served as a missionary in Cuba and was deeply involved in the entire foreign mission enterprise of Southern Baptists. In his notes he allowed that he was not so much concerned with the handful of pastors who had been driven from their pulpits by racists as with the thousands who raise the white flag and flee from the issue out of fear of some minor personal consequence.

Sitting alone in the late-night of his reverie, writing words intended for his eyes alone, the lonely shepherd penned:

> When the time comes that I cannot speak what I believe to be God's word to my day for fear of what the result may be to the offering plate, I'll step out of the pulpit and go to digging ditches or doing whatever it may take to keep body and soul together where I can keep my self-respect.

Then, as if in a moment of unquiet anger, indulging an emotion generally bridled, he lashed out at the most odious of all the excuses and rationalizations used by those determined to keep Negroes from entering the doors of Mercer University—the claim that Mercer belonged to the Georgia Baptist Convention and any change in policy should be referred to that body by ballot. One can hear his forlorn cry: "Mercer doesn't belong to Georgia Baptists! It belongs to the Lord!" Then finally to fitful sleep.

On April 18, 1963 Walter Moore's committee met again to make its final recommendation. Much had happened in the interim.

On December 20, 1962 Mr. John Mitchell, director of admissions, sent a letter to President Harris advising him that Sam Jerry Oni, of Takoradi, Ghana, had applied for admission to the Mercer College of Liberal Arts. The application procedure had begun in October and was completed on December 11.

Mr. Mitchell's letter was a long and heartfelt appeal for the admission of Mr. Oni.

"Mr. Oni is a Christian and a Baptist," he wrote. "He was converted to the Christian faith three years ago through the work of Southern Baptist missionaries."

The letter continued that Oni's parents were too poor to finance his education in secondary school and that "Mr. Harris Mobley [a Mercer alumnus], one of the Southern Baptist missionaries instrumental in Oni's conversion, helped secure enough financial support to enable him to finish secondary school. Much of this support came from Mr. Mobley's personal resources."

As to why the applicant wished to attend Mercer university Mr. Oni was quoted as replying, "I am so anxious to come to Mercer not only because it is a Christian institution, but it would afford me the opportunity of meeting many of the good people of the Southern Baptist Convention who have done so much for my own people."

Mr. Mitchell informed President Harris that, although Mr. Oni was introduced to Mercer by Missionary Harris Mobley, the application of Mr. Oni was unsolicited. Mr. Mitchell, as director of admissions, said that Mr. Oni was the most able international student to apply in recent years and that except for his color he would have been admitted without question:

> Mr. Oni was converted through the work of a young man who was graduated from our university. Would this young Christian understand that the doors of the university which prepared the missionary who brought the Gospel are closed to his converts? Indeed, he has a closer relationship to our university than the Negro of Macon, Georgia. He is one of our constituents.

A concluding lengthy paragraph of Mr. Mitchell's letter discussed the warning of the Woman's Missionary Union about the plight of foreign missionaries trying to explain a segregated system to dark-skinned people they sought to convert. He spoke of national interest: the need to influence emerging nations if they are to be loyal to American democracy and not Soviet communism. He pointed out that Mercer had three Japanese students, a Jordanian, an Arab Christian, and an Iranian in its student body, and a Korean teaching political science.

Rufus Harris included Mitchell's letter in full in his "President's Report to the Trustees."

It was a banner ace. For 120 years, foreign missions had been the raison d'etre of Southern Baptists. Consistently it was what brought in the largest offerings. Sunday schools, from cradle roll classes to aged adults, prayed for missionaries on the home and the foreign fields. I myself recall thinking the prayer object was one word, "homanforinfeels," wondering as a child precisely what I was praying for, yet uttering the words nightly with great fervor. I had been taught to pray for missionaries.

Many young boys and girls had nightmares from Sunday school pictures of missionaries in "the dark continent" suffering death in boiling cauldrons of oil by half-naked savages with bones in their noses and hoops in their ears. And many responded forgivingly by zealously placing their entire Christmas allowance in the Lottie Moon Christmas Offering for Foreign Missions. Unquestionably some of those young boys now sat as men to decide what to do with one of the converts who wanted to go to school with their children.

Surely the Reverend Walter Moore had such recollections as he entered the Administrative Conference Room of Mercer University on April 18, 1963. In a divine rage against the shame of religio-cultural polygamy he did not call upon another to open the meeting with prayer but did the praying himself. But he did not use his prayer as a lecture to persuade. Asking only for heavenly guidance he turned to the business at hand.

After a brief statement Chairman Moore suggested that the committee had five options. They could recommend that only the Ghana student be accepted. (He had previously read a letter from Dean Oliver Littlejohn of the College of Pharmacy stating that he had an application from a Negro student at Morehouse College. The Southern College of Pharmacy, while a Mercer school, was in Atlanta and this news did not arouse the passions that admitting Negroes to the College of Liberal Arts in Macon did. Nevertheless, to admit the pharmacy student was a second option.) Third, they could recommend that the Law School be integrated. They could recommend any combination of those three or they could recommend the dropping of all racial barriers throughout the institution.

There had been considerable support to admit Mr. Oni as a foreign student, on the same basis as other foreign students were admitted, thus not acknowledging that a Negro was afforded entrance to Mercer's halls of ivy. John J. Hurt, editor of the state Baptist paper, the *Christian Index*, had advocated such a policy editorially and had received sizable agreement.

It was clear that the chairman preferred the last alternative: the dropping of all barriers. The Reverend Dr. Moore had not been idle since the January meeting and felt that he had the votes for it. But as the meeting progressed he sensed defections. Two members were absent. Many of the same heated arguments that had been stated on 4 January were resurfacing. His advantage was that they had agreed to give their report to the board of trustees that day. The trustees would begin their meeting at eleven o'clock. That hour was near. Still he let the debate go forward. If he could not succeed in eliciting a recommendation to drop all barriers, he felt sure he had the votes, with the backing of Hurt's editorial, to admit Oni as a foreign student. At least there would be that crack in the parapet of bigotry, precursor of a day when what he saw as spiritual concubinage would abate.

Forty minutes had gone by and there was no meeting of minds. Finally, without prologue, Mr. G. Van Greene arose and faced the committee. "I move the following: The Committee recommends to the board of trustees at their meeting today, April 18, 1963, that Mercer University consider applicants for admission based on qualifications, without regard to race, color of skin, creed, or place of origin."

Mr. C. C. Giddens seconded the motion. The question was called and the vote taken. By voice vote Mr. Greene's motion carried. Five affirmative. Two negative.

It was not the unanimous victory Chairman Moore wanted. After brief discussion Mr. Claude Christopher moved that the above action be amended to accept the applicant from Ghana as a foreign student and remove all racial barriers to the graduate, pharmacy, and law schools of the university but not the College of Liberal Arts, historically the backbone of the university. This motion was seconded by Judge Eberhardt and failed to pass on a vote of two to five.

It was five minutes till eleven. Mr. Haywood, secretary of the corporation of the University, left the room immediately to inform President Harris. Walter Moore wept softly, tarrying behind while the others walked to the Economics Building where the rest of the trustees waited in the Faculty-Trustee Room.

❐

Chapter 6

In their own bailiwick . . .

In the spring of 1958 two students, Marty Layfield and Beverly Bates, took a leave of absence from Mercer University to debate students in Northern colleges on the issue of racial segregation. While describing themselves as "Southern liberals" they took the affirmative side of the topic "Resolved: That Racial Segregation in the South Should Be Maintained." Attracting coverage from *Time* magazine and numerous newspapers, they took their arguments to Princeton, Brandeis, Williams, and even the historically black Lincoln University in Pennsylvania. Back from their tour of thirteen appearances, they told a Mercer chapel audience that "[Northerners] are not extreme about how fast we are going to see acceptance of colored people in the South. But they are extreme in wanting to see some progress."

They warned their fellow students, and the administration and faculty as well, that "If we don't take the responsibility for the problem, then we will have other people taking it for us."

That statement alone was enough in 1959 to justify their self-claimed label of "Southern liberals," for the prevailing political climate in Georgia was still "Never in a thousand years!"

Response to the young forensic scholars' warning was mixed among the students. As was often the case at compulsory chapel attendance, many were reading the morning paper, preparing for the next class or dozing, and didn't even hear what the two debaters said. Some ridiculed them, joking that Mayfield and Bates had taken the affirmative up north and the negative down south. Others pointed to an article in the *Mercer Cluster* of that week, on the same page as the report of Bates's and Layfield's journey, that proved race relations in the South were already superior to what could be found in other sections of the country. It was a long story headlined: "Negro Janitor's Portrait Is Presented: Newton Speaks."

Lee Battle had been a janitor at Mercer for forty years. When he died in 1939 his body lay in state in Mercer's Willingham Chapel, an honor generally reserved for university presidents. Now, twenty years after his death and still remembered, a portrait would hang in the Student Center. Dr. Louie Newton, Mercer graduate, friend and mentor of Rufus Harris, pastor of the prestigious Druid Hills Baptist Church of Atlanta and former president of the Southern Baptist Convention, had spoken at a service near Forsyth when a monument was erected at Battle's grave. The ceremony was broadcast nationwide on radio. The *Mercer Cluster* reported that Dr. Newton was returning for the presentation of the portrait.

Lee Battle was, indeed, a favorite among students. While sweeping walkways or emptying trash cans he would attract students for an impromptu lecture on campus deportment. They would cheer him, shout "Amen," pat him on the head, and move along, leaving the grinning janitor to his chores. An avid Mercer sports fan, he gave pregame pep talks to the team and led cheers during the games. He accompanied the football team when they played Army and Navy.

The *Mercer Cluster* said, "The portrait depicts Battle in his customary attire of white cap and apron and with his brush broom, delivering one of his spontaneous speeches on the campus."

For the reader unfamiliar with collegiate life in the South of 1939, beloved in whatever fashion, Lee Battle was the college mascot. But in 1958, the bountiful and flowery oratory of Louie Newton about the integrity, sincerity, and fidelity of Lee Battle, at the presentation of a "portrait of a real Mercerian and of a Christian gentleman," was enough to deflect the judgment of Marty Layfield and Beverly Bates that all was not right with the Southern system.

Nor was their warning that "If we don't take the responsibility for the problem, then we will have other people taking it for us" heeded by Mercer or Georgia Baptists for another four years. It was only when the inevitability of their prophecy was within view that the Georgia Baptist Convention had race on its agenda at all.

On October 18, 1962 the board of trustees and the president's council of the corporation of Mercer University met. It was a gathering that would set in motion what President Harris had wanted done since he arrived two years earlier from Tulane University: the process of accepting students without regard to race.

President Harris had sent his semiannual "President's Report" to all trustees one week in advance of the meeting, long enough for them to know what to expect but not long enough for rumors to spread and a campaign of opposition to be mounted.

The matter of changing admission policies was not hinted at until there had been fifty-eight pages of details on the affairs of the university.

But a preliminary storm had already blown over Macon following an article that appeared in the *Atlanta Journal* on July 23, 1962, written by Walter Rugaber, a state correspondent. With a Macon byline and a headline reading "Mercer's Head Okays Negroes," the long story reported that President Harris said he favored the admission of Negroes to the 129-year-old institution. It quoted Harris as saying he would "support integration before the trustees," and that as far as he was concerned "their decision will be final."

Since Mercer is owned by the Georgia Baptist Convention, that statement alone would infuriate many Baptists who defend their ownership of Mercer University with considerable zeal. Nor would they look with much favor on Dr. Harris's statement that if the convention disagreed with the trustees' decision to integrate it would have to move on its own to reverse the integration move. The article was sure to create the upscuddle that followed.

For the article to appear in an Atlanta newspaper instead of in Macon was not without design on the part of President Harris. He was given to the most precise strategy. Following the April meeting that authorized a special committee of the trustees to study the matter of desegregating the university, and knowing full well what the final outcome would be, he took remarkable care to prepare rank-and-file alumni and Georgia Baptists for the admission of Negroes to Mercer. He was a close friend of Ralph McGill, publisher of the *Atlanta Constitution* and the *Atlanta Journal.* By then McGill, because of his moderate racial views, was exceedingly unpopular among the bitter-enders. (As an intended insult to McGill his enemies had dubbed him "Rastus" McGill. Instead of chafing at the slur, McGill appropriated it to his own benefit. He named his dog "Rastus" and taught the dog to bark into the telephone. When a hate caller asked to speak to "Rastus" McGill he would say, "I'll get him," then promptly put the phone to the mouth of the barking dog. It is said the calls ceased.)

President Harris knew a public endorsement from Ralph McGill would do Mercer's cause no good. However, Harris valued the counsel of his foxy and legendary friend.

William Haywood recalls an occasion during the summer of 1962 when McGill visited Dr. Harris at the president's residence. It appeared to be no more than an afternoon of socializing on the front porch.

Harris and McGill discussed little except skillful management of the desegregation affair. Haywood took careful notes on their strategizing.

President Harris felt that if the story first appeared in the local press it would attract little attention beyond the Macon area. Rumors, half-truths and falsehoods would filter throughout the state. If the story was carried in the Atlanta paper, with a statewide circulation, everyone would get the same news at the same time. Because McGill, in the minds of most, was more closely associated with the *Constitution*, it was decided to break the story in the *Journal*. Also, Macon was covered by Rugaber, a well-respected journalist for the *Journal*. McGill could have the *Journal* assign Rugaber to interview Harris.

When William Ott, editor of the *Macon Telegraph*, censured President Harris for not first giving a story of such local import to his paper, Harris could truthfully reply that he had not sought the interview with Rugaber and had in the past and would in the future grant an interview to a *Telegraph* reporter or anyone else.

Complicating the exchange was a minor altercation between Harris and a *Telegraph* reporter, Miss Lisa Hardie, in which Dr. Harris thought his position was not reported accurately. His reply to the *Telegraph*, following Ott's letter of chastisement illustrates the uncanny knack Rufus Harris had for combining his Southern gentility, flattery, and feigned innocence and naivete to wield the rapier with exactness:

Dear Bill:

I have your letter of August 10, 1962. I regret that you are "keenly disappointed" about the article which appeared in the *Atlanta Journal* last month. The purpose of this letter is to set the record straight on several points. I did not "choose" the Atlanta paper, as your letter states. Mr Rugaber for a period of three weeks actively sought this interview with me. When he came to my office, I responded to his questions as honestly as I knew how, as I always do in any situation. Any reporter from any newspaper requesting such an interview would have been granted one, and would have received exactly the same answers as did Mr. Rugaber.

It just happened that he represented the *Atlanta Journal*. I never sought the interview.

In this connection, I remember most pleasantly Miss Hardie's visit to my office several months ago. She called seeking an interview, to which I gladly agreed, and when she came to my office we talked at length about various University matters. Your statement about "her version of attempts to develop several stories at Mercer and of delays that have occurred" puzzles me because I am not aware that there have been any such delays. There have been no such occurrences known to me.

Your statement that the story which appeared in the *Atlanta Journal* "was of major importance" is surprising to me. Indeed I saw nothing in the least sensational about it, since it did not contain anything which I have not formerly said over and over again. You know of my great admiration for Macon newspapers and their leadership, and I feel sure you know that Mercer University would not release to any other newspaper any story which I considered "significant."

My letter of July 30, 1962, to Miss Hardie was written solely to clarify one item of information contained in her article which appeared in the *Macon Telegraph* on July 24, 1962. I have long been accustomed not to bother over reporters missing the point. I respect them so much that my feeling is to wonder, with all they have to put up with, how they do so well. But in this case it was obvious that Miss Hardie's sole purpose was to make herself look good, of which I took a dim view, under the circumstances.

All of this is said, as stated above, merely to set the record straight. I have proclaimed my admiration of the Macon newspapers, which I have earnestly come to respect since I returned to Georgia. I cannot adequately express to you my deep appreciation of the excellent treatment accorded news releases from Mercer University. I am, I hope, a person of extremely good will, and assure you that I speak for the University when I offer our complete cooperation in your effort to present the news fairly and objectively.

> Yours very truly,
> *Rufus C. Harris*

At the October meeting of the trustees President Harris felt it necessary to defend his action with the press. It was more defensive than was his practice. The *Atlanta Journal* article had drawn widespread criticism from around the state, something he surely must have anticipated and must have done deliberately to begin clearing the air. Now he used the exchange once more to let his personal views be known to the trustees.

Then in one brief paragraph of his report he made his pitch:

> It is my opinion that the chairman of the executive committee, Mr. Heard, should appoint a committee of five trustees to study this matter of Negro eligibility for admission and report its conclusion and recommendations at the next regular meeting of this board in January 1963.

That was all the "President's Report" said directly. But without relating the two, the next item in the lengthy document was entitled: "Ford Foundation Announcement." In two sentences it was reported that the Ford Foundation had recently handed out $74 million to fourteen small schools to help raise their academic standards and had another $50 million ready to go. The grants were going to schools that admitted students "without regard to race, religion, or creed." No trustee could miss the delicate message.

There followed immediately long passages on student conduct, lines of authority, fraternity and sorority rights, health services, athletic events, and the Student Government Association.

Twenty pages later, without relating it to his earlier recommendation, the "President's Report" listed those schools that had recently desegregated. Vanderbilt, Duke, Davidson, Rice, and Sewanee were among the private and denominational institutions mentioned. The president added, "While I would prefer to consider the issue from the point of view of moral and educational standards, it seems clear that financial considerations are also relevant." That gathering of men and women acquainted with the world of capital needed no translation.

The "President's Report" was seventy-eight pages long—enough tedious business decisions to mildew the most lissome boardroom, all to be done in one morning meeting. The most momentous piece of all was contained in one brief paragraph. But the die was cast. It was not the style of Rufus C. Harris to argue a board into the right, but to assiduously steer, sometimes the steerage seeming no more than listless and innocent sauntering, sometimes bordering on deviousness, leading with the voice of doves.

His recommendation that a special committee be appointed to study racial desegregation was passed unanimously. The president, acting in his capacity as trustee, made the motion himself. At the luncheon that followed the trustee meeting, President Harris, acting for Chairman Heard, announced the members. The Reverend Walter Moore, pastor of the Vineville Baptist Church of Macon and a former foreign missionary, was appointed chairman. Others were Mr. Claude Christopher, Judge Homer Eberhardt, Mr. C. C. Giddens, Mr. G. Van Greene, Mr. B. A. Lancaster, Mr. T. Baldwin Martin, Mr. C. O. Smith, and Mr. J. W. Timmerman. Instead of the five members the president had recommended, there would be nine.

President Harris described the significance and difficulty of his maneuver in a letter to his friend Nathan Pusey, president of Harvard University. Addressing the Harvard president as "Nate," Harris's letter was an almost toadying bid for understanding of so modest a process. After greetings and pleasantries, and telling his colleague what he planned to attempt, Dr. Harris wrote:

> Geographically, Macon is located in line with Montgomery, Alabama, and Jackson, Mississippi, which means it is in the center of the "segregation belt." Altanta, though likewise situated in the Deep South, has a tremendous infiltration of people from other areas composing the industrial buildup there. Likewise, Florida has this infiltration of people from the North which has served to dilute, so to speak, the traditional feeling there. The border states have had it relatively easy for several reasons.
>
> Macon, on the other hand, has had practically no adequate preparation nor infiltration of outsiders to aid in paving the way for the decision. Moreover, the decision of the Mercer trustees was not pushed on them by the compulsions of the policies of the federal government. . . . In my opinion, therefore, it is a much more important and significant step than has been the case in many other places.
>
> I need your help, please, to have this significant step by Mercer understood wherever you may have an opportunity to do so. I would be very grateful if you could do this.

This letter goes far in explaining the zeal of President Harris in taking the risks he took, beyond his oft-stated reasons of it being legally mandated and morally imperative. President Harris was a proud man, with established credentials as an educator behind him. He had a doctor's degree from Yale University, and he had mingled and lived for years with the carriage trade of New Orleans and they had made him their King of Rex. He had presided over that city's finest university. He had traveled extensively in Europe and had represented American higher education in the highest councils around the world. He would not be patronized by his colleagues of the academy as the head of some Podunk denominational school down South ruled by woolhat bigots, nor be embarrassed by a recalcitrant constituency.

In November 1962 the Georgia Baptist Convention met in annual session at the Mabel White Baptist Church in Macon, not far from the Mercer campus. Since the trustee meeting in October, rampant rumors had it that a vote on the desegregation of Mercer would be on the agenda.

Adding to the furor was the knowledge that President Rufus Harris, who had been installed two years earlier, favored changing admission policies. Messengers—the Southern Baptist name for delegates—who would otherwise have stayed in their fields or shops crowded into the church sanctuary in record numbers, a majority of the almost 2,000 prepared to cast a negative vote. The racial issue was the dominant topic in lobby conversations. A small airplane, visible to everyone entering the building, circled overhead towing a streamer: "Keep Mercer Segregated."

The crowd grew quiet and more tense on the second day as the time for the various committees to make their reports grew near. The Reverend James W. Waters, pastor of the host church, Mercer graduate and later a trustee, and a passionate segregationist, worked the crowd.

Instead of allowing open discussion of the issue, the executive committee reported that a five-man group would be named to "counsel" with the trustees. Seventy-five-year-old Dr. James W. Merritt, former pastor of the First Baptist Church of Gainesville and treasurer of the Georgia Baptist Convention, would head the group. Then the issue was avoided completely when the convention accepted without debate a report from the resolutions committee saying: "We believe it unwise for this convention to take further action before these groups have completed their work."

The Machiavellian maneuver had worked; it was church politics at its best. One stance of Southern culture has long been oriental—reverence for its elders. Few would challenge the venerable Dr. Merritt. They also knew what the "counsel" to the trustees would be: "The time is not quite right." A serious split in the ranks had been avoided by the adoption without debate of the resolutions committee report. The forbidden fruit was left untouched.

Back at Mercer, President Harris sat in stoical approval of what most saw as a personal defeat for him. Although the issue of race had been defused, a closely related matter had erupted in a two-hour debate on the floor. Mercer University was in the process of borrowing $8.5 million from the federal government. Opponents, publicly reminding the messengers of the historic Baptist principle of separation of church and state, but privately knowing the use to which Harris and the trustees could later make of it, sought vehemently to defeat it. They lost. The god of Mammon prevailed and Rufus Harris was pleased.

The argument that the Brown decision did not apply to "private" institutions was now dead. Any institution surviving on federal funds was a public one, bound by the law of the land. Those of the law who opposed Harris would be defeated in their own bailiwick. It was now in the moral and ethical arena, the domain of the preachers, exactly where Rufus Harris wanted it. He was prepared to meet them there as well. Thirty years as a Baptist deacon had not left the crafty barrister unacquainted with the tree of Calvary. The Convention sermon had warned against "dealing with issues that are not vital." The preacher declared that "missions and evangelism are the fundamental notes for Baptists." Rufus Harris would test the preacher's understanding of missions and evangelism.

So the battle lines were drawn. A spring freshet on the Flint River would pale as a schoolyard scuffle compared to the broadsides that would be directed at Walter Moore and Rufus Harris during the next six months.

□

Chapter 7

Protest and be damned . . .

Daily stacks of mail arrived for Rufus Harris and Walter Moore, chairman of the special committee. Opposition was generally from college-educated people. It came from lawyers, doctors, ministers, business leaders. Only a small number of those opposing plans to desegregate were women, whereas women writing to commend the move far outnumbered men. Trustees and former trustees were prominent among both supporters and opponents. However, by the time the special committee reported and the board of trustees voted, those opposing the change were in a decided minority.

Rufus Harris was first of all a lawyer. Most of his years as an educator were spent in that arena, first as dean of the Mercer Law School and then as law dean at Tulane. Doubtless he would have signed a treaty with the bar members, many of whom had come up under his tutelage, to escape their censure. It was not to be. The most caviling words seemed to flow from their pens. While not suggesting that barristers would toady to their pontiffs it is worth noting that Judge Carlton Mobley, a justice of the Georgia Supreme Court and a prominent member of the Mercer board of trustees, was among the most unbending critics of Harris's position. Many letters from the pen of attorneys showed copies being sent to Judge Mobley.

A handwritten note from Attorney Louis L. Brown of Fort Valley stated that he regretted not seeing Dr. Harris at the "recent Phi Beta Kappa in Macon." Mr. Brown enclosed a twenty-four-page document entitled "Oxford: A Warning for Americans," published by the Mississippi Junior Chamber of Commerce. The paper argued the illegality of James Meredith's admission to the University of Mississippi by the Supreme Court and the legal rightness of Governor Barnett's defiance.

What must have been a disappointing and painful exchange was one between J. Douglas Carlisle and President Harris. Carlisle was one of Macon's best-known lawyers, a longtime law partner of Judge W. A. Bootle, a graduate and sometime trustee of Mercer, and a friend.

Addressing him as "Chunk," apparently a nickname from their college days, Mr. Carlisle, after referring to "your friend, Ralph McGill," asked:

> If it is not a secret, do you mind telling me about any membership you have had, or now have, in NAACP, CORE, COPE, or any of their fellow traveling groups. I don't recall for the moment the name of the group in which Martin Luther King is active but wish to include that in my inquiry.

Harris replied with a bit of humor:

> I am reminded of the old Maine story where two old friends from Bangor met after a long separation. Jonathan asked of Eben after the greeting: "Well, Ebe, how are you feeling?" Ebe replied, "It's none of your durn business, and if you were not my best friend I would not tell you that much!"

Harris concluded his letter on a more serious note.

> You correctly mention my warm regard for Ralph McGill. We have been friends for a quarter of a century or more, which I have greatly appreciated.

Carlisle's next letter was a stinging indictment of Mercer's plan to accept Negro students, employing legal and sociological arguments. He concluded the long letter by saying, "Chunk, I am distressed that you have turned out to be like you are and I wish I knew—how I wish I knew—how to help you. And Mercer."

President Harris sent a friendly response, closing by saying that if Carlisle wanted to help him, "Maybe you should pray more for me."

The letter that seemed to get the most attention and draw the most serious and sustained response was one from Robert L. Steed of the prestigious King & Spalding law firm of Atlanta. One of the reasons might have been that Steed was already, though quite young, one of Mercer's most celebrated alumni. As an undergraduate he had been editor of the *Mercer Cluster* in 1956–1957, following such journalistic giants as Jack Tarver, Bert Struby, and Reg Murphy. While a student in the Walter F. George School of Law, from which he graduated cum laude in 1961, Steed was editor of the *Mercer Law Review*.

Another thing that attracted many people to Steed's position on any issue was his reputation for his *Cluster* column, "Willard Clutchmyer." Steed, as Clutchmyer, was as funny and perceptive as Mark Twain and as caustic as H. L. Mencken. To the brilliant iconoclast, nothing was sacred. Not the Georgia Baptist Convention, pietistic ministerial students, compulsory chapel, women deans, faculty, such prohibitions as campus dancing . . . nothing, including Bob Steed, escaped Clutchmyer's scathing satire. Because most iconoclasts are considered "liberal" on every issue, many were surprised that in this case Steed/Clutchmyer appeared in the canton of conservatism.

Steed's July 25, 1962, letter to President Rufus Harris, following the Rugaber article in the *Atlanta Journal*, as well as Harris's reply, was circulated to all members of the trustees, the president's council, and officers of the university. That might also account for the widespread attention it drew.

When interviewed in his Atlanta office, Mr. Steed said that his opposition to the desegregation plan did not have to do with race but with the matter of procedure. His law firm, and Mr. Steed personally, were in the forefront in the recruitment of minority lawyers, supporting his claim. In addition, when he became a Mercer trustee in the late 1960s his maiden speech was in defense of the activities of Mercer's student activists, a matter of grave concern to several prominent members of the board.

Whatever his differences with President Harris, the trustees, and Mercer, they must have been short-lived. Over the years Mr. Steed has been one of the university's most loyal friends, serving actively on the board of trustees, more than one term as chairman.

A major part of Mr. Steed's letter and of President Harris's reply of July 31 are presented here because the two together succinctly demonstrate the emotional intensity of the times, the various aspects of the controversy, and the style of two lawyers' clash which nonlawyers seem to enjoy watching.

Subsequent developments suggest the manner in which two people dedicated to the same institution adjust to change and walk on in tandem. Robert Steed and Rufus Harris are two of the most distinguished players in all of Mercer's history.

It should be noted that Mr. Steed was responding to Walter Rugaber's account of President Harris's position that appeared in the *Atlanta Journal*. This was stated in the early paragraphs of his letter in which he pointed out his strenuous objection to the manner in which the matter was handled. Steed continued:

> It would seem that a contemplated program which so obviously amounts to a radical departure from 129 years of policy and tradition would be taken under advisement with the trustees and alumni and with

the Georgia Baptist Convention rather than presented to them and to the public as a virtual fait accompli.

In other words, while I hope the trustees will never permit the integration of Mercer, I feel that the announcement itself has done irreparable harm to the University and has permanently damaged the public image of the school and its alumni in the eyes of a great majority of the people living in this state. For this reason I feel the press release was ill-timed and unfortunate.

Secondly, I object to the program itself. It is, I believe, hostile to the views of the alumni of Mercer, hostile to the churches belonging to the Georgia Baptist Convention, and a gross affront to the vast majority of the people of this state whose thoughts on the question have been made clear by their eight-year struggle in opposition to an involuntary imposition of a condition which you urge for Mercer on a voluntary basis.

While many of us watched in dismay as public schools and universities were forced, some at point of arms, to integrate, we were secure in the knowledge that our University would never be the object of such coercion. Now that which we thought so secure is being supinely surrendered with apparent disregard and indifference to the thoughts of what surely must be a substantial number of alumni.

Mr. Steed's letter went on to point out, correctly, that none of the churches that were supporting Mercer had an integrated membership. He continued:

It is hard however to find justification for the integration of Mercer's student body. In my view the administration of Mercer should concern itself solely with the quality of education offered there and, while integration might give some comfort to those members of the faculty and administration who, because of our conservative policy, feel less sophisticated than their fellows at Emory and Agnes Scott, it will not improve the quality of education at Mercer.

The problem of school integration is sociological and political rather than academic and it is my feeling that no possible good, from an academic or any other standpoint, can come of this proposal.

They were strong words. If one accepted, then or now, Mr. Steed's premise that it is the status quo of the academy, in this case Mercer University, that is preeminent, one would have to concede his argument.

Rufus Harris, however, did not concede. Lawyers seldom do. Instead he chipped away at Steed's allegations regarding Harris's position. He cleverly parlayed each point against the next, carefully pitting what he

actually said against Mr. Steed's understanding from the Rugaber news
article.

Then Harris, counsel for the defense, met the prosecuting attorney on
common ground—the law.

> It seems obvious that I do not think as you do about the Supreme
> Court's decision. The reason I personally favor admitting qualified
> Negroes if they apply is because I believe the law requires it of us,
> since the decision outlawing segregation. Some argue that the Court was
> wrong. Maybe it was, but until the decision is changed it is the law of
> the land, in my view. It being the law, I do not wish to be defiant, nor
> do I wish to be an anarchist. It is true that the decision applied directly
> to public institutions, not to private ones. But what are the private ones?

Harris did not answer his own question, knowing that his opponent
knew the answer as well as he. Both knew that an institution operating
programs such as ROTC with federal funds, accepting scholarship grants
and huge loans, which Mercer had recently done, for construction of new
buildings, accepting police and fire protection, and operating with the
guardianship of a tax-exempt charter, could hardly claim to be private
and above and outside the law. Instead of dealing with his question he
adroitly shifted gears and addressed a matter not mentioned by his adversary, as if in summary before a jury and about to rest his case. What of
morality?

> Moreover, as a Christian, there is with me a matter of conscience
> involved in the obvious lack of Christian amity in the indignity of an
> educational color line. That very simply is the way I think about it.

Mr. Steed had said that he was sending his letter to the Mercer
trustees, something President Harris had probably preferred he hadn't
done. He would try subtly to outdo Steed there. He would send copies of
the exchange to Steed's colleagues at King & Spalding. He concluded his
letter by saying:

> I noted your decision to send copies of your letter to the Mercer
> trustees. I feel sure they are interested in the expression of your views.
> I shall send to them, consequently, and to others at the Trust Company
> Building copies of both your letter and my reply.

The following day, August 1, 1962, Mr. Steed sent a brief but conciliatory letter to President Harris in which he accepted the offer to meet,
at his convenience, sure that an exchange of opinions would be benefi-

cial. Mr. Steed stated that he was in law school during the early part of President Harris's administration and was the beneficiary of many of the significant improvements he had made. Mr. Steed also said that he felt remiss in not having conveyed his approval of most of the changes and regretted that his first communication was negative in tone.

The exchange incited an imbroglio of significant proportion. Van Greene, trustee and businessman of Decatur, lashed out in conspicuous anger:

> [H]ow could you possibly answer his [Harris's] letter of July 31 with your letter of August 1 without beginning it with an apology for accusing him of saying things which he did not say?
>
> . . . We trustees will handle the matter of deciding whether or not to admit negroes when the proper time comes to make a decision. In the meantime I should like to hear from you now as to how you justify answering a letter calling your hand with what you lawyers call evidence, and in writing at that, and you answering the letter without making any reference to the matter. Why no apology? Why?
>
> Looking forward to hearing from you on just this one matter, without launching into a discussion of any other matter, . . .

Walter Moore, chairman of the special committee answered Mr. Steed in a much more conciliatory fashion, yet gave no ground at the end. Stinging under Steed's reference to Emory and Agnes Scott, Reverend Moore concluded his letter with a testy rejoinder:

> I should add that there are many of us who have no interest in feeling "sophisticated," and who consider ourselves to be conservative, loyal Georgia Baptists, and Bible-believing Christians. who believe that it will not hurt Mercer in any way to try to give quality Christian education to the small number of qualified Negroes who may wish to come to us and who can become leaders of their own people at a time when they need the wisest and best leadership possible.

A further setback for President Harris from his colleagues of law was a resolution passed by the Alumni Association of the Walter F. George School of Law. Dated November 2, 1962 it read in part:

> BE IT RESOLVED, we do register our objection to the integration of the educational facilities of Mercer University, it being the feeling that to so act would be contrary to the best interest of the University and student body.

> We do not propose to burden those assembled with arguments in behalf of this resolution, but we do call attention to the many intelligent, logical, and uncontroverted arguments supporting our stand.

The resolution was signed by Malone Sharpe, Lee Grogan, Robert L. Steed, and Robert Barfield.

One week earlier, one of the signers, Robert E. Barfield, had written as an alumnus of Mercer University to Walter Moore, chairman of the special committee, protesting. Among other things Attorney Barfield wrote:

> Please accept this as the strongest possible protest to this proposed race mixing.
>
> I have been given to understand that Dr. Harris has convinced a number of the members of the board of trustees that Mercer is compelled to accept negro students by recent decisions of the federal courts. As a lawyer it is my legal opinion that there is nothing in the decisions rendered up to this time which would require a private institution such as Mercer to accept anyone they did not consider desirable.

By late summer 1962 there appears to have been a full-scale campaign by Georgia lawyers against President Harris and his plan. Milton Harrison of Atlanta wrote, "It is my considered opinion that quite enough encouragement towards events which cause racial strife is being supplied by President John F. Kennedy, Dr. Martin Luther King, Jr., and many others whom you know." While expressing admiration for Dr. Harris making public his viewpoints, Mr. Harrison added that he felt "certain your comments have alienated many of Mercer's friends and supporters and, also, I doubt seriously that the NAACP or any similar group will contribute anything of value to Mercer in the foreseeable future." Again, a copy was shown to Honorable Carlton Mobley, justice of the Supreme Court of Georgia.

There was not, however, a solid front of opposition by Mercer law graduates. There came an immediate disclaimer from Attorney Daniel E. C. Boone, Jr. of Tifton, Georgia, stating that he had opposed the resolution of the Law School Alumni Association and that it did not speak for him. He offered his full support on the matter of desegregating the University.

Tommy Holland, who had graduated from Mercer's law school a few months earlier, discussed the several practical arguments for the admission of Sam Oni, then dismissed them as of no account in the face of

Christian sensibilities. For Mr. Holland, it was morality that argued for integration.

Likewise, B. Carl Buice of Gainesville noted that a Christian institution should be willing to follow the dictates of its faith even when it is not "practical" to do so. "For years the Southern Negro has been confined to something of an intellectual desert. It would seem that Mercer now has the opportunity to be his Samaritan, or the Pharisee who simply passes by on the other side." Apparently Mr. Harris liked the analogy for he used it often in subsequent correspondence.

Alumnus David Mincey, whose family ties with Mercer stretched back to the nineteenth century, also declined to participate in estimates of the Supreme Court's decision and instead quoted scripture to reprove the South for her bigoted ways, after first acknowledging his complicity in it all.

John A. Smith wrote from the small town of Talbotton. He claimed no right to speak except that he was on his way to Mercer in 1903 but got no farther than Athens. "I am a Baptist and as a Christian who believes we should convert the savages of Africa, if possible, I think our work there would be hurt not to admit this man."

In addition, there was Judge Bootle, who chose to remain aloof from trustee deliberations but whose position was well established. Attorney and trustee T. Baldwin Martin, while not always agreeing with some of Dr. Harris's public statements, remained resolute as a backstop of support. Justice Mobley was the chief dissenter.

Most of the letters were prefaced with staunch pledges of fidelity to the rebel stand. Not one person whose letter I have seen wanted to be identified as an integrationist. Yet in most cases their arguments for the admission of Negroes to Mercer brought into question their allegiance to Dixie.

Like the lawyers and their leagues, the preachers and their associations expressed their opinions in divers ways. Letters and resolutions of protest poured in soon after it was announced that a committee would be appointed to make recommendations to the board of trustees regarding Mercer's admission policies.

From the Reverend Kenneth Youmans, pastor of Sweetwater Baptist Church, Thomson, Georgia:

> Our church voted unanimously in Church Conference on November 14, 1962 to inform you, that we object to the possibility of intergration [*sic*]

at Mercer University. We are registering our disapproval with you and the others who are studying this problem.

George C. Gibson, who was awarded the Doctor of Divinity degree by Mercer in 1941, objected to the proposed study on the ground that it would hurt the program of giving to the church. His handwritten letter from Tifton included an interesting statement: "I for one, even as a Christian, am opposed to any integration of Mercer."

Many local congregations made their contention known through formal resolutions. Among them were the First Baptist Church of Bainbridge, Windsor Baptist Church of Savannah, Russellville Baptist Church of Forsyth, and Mt. Pisgah Baptist Church of Butler.

Others expressed their opposition through their judicatures or associations, generally composed of all Baptist churches in a given county. While some of the resolutions were in the style and grammar of the benighted of rural Georgia, integration often spelled as "intergration," one from the Mallary Association that met in Sylvester in October of 1962 showed no such deficiency:

WHEREAS the Board of Trustees of Mercer University through a committee of nine of its members is studying "the matter of admissions to the University without regard to race or color," and

WHEREAS the University has admitted students of the yellow race for many years making it evidently clear that the present study is to consider admitting as students to the University members of the Negro race, and

WHEREAS the harmonious relationship between the white and Negro races has been disturbed seriously in recent years because of self-seeking agitators and political opportunists, and

WHEREAS we believe the admission of Negro students to Mercer University will be precipitous of ill-will, misunderstanding, and sociological deterioration within the ranks of our Georgia Baptist life just as such have taken place in Washington, D.C., New York City, Chicago, Los Angeles, and other areas where integration has grown to fruition within the respective communities, and

WHEREAS no evident good for the races of mankind in spreading the Gospel of Christ, which was the foremost purpose of the Founding Fathers of Mercer University, can be accomplished by admitting Negroes to the University,

NOW THEREFORE BE IT RESOLVED by the Executive Committee of the Mallary Baptist Association:

1. That we deprecate the study of the Board of Trustees of
   Mercer University as portending serious consequences to the
   fellowship of Georgia Baptists.
2. That we call upon said Board of Trustees to desist from this
   unwise course of action.
3. That we call upon the Georgia Baptist Convention to join us
   in these resolutions.

BE IT FURTHER RESOLVED that copies of these resolutions be transmitted to
each member of the Board of Trustees of Mercer University and to the
officers and resolutions committee of the Georgia Baptist Convention.

In addition to a barrage of letters there was verbal cannonading.
Death threats and harassing, late-night calls became commonplace for
President and Mrs. Harris. When Amelia Barclay pointed out that as he
sat at his desk his back was exposed to a clear window, he dismissed it
with a flick of his hand. On November 22, 1963, Columbus Posey,
Mercer's registrar, came rushing down the stairs where he met Tom
Trimble, assistant dean of the College of Liberal Arts at the time and also
a teacher in the philosophy department. "The President's been shot,"
Posey exclaimed. Without meaning to be funny—unusual for Mr.
Trimble—he replied, "Which one?" He later reported that he would have
been less surprised if it had been President Harris rather than President
Kennedy who had been assassinated.

All communications addressed to President Harris were answered
promptly and with amenity. Occasionally he could not resist a response
of humor or subtle put-down. When a former trustee, president of Burgin
Manufacturing Company, a large producer of pine lumber—100,000 feet
daily capacity according to the letterhead—wrote as executive secretary
of the Friendship Baptist Association, regarding "our unanimous opposition to any further integration of Mercer University or any other Baptist
institutions in the State of Georgia," President Harris replied: "I hope you
will understand that [your resolution] puzzles me, since there has been no
integration of Mercer University, which I personally think is a mistake."

Rufus Harris's patience was not without limits. Once when a North
Georgia churchman wired him, "PROTEST JUDGE GUS BOOTLE ON MERCER
BOARD," he told his secretary to "Just wire him back, 'Protest and be
damned'." When be began receiving complaints about his use of foul
language to an alumnus he explained to the secretary that when he gave
such instructions she was supposed to hold it a day or so, then check to

see if that was still what he wanted to say, as was his practice when he was president of Tulane.

On another occasion when someone wrote to say his church was withholding its offering to the Cooperative Program, President Harris determined that Mercer's percentage of the withholding would amount to fifty-seven cents. He wrote that he was sorry for the action and was going to make up the loss to Mercer personally.

While it is easy for the sophisticates of today to assume the objection to racial integration came only from uneducated woolhats, that was not the case. It was Senator Walter F. George, an alumnus for whom the law school is named, who not many years earlier read into the *Congressional Record* the "Southern Manifesto," using language that today would be considered inflamatory. And it was the Reverend Dr. Montague Cook, a Mercer graduate who had been awarded the Doctor of Divinity degree twelve years earlier, who preached the widely distributed sermon series entitled "Racial Segregation Is Christian" at Trinity Baptist Church of Moultrie, the hometown of Columbus Posey. In the last of the sermons Dr. Cook addressed the president of his alma mater directly:

> Dr. Aderhold [president of the University of Georgia] and the University can be excused of fault in this sad situation, for the negro girl was at the University under Federal court order and not by invitation. Not so with Dr. Rufus Harris, President of Mercer University. He is under no court order forcing him to integrate Mercer. It is Dr. Harris's invitation against the advice of some of his trustees; against the advice of an Advisory Committee from the Executive Committee of the Georgia Baptist Convention. . . . Do you realize, Dr. Harris, that in opening the doors of Mercer to negro students you are setting up a social situation that experience shows leads to the amalgamation of the races?

But President Harris was by no means left comfortless by the Georgia clergy. Some churches and many pastors from around the state sent messages of support. Sometimes they were so modest they barely registered. Sometimes there was a faded timbre of Joshua's trumpet. Occasionally there could be heard the solemn procession around the rooted walls of segregation. Rufus Harris and Walter Moore dealt with each step as it came, never in doubt that the walls would crumble.

The First Baptist Church in the Old South town of Manchester, where Tom Holmes had been pastor twenty years earlier, led the way. After the WHEREASES regarding the missionary movement and Christian education the board of deacons resolved to encourage the admission of Sam Jerry

Oni. Even here, however, it was reckoned necessary to say, "While we cherish our Southern traditions and way of life we recognize that the greater allegiance belongs to Him who is our Maker and Redeemer."

Rufus Harris and Walter Moore would ask nothing further. They, too, were very much of the South.

Just east of Athens, where riots had broken out over the admission of two Negro students, is Winterville, a town with just a few more than 600 people. To name a Baptist church in Winterville as First Baptist would have been redundant. It was the Winterville Baptist Church. There the Spurgeon Coile Sunday School Class voted unanimously to commend Dr. Harris "on your stand to admit the Ghana student and all other Negroes who qualify to Mercer University." The signer of the letter identified the class as consisting of fourteen male members. This was the kind of endorsement Harris wanted—the little people, rural, small town, menfolk.

The applause of women had already been heard. When Miss Janice Singleton, executive secretary-treasurer of the Baptist Woman's Missionary Union of Georgia, wrote urging President Harris to hold to his conviction to accept the Ghana student, and all other qualified Negro applicants as well, he knew he had a potent ally. Though women were not allowed to be deacons or pastors in their churches, Rufus Harris was conscious of the sway they had when race was a factor. It was church women who had virtually stopped lynching in the South through their organization, the Association of Southern Women for the Prevention of Lynching. Standing as quiet onlookers in courtrooms, calling on Southern sheriffs and chiefs of police, wearing their sashes of solidarity, they monitored the system and let it be known that white women did not need their menfolk to protect them by torching and dismembering black males.

The men began to speak too. From Chickamauga: "Admit the man. To be Christian you can do nothing else."

Clayton, Thomson, Gainesville, Dexter, Monticello, Albany, Lindale, Bowdon, Lawrenceville, Dalton, Duluth, Sarepta Association. The little places. When letters and resolutions came from major cities they were generally from churches with names like Southside, Fifth Street, Capitol View.

The demographics were revealing. Someone was at work. Only the most careless researcher would assume that the outpouring was accidental. Although the sentiment was out there, someone was priming the pump. Who? It is a rare tree that puts forth its fruit without the prophecy of leaf or blossom. The thunder-winged spray of teachers like G. McLeod Bryan, Marguerite Woodruff, Das Kelly Barnett, Ray Brewster, and Joe Hendricks was forming a rainstorm. Most of the preachers writing favorable letters were of the classes of the 1950s. Those who had prepared the newground and dropped the seeds were waiting for manna to fall with the dew and encouraging it when they could.

Joseph M. Hendricks was then dean of men at Mercer. His position was not a very strong rung on the establishment ladder of command, but he knew the young preachers. All of them. And they knew him. One phone call from Dean Hendricks was often enough to prompt a nudge to the trustees. From his home on the Mercer campus or the family farm in Talbot County his pickup covered the state.

"Cap'm" was his sobriquet for President Harris, and "Cap'm" and Mercer were in trouble. Hendricks's devotion to both was immeasurable.

Driving up to a small-town Baptist parsonage and knocking, or standing in the dooryard of a country church, usually unannounced, he would engage in a few minutes of reminiscing. Then make his pitch. "Cap'm needs our help back on the yard." Without pleading the case for racial integration he would tell the recent graduates, "That same old crowd is trying to ruin us this time." The mention of "that same old crowd" brought back memories of petty rules, real and imagined, and other grievances. Often it was enough to prompt the young preacher to do battle with anyone seeking to stymie the new administration. If pressed to identify the "same old crowd" Hendricks would mumble the name of some well-known rapscallion, then hum, recite, or sing, always off-key, the chorus of Mercer's "Alma Mater":

> *Forward ever be thy watchword*
> *Conquer and prevail.*
> *Hail to thee, O Alma Mater!*
> *Mercer, Hail, all Hail!*

Then he would be off to the next town. He was not riding the backroads of Georgia to convert but to open the gates of morning.

But more than the lawyers and preachers had to be dealt with. Mercer had been founded in an era when its constituency *owned* black people. Now that same constituency was being asked to send their children to school with blacks. In its infancy Mercer had lost one out of eight of its alumni to federal swords and muskets. Now the heirs of the same alumni were being asked to bow the knee to federal court decrees. The most

Southern of the original colonies, stripped of all but pride by the ravages of war and reconstruction, was being called upon to swallow that.

The Anabaptist pacifist tradition, the persecution of English Baptists for nonconformity, and the inflexible separation of church and state championed by Roger Williams, who organized the first Baptist church in America, were unspoken memories. The Baptists of Georgia and Mercer had gone to Baal-peor and become like unto the things they detested. They were Southerners, Georgians, Confederates, and any appeal to what it had meant to be a Baptist in the seventeenth, eighteenth, even nineteenth centuries was lost to the undiluted fealty to the Lost Cause. That allegiance was reflected in the daily mail of Rufus Harris and Walter Moore.

These words from Augusta were typical:

> Why admit a Negro is my question. Why wreck the morale of the other students? Best yet, why not rid our Mercer of one Rufus C. Harris? I am sure that would do more good than anything else. Yes, they have tried to come into our church. Not for worship but to cause trouble. They have been refused and will continue to be refused.

The rank-and-file dissenters had two concerns: marriage of Negro males to white coeds and Russian Communism. The former was reinforced by the marriage of Charlayne Hunter, the Negro woman admitted to the University of Georgia by order of Judge Gus Bootle, to Walter Stovall, a white man whose brother-in-law would become a teacher at Mercer.

A postscript of irony is that after thirty years of desegregation at Mercer not one African-American male has married across racial lines. And, at least for now, Russian Communism is no more.

The hand of the Macon Citizens' Council, an organization formed soon after the Brown decision to short-circuit its implementation, was apparent in much of the mail opposing the admission of Sam Oni. The Council sent thousands of letters to every part of the state urging the recipients to talk with their ministers about writing to the trustees. "Demand your preacher or church to withhold funds from these integrated institutions or you will discontinue contributions to the church. Be firm, and by no means promote or support integration in any form as it is a sin and crime towards God and His teachings. Let's write today to save our churches, communities, and our country from Communist-inspired integration."

A number of alumni wrote that they had changed their will when Mercer was included. Robert S. Roddenbery, Sr., who identified himself at ninety-five as Mercer's oldest alumnus, sent a well-worded and long letter of vehement protest, returning his pledge card. Three of his brothers, his son, his grandson, four nephews, and two great-nephews were Mercerians. To suggest that they were not of plebeian stock Mr. Roddenbery added, "All the above paid their own way at Mercer; none was the recipient of any subsidy."

Mr. Roddenbery might have been the oldest alumnus but there was correspondence from an earlier class. Mr. George Pinckney Shingler sent a warm letter of praise for Rufus Harris and his plan for admitting applicants on the basis of merit alone. Mr. Shingler compared the battle President Harris was fighting over race with his own confrontation with the antievolutionists fifty years earlier. A chemist, Mason, and Episcopalian, Mr. Shingler had graduated from Mercer in 1900.

Strong messages of resistance came from the heads of Willingham Cotton Mills, McNair Building Supplies, and other leading industries. Some members of the trustee board did not wait for a report of the special committee before voicing their own opposition. A former national president of the alumni association, Dr. John M. Martin, communicated with Walter Moore, President Harris, and the trustee chairman, stating that he would do no more for Mercer University if Oni should be admitted. It would be a rare administrator, charged with the solvency of a privately funded institution, who would not take such advisement to heart. But it seems doubtful that President Harris took another sounding after his mind was made up.

Students were also taking up the cudgel against their president, generally in the form of restroom graffiti. "Rufus Harris is a Methodist," was found on several restroom walls. (Methodists were assumed more liberal on race at the time.) A favorite seemed to be "Mercer loves niggers and queers." When another student made the rounds of the stalls and penciled underneath that epithet, "So does Jesus," the hector desisted.

Sometime in early 1963, at the end of a week mixed with trenchant assaults and sweet encouragement, Rufus Harris was sitting alone in his office, staring out the window at trees that were already big when he arrived on this campus as a student in 1915. And across a campus adorned with architectural symmetry, buildings that had not stood when, in 1926, he was appointed dean of the Law School with a salary of just a little more than $4,000 per year. Before him were two stacks of mail, marked favorable, unfavorable. All had been appropriately and patiently answered and would soon find their way to the tall filing cabinets that lined the walls of an outer office. The corridors were quiet, the class-rooms empty, students were scattered from Catoosa County to Sea Island.

"Amelia, will you come in here for a moment." In a voice of aristo-cratic affability and collegial pride he read to his treasured executive assistant and friend:

Dear Dr. Harris:
    You are on solid ground with both feet in this issue. Stand pat and fight it out. Your side is sure to win in the final. And what happens to a great cause is always more important than what happens to an indi-vidual sponsoring the right. The fine statement in your stand is the fact that you say there is a moral issue involved. To say we should accept it because we just abide by the law is mighty poor support for integra-tion, if it is a support at all. To say we must accept the Negro as a brother, because we want to do so, is better than most people are yet willing to do. This letter is likely due to the seed sown in English class at Mercer where I sat under Professor Carl Steed. He was a great advo-cate of the rights of the Negro even then, and did not wait until Sunday to say so.

                Sincerely,
                J. M. Etheredge, Jackson, Georgia.
                Mercer Nineteen eleven.

Chuckling with satisfaction Dr. Harris put the letter on top of the "in favor" stack. "Amelia, I couldn't have said it better myself."

There had been three letters from the class of 1911 that week. All of them were friendly, all had mentioned Professor Steed. Two referred to him as "Baldy" Steed. He must have been a fine teacher. The bread he cast upon the waters had been well flung. Now it had returned to rescue one of his students of the class of 1917, one who also spoke of "Baldy" Steed with reverence.

There were other letters that week that pleased Rufus Harris. From a former student teaching at Stanford, an old New Orleans friend, then a Rabbi in Chicago, a Catholic U.S. Army officer in Maryland, a geology professor at Emory, the presidents of Vanderbilt, Columbia, Tulane, Harvard, and Louisiana College. All accolades and Godspeed.

Even so, it must have tried the patience of Rufus Harris, a man not given to dealing with trivialities. "Protest and be damned" was his essential impulse. But Rufus Harris could discern the face of the sky as well as the signs of the times. The 1960s were in their morning and the sky was red and loading. The crafty barrister and educator knew that it meant foul weather. His superlatives were a luxury that could await another day. Right now his Scotch called. Despite other excesses he was a moderate user of alcohol. But this was one of those occasions.

❐

Chapter 8

A journey not yet ended . . .

When elephants fight it is the grass that suffers.
> —an African (Kikuyu) proverb

Exactly two weeks before the special committee and the Mercer board of trustees met, Harris Mobley, the missionary who had recruited Sam Oni, spoke in Willingham Chapel to the student body. Dr. Robert Otto, Mercer's dean of the chapel and a man of radical naivete, had brought Mr. Mobley from Hartford, Connecticut, where he was attending graduate school while on furlough from the mission field.

It was not Mr. Otto's intent to lance the boil that had been festering since the first hint of admitting Negroes to the university. Otto, though deeply committed to racial justice at every level, was a product of Swedish Baptists, by way of Connecticut and Minnesota, and not given to the kind of subterfuge liberal Southerners were finding it necessary to employ at times. His thinking was that the foreign mission endeavor was indigenous to Georgia Baptist life, Harris Mobley was a foreign missionary, Sam Oni was a product of Georgia Baptist missions and might become a student of a Georgia Baptist school. To Otto, a man trained in logical empiricism, Harris Mobley was an appropriate speaker for a Georgia Baptist college in such a time. What Mr. Otto had not considered—and would not have demurred if he had—was a south Georgia boy's penchant for, as they say, "poking a wasp's nest." That was what Harris Mobley, who had graduated just eight years earlier, had come home to do.

Already disappointed with the empty brand of Christianity he found peddled by much of the American mission enterprise, Mobley was ready to do battle.

If ever there was a time when the ancient proverb "The fathers have eaten sour grapes and the children's teeth are set on edge" might have been quoted, it was among Georgia Baptists in 1963 when this former Mercer student mounted the dais to address those who had taught him and the new generation of students, all knowing that the issue of race could no longer be sidestepped.

Almost exactly 100 years earlier, the yearling Georgia Baptist Convention, meeting in Athens, upon receiving a committee report on secession, voted as cheerleader for the Confederate cause. The members of the Convention considered it "a duty to approve, endorse, and support the government of the Confederate States of America, and as citizens to urge the union of all people of the South in defense of the common cause by joining their fellow citizens in maintaining the independence of the South by any sacrifice of treasure or of blood."

"All people of the South," of course, did not include Africans owned by the spiritual descendants of Roger Williams, John Leland, and the European Anabaptists who would have been horrified at their progeny involving themselves in a political crisis. Though still in its infancy, in 1861 the Southern Baptist Convention had already strayed far from its Baptist heritage, from Roger Williams and before him John Smyth and Thomas Helwys, whose singlemindedness regarding the separation of church and state was typified in article 84 of "Propositions and Conclusions concerning True Christian Religion, containing a Confession of Faith of certain English people, living at Amsterdam" (1612–1614):

> That the magistrate is not by virtue of his office to meddle with religion, or matters of conscience, to force and compel men to this or that form of religion, or doctrine: . . . for Christ only is the king, and lawgiver of the church and conscience (James iv.12).

But one month after Georgia Baptists had set the tone for church involvement in state matters, without even being asked by civil magistrates, the six-year-old Southern Baptist Convention, meeting in Savannah, the town where Harris Mobley was born, and where Charles Wesley had written and published his first book of hymns—many of which call for justice and righteousness—followed the lead of Georgia Baptists without a dissenting vote. It was their conviction that secession was just, right, and necessary if subjugation and devastation were to be avoided. The Convention closed its session by appealing to the churches and their members to follow the example of "the noble army of saints and heroes who labor not in vain in the work of the Lord." The things they abhorred, subjugation and devastation, were the harvest of their resolve. But manumission of the Africans was a certainty, once the war began.

Many in 1963 saw the prophecy of "sins of the fathers" being ful-filled in their midst: "We have it coming and there is nothing we can do." Harris Mobley was not among them. His teachers at Mercer, especially Professor G. McLeod Bryan, had taught him well. So he stood in the lineage of Jeremiah and Ezekiel. The sins are *our* sins.

The young furloughed missioner made no mention of sour grapes or teeth set on edge. Instead he thundered that the fault and responsibility was in their hands:

> Neither the NAACP nor the Kennedy administration is responsible for the moral aspects of the race problem. We are. It is the problem of the church because it is basically a problem of human dignity and self-respect, values which you cannot long deny to others without losing for yourself. . . . Christian compassion and segregation will not mix; they are like oil and water.

Such words would cause not even a ripple today. But in 1963 in Macon, Georgia, they were words of one demented. Such outrageous thoughts were spoken at one's peril. Mercer University had produced a prophet. And now he had returned from afar to prophesy to those who had sent him forth. No one slept in chapel that day. Some faculty cheered in the depths of their hearts. Others wished he would be more circum-spect. Students wondered what manner of man they were hearing. They had been Baptist Christians all their lives and had never heard such mad-ness. Harris Mobley was not through.

Using the metaphor of Jesus as servant—washing the disciples' feet, giving himself to the hurt of the world, involving himself with the least—Mobley went on:

> So then, let us be Christian in our world mission today. Let us cease peddling pious piffle and plunge into the needs of our brother and sister. But in Africa I am afraid involvement is the least applicable word to describe the missionary's relationship to the African. Unlike the good Samaritan, we have simply refused to dismount and get involved in the wounds of the African.

To that point Mobley had trifled with hangnails. It was when he turned to dispelling the myth of the suffering, sacrificing servant that the church bureaucrats were speared to defensive and angry rebuttal. Though a man of middling size his voice filled the chapel, crossing and rising to the cupola and beyond. Law students, not required to attend chapel, milled around outside, sometimes scoffing, sometimes with angry rebuttal, as the preacherman emptied his scalding wrath, singling out the cursed tariff exacted of the poor for the mollycoddling of missionaries alleged to be living like mendicant friars.

> Look at our houses. Where do you find a missionary? Perched pretentiously on some imposing hilltop, isolated from the African community, in colonial fashion, high above the tin roofs of the villages below, or out in the exclusive suburb for Europeans, or crowded together in an insulated island transplanted from the Southern United States and called a missionary compound.
>
> Hear me well. I am not dealing in missionary methods. What I am saying is that our methods have reflected our theology, and the image has emerged *un*christian. Let the missionary have his houseful of servants, his "boy-master" relationship. Let him mimic the colonial past. Let him have his big American car, horn blowing, dust flying, Africans running off the road covered in dust or mud, but let him also know he is thereby distorting the Christian Gospel. Let the mission boards also understand well that their reluctance to radically alter this tradition has already set in motion movements for their ejection. The countdown has begun. Only some drastic steps will stop the explosion.

Whether he intended it or not, the young missionary was starting an explosion at home. His address that day would be reported throughout the South and nation. An angry Dr. Louie Newton would write him to "send me a copy of that speech you made and that was reported in the *Atlanta Constitution*." A concerned Foreign Mission Board executive would caution him about his indiscretion, alluding to one biting the hand that fed him, not even hearing the knock on the iron gate of the sepulcher of spiritual death. The Foreign Mission Board official wrote Harris Mobley that the consensus at Board headquarters was that the sermon in Willingham Chapel was "sophomoric."

This sprout of Jesse Mercer had, for certain, raved, warning his segregation-minded people of the hazards of flowerpot Christians, filling the atmosphere with the aroma of cheap and worthless piety. He talked of the missionary refusing to learn the language of the African, declining a drink of water from an African home lest it give him dysentery, and ridiculed returning missionaries who boasted of converting a witch doctor. "Ah, *we* are the witch doctors!"

He lamented the practice of sending mediocre intellects, with no more creativity and sensitivity than to load a Chevrolet with literature from Nashville and traipse around the country with nothing more to offer than a rubber stamp of the Southern Baptist program. "Stay at home!" he screamed.

> The University of Ghana has 600 students from all over the continent, inquisitive, Marxist-minded, critical of the missionary. Not one of our missionaries is there. Why? Few are capable. It is much easier to hightail it to the nearest bush village, gather the children under a mango tree, sing "Jesus Loves Me," and go back to the suburb.

Mobley's most stinging words had to do with subchristian racial segregation at home. He dismissed legally mandated integration as political expediency. The Christian must do it because it is right. "Let the Peace Corps worry about the American image abroad. We have a higher motivation." He rebuked churches of Georgia for parroting the culture, saying it is their task to *transform* culture.

His altar call to the students was a converse of any they had ever heard.

> For this reason I would not ask any of you to go to the African or Asian mission field. You're in one here! You need to go home. Go to your homes and communities determined to demonstrate Christian brotherhood for God's sake.

The students were accustomed to drawn-out harangues at protracted meeting or the closing evangelistic service at church camps, where every string on their emotions was plucked until they, sometimes exhausted, went down the aisle and vowed they were dedicating themselves to a life of service and sacrifice in some distant land. Now here was someone telling them there was no service, no sacrifice, and that if they wanted to be missionaries they should stay at home for, "The harvest truly is plenteous, but the laborers are few."

It is no wonder that this speech in Willingham Chapel pretty much finished Harris Mobley's missionary career. He got a Ph.D. degree in anthropology, taught for twenty-five years at Georgia Southern University in Statesboro, Georgia, and today operates a chain of Huddle House restaurants. A prophet is not without honor, save in his own country, and in his own house.

Harris Mobley had sown the whirlwind. Two weeks later, on April 18, 1963, the reaping was at hand. The Mercer board of trustees was in session, convened by Chairman J. M. Heard at exactly eleven o'clock.

After brief formalities Chairman Heard asked President Harris to assume the chair, a move not only welcomed but expected by the president. As captain of the ship, he chose to be ever near the helm.

Although the guests had already been welcomed by Chairman Heard, President Harris did it again. Then he introduced those of the administration who were there at his bidding. Knowing that an important decision was about to be made, he had brought Mr. James Arnall, director of the University news bureau; Mr. John T. Mitchell, director of admissions; Dr. Robert Spiro, dean of the Liberal Arts College; Dr. Oliver Littlejohn, dean of the Southern College of Pharmacy; Mr. Thomas Holmes, director of University Development; Mr. Mike Murphey, assistant director of Development for the College of Pharmacy; James C. Quarles, dean of the Walter F. George School of Law; and Mrs. Amelia Barclay, executive assistant to the president. Not one was there without purpose. In addition to those staff persons, President Harris had invited Dr. Walter P. Binns, his roommate during student days, an alumnus, and a former member of the board of trustees who had recently retired as president of William Jewell College, a Baptist school long integrated.

The president presided in his usual formal and inoffensive fashion, giving no impression that this was anything more than the "third Thursday in April" board meeting.

Judge Carlton Mobley, justice of the Georgia Supreme Court, had resigned from the board because of his disagreement over desegregation. It was handled routinely, with President Harris expressing "everyone's appreciation for Judge Mobley's service to the University." What was not said was that President Harris had taken every route he knew to dissuade Judge Mobley, knowing the widespread influence the judge had with Mercer's law graduates. Instead, President Harris expressed enthusiasm over the nomination of Dr. W. G. Lee, already present, to fill the unexpired term.

There were matters of the operating budget for the coming year, faculty promotions, and a lengthy resolution memorializing Dr. Spright Dowell, the esteemed, long-termed president of Mercer, who had died less than one month earlier.

President Harris asked his special guest Dr. Binns to speak to the trustees regarding Dr. Dowell. Dr. Binns did so briefly, then commended the trustees for the appearance of the campus and for the outstanding faculty, and concluded his remarks by observing that these are difficult times for church-related colleges, and that the role of the trustees is an increasingly important one if the college is to find the funds it needs. His role was competently played. It was well established that private institutions denied grants for reasons of discrimination would suffer.

More business matters: tenure, maternity leaves, enrollment limitation, student financial aid, monetary problems of the College of Pharmacy, the report of the Committee on Honors: the Reverend Mr. J. Thornton Williams, president of the Georgia Baptist Convention for the Doctor of Divinity degree; the Reverend Dr. Roy O. McClain, pastor of First Baptist Church, Atlanta, for the Doctor of Divinity degree; Dr. Hoke S. Greene, vice president and academic dean of the University of Cincinnati, for the Doctor of Science degree; the Honorable Ernest Vandiver, former governor of Georgia, for the Doctor of Laws degree; and finally the Reverend Mr. James S. Waters, pastor of Mabel White Baptist Church of Macon and an ardent segregationist, for the prestigious Algernon Sydney Sullivan Award. None of the choices for honors was fortuitous.

So far, everything was legitimate, forthright, inculpable. Just a university board of trustees at work. But somehow each item seemed to prepare the way for item 6 on the agenda, the report of the special committee appointed to study and recommend a policy for the admission to the university of students without regard to race.

Then, according to the official minutes of that meeting, the calm was over. Mr. Moore was summoned to give the report of the special committee. He began by saying he had understood that his committee was instructed to recommend how, not whether or not, to do so. He carefully outlined how they had gone about their work, making prominent mention of the application of the missionary convert, Mr. Sam Oni. Then, amidst nervous clearing of throats and shuffling of feet, Mr. Moore, as if reporting on some minor routine, announced that it was the committee's recommendation that Mercer University consider applicants for admission based on qualifications, without regard to race, color of skin, creed, or place of origin. He moved its adoption. His motion was quickly seconded by Mr. J. Warren Timmerman.

Just as quickly Mr. Guyton Abney moved that action on the report of the special committee be postponed for sixty days. His motion was defeated by a vote of thirteen to six.

Rufus Harris remained poised. Seeing the trend he left the gavel at rest, not even exercising his parliamentary skills by ruling Mr. Abney out of order for making a motion when another motion was on the floor. Giving rope. Lining the dominoes.

Mr. Abney challenged the moral right of the Mercer board to take such action since it would affect the admission policies of all other Georgia Baptist schools, a strange interpretation since each school had its own trustees. But Mr. Abney spoke as one charged with the unrolling of an apocalypse.

Dr. Trimmer referred to the explosive racial situation in Macon and cautioned that this was not the opportune time for such a step.

Mr. Smith spoke of the Negro's inability to support his own elementary and secondary education. "Georgia has thirty percent Negroes," he told the group. "The more Negroes you have in a community or state, the more violent the crime rate goes up. The percentage of murders committed by the Negro race is two-thirds. I do not want to submit our young women to schoolroom contact with people of that character. We have forty to fifty times as many to integrate in Georgia as in other states." He stated that when the voting time in this matter is appropriate, he wishes his negative vote to be specifically recorded.

Rufus Harris calmly presided. Walter Moore said no more, heartened by the defeat of Abney's motion.

To that point only those against the motion had spoken. Now those favoring changing admission standards began to express themselves.

Reverend Douglas Jackson stated that he was a product of the segregation concept but he could not vote to exclude anyone because of color of skin.

Dr. Trimmer, with distinct anger in his voice, declared that anyone saying segregation is unchristian is saying Mercer has been unchristian for 130 years, including Dr. Dowell, and that is not fair.

Reverend Jackson apologized if what he said was interpreted as accusing anybody of being unchristian, then quickly drove the nail more deeply by saying he could not conceive of Jesus refusing to recognize any man because his skin is black, white, red, or any other color, and that he must vote that conviction.

The cacophonous passion continued for almost two hours. It reached its peak when a substitute motion was made to admit the Ghana applicant as a foreign student but to make no further changes in admission policies in the College of Liberal Arts.

Mr. Abney stormed that if they had to admit a "nigra" from anywhere he would prefer that it be a homegrown "nigra," not a foreign one. The substitute motion failed by fifteen to four.

Mr. Martin said that he had problems with desegregation but was going to vote for it because he trusted the president, and Dr. Harris had asked that it be done. Dr. Harris had said so in his written "Report to the Trustees," anticipating a favorable recommendation from the special committee. After two pages under the heading, "Negro Admissions," in which he said that the admission policy was a great barrier to Mercer's future, he predicted a sure deterioration if the policy was not changed. "I feel sure that we will be unable to deeply touch the more sensitive students," he wrote. "They will be on the critical side of our Christian pretensions." His appeal was personal and compelling, until finally the report said:

> Now, I would ask you to do a brave thing. I would ask you to remove the barrier because I believe it is the right and Christian course to take. I ask it also because the discrimination is, I believe, a barrier to Mercer's progress.

Following Mr. Martin's statement that he would vote for the motion because of his trust of the president, President Harris, finding the entire embranglement increasingly distasteful, felt it was time to exert himself. Three members of the board had resigned during the meeting, although two would later reconsider. If the acrimonious debate continued and more members seceded, it was possible that a quorum might not be present and the mission would be aborted. Still the old soldier was not deterred from his purpose.

With feigned caducity he arose slowly, and after a courtly bow to Mr. Martin, followed by another to the others, he took a mildly palsied stance and began to speak. He asked that the decision not be made out of deference to him. Then he spoke a few words that probably carried the day.

> I work hard to do the best I can. I pray for guidance. I can be useful to you if I state to you precisely what I think on all our issues. This is what I propose to do. If ever you reach any point where you don't agree with my views, that will be all right with me for that is the democratic way. I try to be infinitely fair, and at the same time to state what I think is right. If I must be called bad names, that is all right, too. I want you, my brethren, to be able to work with me in love and in interest. Such is my regard for you.

And he sat down.

It was vintage Rufus Harris, a blend of ill-fitting modesty and piety, words of finesse and flattery, capped with gracious Southern manners, all predicated to do just what it did do: stop the debate. All with the resonance and cadence of a patrician. Prevailing ascendancy.

When President Harris took his seat the question was immediately called. The vote was thirteen for, five against, three abstaining.

By morning, Sam Oni, in far-off Ghana, would start packing for a long journey, a longer journey than he, or any member of the board of trustees of Mercer University, had the faintest inkling. A journey that has not yet ended.

❑

Chapter 9

Except the Lord build the house . . .

With the loose-jointed vote of the trustees, Mercer University would now have black students.

Still the intractable question asked by Dr. Trimmer at the trustee meeting remained. Had Mercer University, he asked, been unchristian for 130 years by being racially exclusive?

Dr. Trimmer had raised the question rhetorically. The apology given by Reverend Jackson was perfunctory. The issue, however, was neither rhetorical nor perfunctory. The issue was real.

If President Harris and those who voted with him were correct in their claim that Mercer should be desegregated in 1963 because it was the Christian thing to do, when exactly did it become the Christian thing to do? Would it have been the Christian thing to do on the fourteenth day of January in 1833 when Mercer Institute was opened at Penfield? Was it not black people who planted, hoed, and gathered into barns the crops that bought the timbers and nails, furnished the library and laboratory, paid the meager salaries for the teachers?

What if Jesse Mercer had stood in the church house door and cried out, "We are disciples of the one of whom it was said 'in Him there is neither bond nor free'"? He might have added, "We, Gentlemen, are Christian. Except the Lord build the house, they labor in vain that build it. We know wherein it is written that we are all one in Christ Jesus. We know the laborer is worthy of his hire, and we know well the laborers in this cause. Their children shall be our children, for this is none other than the house of God. Gentlemen, in the name of Jesus Christ, we open these doors this day to all."

He might have said that . . . but he didn't.

What, then, in light of Dr. Trimmer's question, are we to make of Jesse Mercer? Was he not Christian?

Would it have been the Christian thing to do on April 10, 1865, the day after Appomattox? Nathaniel Macon Crawford was president of Mercer then. His father had been a United States senator from Georgia, secretary of the treasury, and minister to France. Might not his son have spoken an authentic and authoritative word for the Lord?

What of May 16, 1954, the day before the decision of Caesar, *Brown v. Board*, was handed down?

What are we to conclude regarding Billington McCarty Sanders, Gustavus Alonzo Nunnally, James Bruton Gambrell, Charles Lee Smith, Rufus Washington Weaver, Spright Dowell, George Boyce Connell—presidents all? It was of them Dr. Trimmer asked his question in the boardroom. Were they unchristian?

From Abney to Yates, all trustees of Mercer University. Some 400 of them over the years. All known as honorable men, God-fearing, church-going, mission-minded. No one has answered Dr. Trimmer's question. No one, as yet, has institutionally said, "We are sorry. Forgive us."

As the Mercer trustees were debating the admission of an African convert, President John F. Kennedy's New Frontier was being tested most severely by the Vietnam entanglements and the rising tide of racial unrest that had continued to mount since the Brown decision of 1954. Kennedy had inherited both problems from earlier administrations. The judiciary had decreed on May 17, 1954 that racial segregation in public schools was unconstitutional. The executive branch, first under President Truman and later under Dwight D. Eisenhower, had authorized money and a few military advisers to assist the French in their war against Vietnam, a tiny country twelve time zones and 7,000 miles away. Though both previous presidents knew that it was a conflict in which America had nothing more than an ideological and theoretical stake—no economic threat, no ethnic minority clamoring for their people to be rescued—each one had escalated America's commitment until there seemed no face-saving way out.

Both the matter of Vietnam and civil rights for African-Americans were problems of great magnitude. One of America's greatest weaknesses seems to be that its self-image has led it to believe there is no problem it cannot solve. Whether the problems are those of the American South or of Southeast Asia. Or maybe that is the inherent attribute of all humankind, the dividing line between finite and Creator. Hubris. Hidebound pride.

Although civil rights had been on the agenda of African-Americans since the Civil War, the most progressive-minded politician had vacillated when faced with the overwhelming tide of racial discrimination and bigotry. Not even the progressive New Deal of Franklin Roosevelt, despite prodding from his wife Eleanor, acknowledged the bitter fruit the continuation of a rigidly segregated society would inevitably bear.

It was America's wrestling with those two indomitable problems, racism and Vietnam, that would be the crux of Sam Oni's education in the land to which his missionary friend was sending him. What he would gain in library, laboratory, and lecture hall would pale in comparison. His tenure would be at a time when America was experiencing political unrest, domestic upheaval, constitutional conflicts, and radically changing social mores unrivaled since the Civil War.

Oni was no stranger to the blotches on America's soul. He had known of the indecisiveness on the part of Baptist leadership in Georgia as well as the vocal minority on the Mercer board of trustees that opposed his admission. He knew of Emmett Till, Rosa Parks, Autherine Lucy, and James Meredith. Their stories had been heralded on the pages of Africa's daily newspapers. And he would know of Medgar Evers, brought down by a Mississippi assassin's bullet three months before Sam arrived, and the riots that had followed.

He remembered the Gold Coast days, before it was free of British rule and the oppression of his people. He had also witnessed the imperialistic mode of American missionaries and had paid a price for opposing it.

There were things about Mr. Oni that John Mitchell's letter to President Harris presented to the board of trustees did not say. One was that Oni had indeed attended the Sadler Baptist Secondary School in Kumasi, Ghana where Mobley taught. But he had been expelled for disruptive behavior. He graduated from the Figai Secondary School in Sekondi, Ghana, as the letter stated, because of that expulsion. Nor was he a native of Ghana.

George W. Sadler, for whom the Baptist school was named, had been a name in foreign mission circles for forty years. From 1939 until 1958 he had been foreign mission field secretary for all of Africa, Europe, and the Near East. When he assumed that position there were fifty-three missionaries in seven countries. When he retired there were 341 in twelve countries. No doubt his name carried a lot of weight when the matter of admitting Sam Jerry Oni was discussed by Georgia Baptists.

The meeting at Powelton, Georgia, in 1815 had as its purpose "to evangelize the heathens in other lands." The Powelton Baptist Society for Foreign Missions was there established with Jesse Mercer as president and William Rabun as secretary. The missionary zeal of the founders of

Mercer preceded the founding, a dedication bordering on fanaticism. What was happening now would be codicil, or else denial, of their will.

Although there is no evidence that anyone deliberately deceived the Mercer trustees and administration, part of the story of Sam Jerry Oni that was circulated during the admission proceedings was utter mythology.

In the first place, even the name was incorrect. Mr. Oni's given name was Sam, not Sam Jerry. When he was applying to American schools he recalled that all American male missionaries he had known had middle names. Assuming that was the American norm, and not wishing to be different, he searched for a second name for himself and settled on Jerry, feeling that Sam Jerry had a nice, lyrical ring. Although he wore that appellation during the years he was at Mercer, and is still so known, his name is Sam. (The reader will find him referred to as Sam Jerry in places here in the context of time and events.)

The strongest plank in the platform of those seeking his admission to Mercer was that Oni had been a heathen, "led to the Lord" by Harris Mobley, a graduate of Mercer University and of the Southeastern Baptist Theological Seminary in Wake Forest, North Carolina. The story was reported in newspapers throughout the nation. The *New York Herald-Tribune* carried it as an editorial titled "The Missionary in Reverse." *Reader's Digest* reprinted it. Although Harris Mobley had tried immediately to correct the story, by then it had gone around the world. With that kind of coverage it would not be easily dispelled. Mr. Mobley did what he could.

Another version was that Oni had been converted by another Southern Baptist missionary prior to Mobley's arrival but had his faith strengthened in Mobley's classroom.

That version was half correct. Mr. Oni was not converted by a predecessor of Mr. Mobley's but his faith was strengthened by Mr. Mobley, who had not taught him in a classroom but defended him before the Sadler administration and fought to gain his readmission, then supported him financially at another school. Actually, Oni had grown up in a Christian home, Anglican, not Baptist. Oni was converted to the Baptist denomination from the Anglican one, not from heathendom. His father, a trader who had gone to the seaport town of Takoradi, Ghana, from Western Nigeria, had also been influenced by the Baptist missionaries and sent his son to a Baptist school for the same reason Baptist parents send their sons and daughters to Mercer. And doubtless Mr. Oni's parents were as troubled that their son was dismissed from the mission school as Georgia parents would be if a son or daughter were kicked out of Mercer.

Remembering the British years of his youth and seeing the similarity between that and the imperious ways of the Americans, Sam Oni decided to make a statement at Sadler Mission School. In Ghana's secondary schools the examination prerequisite to graduation was given by the government, not by the individual schools. To fail that examination was tantamount to failure in life. Sam Oni perceived that the teaching methods employed by the Sadler Baptist Secondary School faculty were not preparing the students for the required test. He suggested that African teachers be employed, people familiar with the government-mandated exam. The Sadler administration agreed to do so but only if the teachers were Baptists. Such teachers did not exist. Sam Oni organized a two-day demonstration, leading seventy students in a march around the campus. The disruption resulted in a disciplinary hearing. When Oni would not withdraw his demands, he and two other student leaders were summarily dismissed. "They thought Sam might be a Communist," Harris Mobley remembers, chuckling at the thought.

So Sam Oni would be an experienced civil rights activist when he arrived in America. If the recalcitrant trustees and alumni had been apprised of that, their case against Mr. Oni's admission would have been pressed with considerably more vigor. But they didn't know.

Both Mobleys felt a deep affection for the young student, and believed that his dismissal was an injustice. Knowing Oni to be a brilliant and ambitious student, they suggested that he enroll in Figai Secondary School, a government school nearby. When he agreed but did not have the necessary fees, the Mobleys drew upon some of their meager funds to cover them. "Maybe our motive was not altogether spotless," Harris Mobley recollects. "I think we already had in mind asking Sam to face the racial barricade at our alma mater." An impish, yet virtuous grin crosses Mobley's face as he talks about it. "Not all meanness is evil," he adds.

Whatever their motive, when they received a letter from a young Mercerian reformer—whose name no one can or will recall—stating that the best prospect for desegregating Mercer University was to have an applicant from the mission field, Harris and Vivian Mobley were ready to deal. The campaign to integrate Mercer, a university then in its one hundred thirtieth year, had begun.

It was not a new enterprise for the young missionary couple. Two years earlier they had received a similar inquiry from some of Professor G. McLeod Bryan's students at Wake Forest University, a sister Baptist university in North Carolina. Under the name "African Student Program" the students stated that they had raised sufficient funds to pay the transportation of an African student and felt confident they could provide the entire cost of a college education at Wake Forest if a qualified African student could be recruited. Professor G. McLeod Bryan, then at Wake Forest, had taught Harris Mobley at Mercer and gave those students Mobley's name. Mobley arranged for a student named Edward Reynolds to apply to Wake Forest. With that ammunition the students began to pressure the trustees to open Wake Forest's doors to blacks. When the trustees refused the students brought Reynolds over anyway, enrolled him in Shaw University, a Negro college in Raleigh, North Carolina, and continued to lobby the trustees. In addition, more than 700 Wake Forest students declared Reynolds an "honorary student" of Wake Forest. Their position was that students were the raison d'être of any educational institution, that students had admitted Edward Reynolds, and thus he was "a student in exile" from Wake Forest University.

The Wake Forest students had succeeded in putting the Wake Forest board in a ludicrous light. Yielding to this, and doubtless other pressures, the following fall Edward Reynolds was admitted as a student to Wake Forest in full standing, and all racial barriers dropped.

Well aware of all that, Sam Oni—with Jerry as his new middle name—nevertheless received the news that he had been admitted to Mercer University with enthusiasm, embarked on his journey without fear, and anticipated his first day at school with the tingle of a snaggletoothed first grader catching the yellow school bus for the first time.

❏

Chapter 10

The most meticulous preparation . . .

Soon after the trustees made their decision two other Negroes were admitted without controversy. Mr. Cecil Dewberry, a native of Cincinnati, had completed two years at Fort Valley State College and transferred to Mercer because he felt it would offer him a better education. Mr. Bennie Stevens lived in Macon. Both, in effect, were walk-ons and attracted little attention.

Mr. Dewberry would live with relatives in Macon. Mr. Stevens would live at home. Sam Jerry Oni would be the only student of known African heritage residing on campus.

The most meticulous preparation was made for his arrival. Immediately after the board of trustees voted to admit students without regard to race, William T. Haywood, business manager of the University and secretary to the board suggested that a committee be appointed to anticipate any nonacademic problems that might arise and to suggest ways of dealing with those problems.

The substance of the committee's report, sent to President Rufus Harris on August 13, 1963, may seem laughable to today's university student or college administrator but in the summer of 1963 it was treated with utmost seriousness. Others may be outraged that such a study was deemed necessary prior to the admission of one black student to dormitory life. Only by understanding the emotional intensity inherent in the most modest change in racial mores at the time can one be aware of the committee's intent, or comprehend the long hours they spent considering what today would be the most demeaning trivia. Some of those on the committee saw it as institutional drivel but in their staunch commitment to the cause of integration accepted the indignity as part of the price.

Called the Administrative Advisory Council's Special Committee, it consisted of the following members:

> William T. Haywood, chairman
> Joseph M. Hendricks, dean of men
> James C. Clegg, director of men's housing

Helen Glenn, dean of women
Ethel Reeves, dietician
Ida Mae Wright, manager of the snack bar
Arthur Walton, director of student housing
Martha Maddox, university hostess
Robert Otto, dean of the chapel

The Committee discussed the matter with the assumption that there "would be total integration of all facilities at Mercer University for all bona fide students." The agenda included a long list of questions, covering every imaginable aspect of campus life. Some matters were treated with the obvious intent of dispelling any allegation that the NAACP or some other outside organization was party to a maneuver to force desegregation upon the University.

A summary of the committee report follows.

1. Do we anticipate any difficulties with the Negro students themselves?

It was not anticipated that there would be any difficulties with the Negro students. The two day students accepted have been carefully screened by the admissions office and the division of student personnel and it is not felt that they represent any organization or any concerted drive for the integration of the University. Since the dormitory student, Mr. Oni, is a foreigner, it is not felt that he will have any connections on the local scene that would cause him to present any difficulty.

2. Should we expect a concerted campaign to test every aspect of University life to determine whether we are in fact totally integrated?

It was brought out that Mercer University enjoys a good reputation among local Negroes and the local Negro leadership in our voluntary handling of this matter. For this reason, it is not felt that we may expect any trouble from local Negroes or Negro organizations. It is felt, however, that the social life of the campus may pose a problem. Fraternities and sororities have national bylaws that prohibit the pledging of certain minority groups and this would serve to exclude our Negro students from the social fraternities and sororities. All male Mercerians are eligible for membership in the Mercer Independent Men's Association and as a member of MIMA could be expected to participate in social activities of the organization.

3. Possibility of the introduction of Negro guests for overnight stays in the dormitories.

This was recognized as a remote possibility. We used the term "remote" because all indications are that the dormitories will be overcrowded and we will probably not have bed space for visitors prior to the winter or spring quarters. It was recognized, however, that generally students are allowed to have overnight guests on the campus only on weekends, at which time there may be vacant beds in the dormitories which may be utilized for guests only with the express permission of the student normally occupying that room. It was recognized that local Negroes may very well wish to visit with Oni in the dormitory but the dean of men, through counselling, will attempt to keep this visiting down as much as possible and discourage it.

4. Should we anticipate any problems from the Negro employees, with the possibility of certain challenges from these employees?

It was the consensus of the group that with the possible exception of some pressure from employees as a result of encouragement from local Negro leaders for an improvement of certain types of jobs, we should anticipate no difficulties with our Negro employees. It was recognized that one of the current movements of the Negro race is better job opportunities and our Negro employees may very well expect to be elevated into some of the supervisory jobs. The business manager and the superintendent of buildings and grounds advised the committee that some thought has been given to putting a Negro supervisor in charge of the night cleaning crew and that these pressures would have to be handled as they develop.

5. Does the integration of the University include our Negro employees?

This question assumes the use of the facilities of the University and was answered affirmatively. The problem of certain communicable diseases which are prevalent among Negroes and particularly those on the level of our employees was discussed extensively. It was pointed out that all employees in food services are required by law to obtain health cards. It was the unanimous opinion of the committee that all wage employees henceforth be required to secure and maintain current health cards issued by the county health department. This should be required of white as well as Negro employees so as to obviate any charge of racial discrimination.

6. Will Negro employees be required to use separate restrooms?

While no signs on campus indicated colored and white it was acknowledged that by tradition certain restrooms had been set aside for Negro employees. It was recommended that all restrooms be available without regard to race but that no announcement should be made.

7. Will Negro employees be allowed to use the University cafeteria and snack bar?

The answer was yes, but "since the cost of food in these two facilities is rather prohibitive for this group of workers" this was seen as no problem.

8. What is the status of our Negro employees in relation to our white employees?

There would be no change since all Negro employees are wage employees; there are none in the administrative, faculty, or staff categories.

9. What legal questions are raised through city and state laws covering integrated feeding, housing, and social mixing of whites and Negroes?

Advice of the University's attorney was recommended. But it was recalled that at his inaugural ball, Governor Carl Sanders entertained a Negro member of the state legislature and his wife.

10. What will be our policy for leasing of University campus apartments to Negroes?

Negro students would be treated as other students. University apartments are not leased to wage employees. Again, all Negro employees are wage employees.

11. A number of University student organizations conduct their affairs at places other than the University campus. Do we prohibit Negro students from becoming members of these groups where off-campus facilities are segregated?

Those matters would be handled on an individual basis.

12. Can we refuse to sell admission tickets to Negro students wishing to attend dances and receptions held off-campus at segregated facilities?

No.

A photo album

On Sunday, 25 September 1966, Tattnall Square Baptist Church deacons deny Sam Oni entry, stating, "You know our position. . . . We are with the majority of the church."

PLATE 1

Top left. Freshman Sam Oni in 1964 *Cauldron.* *Top right.* Oni speaks at Founder's Day, Mercer University, 1994. *Middle left.* Oni as senior in 1967 *Cauldron.* *Below.* An article by Oni in the 20 November 1964 *Mercer Cluster.* He was a contributing editor.

SAM ONI

a letter home

My Dear Akyeampong,

Many thanks for the very interesting letter of last week. It was most thoughtful of you.

I enjoyed reading the newspapers you sent. The American Press usually doesn't publish anything but sensational news about Africa. So you see why, even though the newspapers were a month old when they reached me, the news was by no means stale .

I was delighted to read of the tremendous strides being made in national reconstruction, but the news of Fijai High (my alma mater) losing the national high school soccer championship was pretty depressing.

It was most heartening to read the special edition of the Ghanaian Times dedicated to the memory of the late President of the United States, John Fitzgerald Kennedy. In a moving tribute the Times called Kennedy "a challenging figure of great resolve, courage and determination" whose assassination "has robbed the world of a dynamic personality." And in its editorial, the Times acclaimed "resourcefulness of this daring personality whose trials, triumphs and tribulations had towered him into the realms of the respected and revered statesmen and leaders of our times."

But nothing was so touching as the news of the Ghanaian who in sheer admiration of the departed great leader named his new-born baby after the late President.

As you will recall, it was soon after my arrival in the States that the terrible tragedy happened. I was knocked cold. It was as though a brother had passed away. Perhaps it was worse than that, for even though I watched every agonizing moment on television—from the assassination to the funeral, I kept convincing myself that John Fitzgerald Kennedy couldn't have been taken away from us like that. No, he couldn't have died like that—in the bloom of youth.

It is almost a year now since the President was snatched away by a cruel fate, but I am not writing this in commemoration of the anniversary; for throughout this past year, I couldn't forget to remember the man whose courage and wisdom had been a source of inspiration and hope to me and the young people of the world.

Friends in various parts of the world have written to tell me what monuments have been raised in memory of this unique world leader. I traveled a little last summer and I saw many of the Kennedy memorials all over the United States. I myself have quite a collection of Kennedy "things"—books, personal papers, articles and other souvenirs.

But I am only too aware that all these are mere substitutes. Whatever monument America and the world raise up for John Fitzgerald Kennedy will only be in memory of the man who served mankind so well by preserving the peace, but who was cut away from us when we needed him most.

Please pray for Mrs. Kennedy, Caroline, and "John-John"—and for America. Write soon.

·Cordially yours,

Sam

PLATE 2

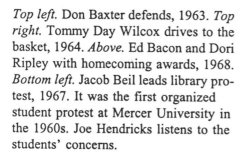

Top left. Don Baxter defends, 1963. *Top right.* Tommy Day Wilcox drives to the basket, 1964. *Above.* Ed Bacon and Dori Ripley with homecoming awards, 1968. *Bottom left.* Jacob Beil leads library protest, 1967. It was the first organized student protest at Mercer University in the 1960s. Joe Hendricks listens to the students' concerns.

PLATE 3

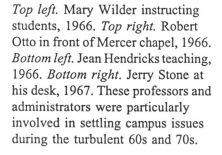

Top left. Mary Wilder instructing students, 1966. *Top right.* Robert Otto in front of Mercer chapel, 1966. *Bottom left.* Jean Hendricks teaching, 1966. *Bottom right.* Jerry Stone at his desk, 1967. These professors and administrators were particularly involved in settling campus issues during the turbulent 60s and 70s.

PLATE 4

Top left. Mercer ROTC company officers, 1966 (left to right): Sgt. David Laney, Capt. Woodrow Fincher, Sgt. Bennie Stephens. Stephens went on to become a lieutenant colonel in the United States Army.

Above middle. Bill Randall instructs students, 1969. African-American professors were rare in Southern universities at that time.

PLATE 5

Top right. Photograph and original caption from 24 May 1968 *Cluster.* These three students were part of the Mercer student body and faculty that participated in the Southern division of Dr. Ralph Abernathy's Poor Peoples March. *Bottom right.* In the city of Macon, more than 200 marchers showed their support.

Joining hands to sing 'We Shall Over-Come" are Mercerians Martiel Babbitt, Betty Jean Walker and Ed Bacon, President of the SGA.

Mercerians preparing to join the S.C.L.C. marchers include Dr. Ebey, Dr. Otto. Dr. Cox, Dr. Jean Hendricks, Mr. Perry, Mr. Miller, Dean Trimble, and a group of students.

PLATE 6

ARGUMENT AD ABSURDUM

DIANA DENTON

"Jesus loves the little children,
All the children of the world,
Red and yellow, black and white,
They are precious in his sight. . . ."

The closing bell of the superintendent bring to an end the final strains of that classic of Sunday School hymnology and supposed affirmation of Christianity's concepts, the little children and their big parents filed freely into church, to seat themselves—with the accustomed pre-sermon irreverence, this time a little more nervous, perhaps, than usual—and await the message of the saving love of a God not dead, who in a few minutes would seek their dimes and dollars for a missionary effort: to carry the gospel "to all ends of the earth".

Outside, a young man stood, awaiting his chance to join the worshipping throng who supposedly gathered inside out of a concern for their own sins and those of others, supposedly to share the sentiments of the missionary-preacher. Outside, the cameras ground, the press and public watched and waited, while on the steps a minion of the law of God stepped carefully before the Negro whichever way he turned, and in a low voice tried to reason with him: "Please leave peaceably," they told him. "We don't want any trouble here. It is your attempts to be admitted, not our efforts to disbar you, that are at fault and cause trouble."

"You are telling me you do not want me." He seemed a bit perplexed. "Then if you do not want me in the kingdom of God, you are condemning me to Hell."

("Profanity!! Blasphemy!!" those standing around him cried. But when the minister used the same four-lettered word inside, they merely trembled a bit and perhaps whispered "Amen!")

"We are not saying God does not want you, or that you are not welcomed to His Kingdom, but merely that we do not want you, and that in this church, His Kingdom here on earth, there is no place for one of your particular color."

"I am a foreign student," he explained. "I was converted by your own missionaries in my Africa."

"It isn't that we don't want foreigners," they kindly answered him. "In fact, we've voted to allow two foreign students to attend our services, and one of them was a Buddhist."

("Vos populi, vos Deii.")

Meanwhile, a little black dog ran up and down the steps, and in and out of the church, with no one to stop or even question him.

A black Christian turned away with the consolation that in welcoming yellow Buddhists these people had done their fair share in the eyes of God and their fellow man. A man quite literally "treated like a dog" while the canine worshipped unhindered. A hymn that now sounds like a TV commercial: "Red and yellow, - -blip, blip- - and white." No contradictions here or paradox!

"Vox populi, vox Deii." The voice of the people is the voice of God. Isn't it great to live in a country where even the divine must yield to a majority vote?

Diana Denton, associate editor of the 1966 *Cluster*, wrote this article on 4 November about the Tattnall Square affair.

PLATE 7

Harris Mobley, Mercer alumnus and
missionary. He recommended that Sam
Oni enroll in the university.

Judge William Augustus Bootle,
U.S. Middle District of Georgia

PLATE 8

Dr. Rufus C. Harris, President of Mercer
University, 1959–1979

Walter Moore, Mercer trustee and
chairman of the special committee
on racial policy.

PLATE 9

MACON NEWS

Metro ★ Edition

Monday Afternoon, May 11, 1970   22 PAGES — 10c

lan

'y

reau
al Asso-
ment of
oday it
an ordi-
permits
470 Ne-
ring the

Flana-
:els the
onal be-
ight of
He said
ther to-
District

irrested
er the
eed on
report-
ents to
ngs for
he $200

ie com-
not be
er Jr.,
court,
rrange-
:harges
ited 470
ay and
demon-

are be-
Dooly
r Pine-
in the
and Ft.

, about
held in
second
s were
demon-
ased to
y then
stration
·d for a

ese of
.a hold
:eep the

ents of
classes
ol this
t after

still do
number
·se said
d close.
er Rob-
by · the
idership

Viet Flotilla Reaches Capital of Cambodia

South Says 200 Foe Killed in River Driv

SAIGON (AP) — A South Vietnamese navy flot.
driving 60 miles up the Mekong River reached the Ca
bodian capital of Phnom Penh today, government he
quarters reported. It said more than 200 enemy tro:
were killed in the drive along the river.

A half dozen U.S. advisers and 13 South Vietnamese s
sailed with the flotilla, South and two Americans and 25 V
Vietnamese sources said. namese wounded.

The flotilla, which left South   The U S Command re;
Vietnam on Saturday, complet- two clashes with enemy tr
ed a 60-mile drive that helped S u n d a y in Cambodian a
secure an important ferry cross- where American troops
ing on Highway 1, in Cambodia. searching out enemy stock;
and base camps.

The arrival of the flotilla at   Eight American soldiers
Phnom Penh was announced by reported killed and 18 w ...
the South Vietnamese, who in those two actions. E
made no mention of U.S. ad- losses were unknown.
visers being aboard the boats.
President Nguyen Van :
The presence of advisers was of South Vietnam traveled
reported later by South Vietna- Tay Ninh, 45 miles northwe
mese informants who are in a Saigon, today for high-l
position to know. · briefings on the operation
Phnom Penh is well past the Cambodia.
21.7-mile limit beyond which · He told newsmen there
President Nixon told congres- Cambodia has set no fint
sional leaders last week Ameri- geographic limits on the cur
can forces would not penetrate actions.
into Cambodia. Whether this ap- He said that if asked by
plies to advisers of the South Cambodian government, S
Vietnamese and aircraft sup- ther into Cambodia
porting them was not clear. ther into Cambodia
But in a communique report- there is no deadline yet f
ing on the river operation on :ing out."
Sunday, the U.S. Command said   Thieu said the South V
today: "U.S. forces yesterday namese can return to Camb.
provided the following support after the current drives are
to the Republic of Vietnam 4th ed, but implied that the ac
Corps operation in the 'Mekong ment of the Cambodian gov
River corridor' — aerial re-sup- ment would be sought if
ply tactical air strikes and ad- was done. Noting that
visers. In addition, approxi- forces provide support for S
mately 30 U.S. Navy craft, U.S. Vietnamese operations, he
Navy helicopters and U.S. Navy said contin. :d or future op
0-10 aircraft are participating in tions in Cambodia "certa
the combined U.S. Riverine will be coordinated with
force. U.S. casualties associated U.S. Command."
with this support were four   Allied headquarters said :
killed." enemy troops have been ki
The navy movement was ac- since operations inside Cam
companied by gains of South dia began April 29.

JOE HENDRICKS, left foreground, dean of men at Mercer University, talks with one of the more than 20 placard - carrying, anti - war demonstrators who sat quietly during the ROTC awards day ceremony today at Mercer. Dean Hendricks agreed to sit with the group if they would keep their protest orderly. The group which sat at one end of the drill field contained, according to a university spokesman, a number of young people who were not Mercer students. They remained seated during the playing of the national anthem. Awards made at the ceremony are listed on Page 3B. (Drinnon Photo by Henry Hulett)

Many Campuses Reopen; Strike Calls Continue

On 11 May 1970, in an effort to maintain order, Joe Hendricks sits with antiwar demonstrators at the Mercer ROTC Honor's Day. As the front-page *Macon News* headlines indicate, there was widespread unrest throughout the nation.

PLATE 10

Headlines from the *Mercer Cluster* between 1963 and 1972.

PLATE 11

ROTC Honor's Day proceeds as Mercer students express contempt.

photo by Johnny Turne

Antiwar activists protest at Mercer ROTC Honor's Day, May 1970.

PLATE 12

photo by Johnny Turner

Faculty tea held April 5, in front of ROTC buildings defaced the night before by unknown vandals.

Graffiti spraypainted on Mercer ROTC building the night before faculty tea, April 1970.

PLATE 13

Harris Defends Federal Aid, Tattnall Square Ministers

Dr. Rufus Harris, Mercer president, said Monday night that he does not believe that federal aid to education will destroy the wall of church-state separation.

Speaking at a Brotherhood meeting at the Second Ponce de Leon Baptist Church in Atlanta, he said that the church already operates under government.

"Churches go hand in hand with government on a great number of matters including tax forgiveness, police, safety, fire, health and construction controls," he said.

He added that cooperation and church-state coexistence in countless forms has flourished since the founding of the republic, and none of them has impaired the essential separation.

"Aid for education is but a form of cooperation since our colleges, including the church colleges, help to provide the nationally needed educational opportunity and help to meet the national crisis in education which the country now faces," he said.

The prominent educator went on to say that "realistically this aid is a form of *quid pro quo*, i.e., payment for a valuable and needed education service, now being rendered."

Dr. Harris further pointed out that millions of dollars of federal funds have been granted American colleges for years, and there has not yet been a single educator who has testified to one instance of attempted control.

"It is only those without experience or opportunity who have cried out the imminence of interference and control," he added.

He went on to say that it is proper that the federal government should prescribe full and adequate provisions to be met before granting federal money.

"The American taxpayers do not wish their money to be given without ample protection and assurance of its legally established use," he added.

Dr. Harris said that "a second alarm is contained in the slanted question asking if Baptists, or the other churches, wish to support colleges 'primarily oriented to the sciences?' "

He pointed out that adequate facilities for science instruction, or any other instruction for that matter, must be met, especially since many church colleges find themselves in this period with its stupendous science upsurge critically needing a modern science building.

"Such a fact does not indicate that the colleges will become science 'oriented,' " he added. "They desire only to handle adequately their modest teaching programs in science as it must be taught in today's world by any good undergraduate liberal arts college."

The Mercer president said "a third alarm is the assertion that if federal aid is accepted it will mean that church-related colleges will become secularized."

"This is not a true consequence," he said, pointing out that religion on the campus of a Christian college is not confined to the chapel service nor to formal instruction in the department of Christianity.

"By the nature of teaching at the university level . . . the Christian liberal arts college serves and establishes the Christian ethic, purpose and faith in everything it does or offers," he added.

Dr. Haris said the federal restriction forbidding the formal teaching of religion or the conducting of chapel programs in a building constructed under a federal grant for a science structure is well understood.

"The law requires it," he said, "and buildings must not be used for activities beyond their agreed purposes. One cannot, for instance, change a science building constructed by federal aid to a chapel or a dormitory for that matter, nor can one change the use of a building given by a private donor for a particular purpose."

Embattled Fonda blasts government policies

by Chuck Jackson

Speaking before a packed Willingham Chapel, Jane Fonda, actress and proponent of radical change in America, delivered the third of this year's Insight lectures amid some feelings of apprehension by both Mercer and the Macon community.

The star of "Barbarella" and "They Shoot Horses Don't They", addressed herself to three basic areas; repression in the United States, focusing on students; increasing criticism of the Vietnam War, focusing on the changing attitude of the American military man and the Black Panther Party, focusing on police assualts on its members.

The 32 year old Fonda prefaced her remarks with a detailed description of her recent arrest in Cleveland because she was sure there had been some problems with the administration "and the trustees and since it pertains directly to what I'm talking about political persecution."

She related her experience in Cleveland directly to one of political repression and said that nothing of this sort had happened to her before she began making her political viewpoint public and wondered if it could happen to her "a white movie actress," what might be happening to persons less fortunate who could not afford expert legal advice.

"I am apparently on a list of people to be watched," she said, and am searched and watched.

"The administration talks about terrorism and violence, I think terrorism on the part of the law enforcement officials against citizens of the U.S. because of their political beliefs is the most terrifying form of terrorism that exist in this country."

Miss Fonda said there are two areas of law enforcement, however, which have broken down which the administration will not go into and which she is very concerned about.

"Nixon has yet to be impeached," she said, and is guilty not only of war crimes but also of violating our constitutional rights. "There is a law which says that if a president of the United States invades a foreign country without a declaration of war from congress he can be impeached."

In case you are worried about being stuck with Agnew," she remarked, "our nations most unguided missile, he has yet to be indicted for crossing state lines to incite to riot."

The adminstration is taking great pains to win over the students she said, because the young people in America are an incredible threat to change. And they are rejecting more and more the principles on which the American way of life is based.

"The American institutions are collapsing; they are obsolete and the government is trying to disguise the institutional collapse by making scapegoats of students under the guise of campus unrest."

On the other side of the coin she pointed out the tremendous power of the students and cited an example of the pullout of U.S. forces from Cambodia as a manisfestation of that power.

The administration, she said, is scared of what is happening to students in this country.

"What would they do without students "for cannon fodder for their wars" she questioned. What would they do without students to fill the jobs of the establishment.

"The problem is that more young people today are realizing that while everyone is scrambling for a better seat on the ship the ship is sinking." And this she said scares the administration.

What the administration is saying is work within the system, but she said the system is closed and cited the example

Cont. on Page 2

Jane Fonda delivered the third of the Insight Series lectures in Willingham Chapel November 17. Photo by Johnny Turner.

Hildebrand speaks here

Assistant Secretary of State for European Affairs Mark Hildebrand told a crowded audinece in Ware Music Hall November 12, that the German Ostopolitik of Willie Brant is crucial to our relations in central Europe.

The secretary, who was invited by Ambassador Dowling, also commented on the U.S.

Insight Lectures at Mercer bring antiwar activist Jane Fonda, 1970.

PLATE 15

Top left. This "blackface" picture appeared in the 1963 *Cauldron.* Did it mock racists, or was it racist? *Top right.* Students show support for Black Studies proposal at Mercer, 1970. The faculty approved the program. *Bottom right.* The Black Student Alliance meets, 1971.

Faculty gathered to discuss and vote on the interdisciplinary Black Studies major (top right photo). Seventy Plus Black students sit outside door and in front of the faculty meeting building to express physical support of the Black Studies proposal. (Top left and above photos.)

Members of the Mercer BSA singing at their meeting Tuesday September 27 in the Connell Student Center. Photo by Lenny Jordan.

PLATE 16

13. Since there is no definite limitation on the student section at basketball games, Negro students and their guests and Negro guests of white students will, of necessity, bring them in direct contact with the general public.

> The committee discussed the possibility of a reserved white section or perhaps reserved seats for regular customers. The business manager was requested to check the advisability of placing a fence across the balcony sections to delineate the student section at ball games.

14. Will we allow any demonstrations by students, either pro or con regarding the integration of the University?

> No demonstrations of any kind—race, food, panty raids—is conducive to intellectual pursuits and should not be tolerated.

The work of the Committee had been exhaustive. The report was dispatched to Dr. Harris in Munich, Germany, where he was visiting Walter Dowling, a Mercer alumnus and the American ambassador to West Germany. Whether Harris ever bothered to read the report is not certain. But no matter. Even if their report had been totally negative it would not have hindered him in continuing what he had set out to do. Rufus Harris intended to stay the course.

□

Chapter 11

Fledglings ready to fly . . .

Now. Who will be his roommate?

Despite the fracas that had ruled in boardrooms and shaken administrative halls, many Mercer students in the early 1960s were nonchalant about it all. Hearing the fractious voices steaming from the trustee meeting, one student was heard to ask another, "What the hell is that?"

"I think it's Darwin's waiting room," his friend replied.

It was an apt metaphor, for not since the academy was accused of ejecting God for the primal germ or tadpole had the pinnacles of Willingham been so shaken. Just as "Origin of Species" generated enmity and mayhem among neighbors, the subject of integration of the races was the hair trigger of the early 1960s.

Still there was a general drowsiness within the student body. They, too, would detonate within a few years, but not yet. Perhaps it was a combination of their slumber, and the gnawing of Old South genes. Whatever it was, those charged with housing found a contrariness when it came to room assignments. Despite the fact that many of the students favored Mr. Oni's admission, and that the student press had reported and editorialized for it, no one wanted to get involved to the point of being his roommate. There was now a determination within the administration to make it work in a dignified and peaceful manner. Those at the level of student personnel were eminently decent men and women. They had witnessed the violence of Tuscaloosa, Oxford, and Athens, and were determined that it would not happen on their watch. While some, in places where there had been rioting following the admission of African-Americans, were content to sit in tight-lipped silence, saying "I told you so" as their world crumbled around them, this academy cadre was dedicated to tranquillity within the compound. Joseph Hendricks was back at work. He had covered many miles, rung many doorbells, and lobbied many gatherings to effect the admission of Mr. Oni. Now he would not have it that the first racist slur to Mr. Oni would be that not one of his American male schoolmates would agree to room with him.

In finding a roommate Dean Hendricks had an ally in Dan Bradley, an outstanding recent graduate who was then assistant director of admissions. Dan Bradley was a remarkable young man. He had grown up in the Georgia Baptist Children's Home, on land where airplanes coming to Atlanta now touch down. A deeply religious lad, he was able to recite almost the entire Bible before leaving high school.

At Mercer Bradley was a popular and excellent student, holding many offices, thoroughly in tune with all that was going on around him. He became a lawyer, not a preacher, and rose in his profession to become president of the government-funded Legal Services Corporation under President Carter. Mr. Bradley protected the Legal Services Corporation from an effort to disband it by the Reagan administration. The corporation secure, he spent his last years as one of the most vocal and effective champions of gay-lesbian rights, traveling the country for the Gay Rights National Lobby. Though a lifelong liberal Democrat, he would as devoutly defend Judge G. Harrold Carswell, another Mercer-educated lawyer and one of Richard Nixon's nominees for the Supreme Court turned down by the Senate, as he would one of his own political persuasion. Or General Edwin Walker, ardent member of a society named for Mercerian John Birch. (General Walker had championed a riot at the University of Mississippi when James Meredith sought entry.) Such was the mettle of Dan Bradley.

Mr. Bradley died of AIDS on January 8, 1988, and was buried in the grace-filled red clay of Meriwether County by one of his mentors, Dr. Joseph M. Hendricks, by then a professor in Mercer's College of Liberal Arts. Dan Bradley, who gallantly served a Democratic president from his native Georgia, lies just four miles from where another Democratic president, Franklin D. Roosevelt, drew his last earthly breath.

But all of that lay in the distant future of five psychiatrists and a successful law career, for it was only after that that he chose to make public his personal sexuality. In the spring of 1963, when Dan Bradley was asked to find a roommate for the first black person enrolled at Mercer University, he was still bivouacked in his fear-ridden closet of loneliness, known only as a dedicated defender of what was best for Mercer University, a cause he pursued until his life's end.

A cast-down Dean Hendricks was alone in his office, piddling with such routine matters as chapel absences. He had earlier crossed out the names of possible roommates for Mr. Oni. Everyone had declined. Dan Bradley knocked on his door, gave a morning greeting and took a seat across the room. The two men sat discussing the scorching, late spring drought and heat wave that had stifled middle Georgia for weeks. Mr. Bradley inquired about "Mr. Charlie," Dean Hendricks's father, who was in declining health. The dean jokingly replied that he thought Mr. Charlie was abiding the heat better than the cows. They talked about a lodge Mr. Hendricks and his sister, Dr. Jean Hendricks, a teacher of psychology at the University, were considering building near their ancestral home in Talbot County.

After several minutes of unrelated and good-natured banter Dan Bradley stood to leave. Starting to open the door, he turned back to face Mr. Hendricks who was returning to his paper work. "Oh, by the way, Dean, Don Baxter is going to room with Sam Jerry Oni."

"Dan Bradley, I ought to kill you," the smiling dean said.

"He'll be perfect," Dan Bradley said. "At six-foot-seven he won't be easily bullied." Then Bradley went on his way.

The nineteen-year-old Don Baxter had listened with rapt attention the day Harris Mobley spoke in Willingham Chapel, and after twenty-five years can still quote much of what he said. Baxter, a rising Junior, was president of his class, a student preacher at the Tattnall Square Baptist Church on campus, and starting center on the basketball team. In addition, he had grown up in Dr. Louie Newton's silk-stocking Druid Hills Baptist Church in Atlanta. All that, combined with his size, did seem to make him a perfect choice.

Though Don Baxter would pay a penalty for his act of humanity he did not see it as a moral crusade. It came about when he attended a housing committee meeting with the head resident, Otis Andrews, a ministerial student and Baxter's former roommate. When the subject of a roommate for the African student was on the agenda as an especially pesky problem and it was asked if anyone had an idea for its resolution, Baxter volunteered.

Changing his vocational plans from the ministry to medicine, Baxter is today one of America's most celebrated orthopedic surgeons, specializing in athletic medicine, and is a professor at the Baylor and University of Texas Medical Schools. He claims no heroics for his collegiate challenge of the status quo. "It was just the way I felt about things at the time." Yet he credits the experience of dealing with those who opposed him with changing his life forever—less doctrinaire in religion, more sensitive to the suffering of others, and more understanding of the essential nature of the human animal.

◻

On September 7, 1963, Dean Joe Hendricks and John Mitchell, director of admissions, waited outside the depot of the Atlantic Coast Line Railroad. Not wanting to expose Mr. Sam Jerry Oni to the "White" and "Colored" waiting room signs which still separated travelers in Macon, Georgia, they chose to greet him along the tracks. Dean Hendricks had called Mr. Oni in Atlanta where Oni was visiting in the home of a professor at Morehouse College. Accustomed to the soft Southern drawl of most new Mercerians, Mr. Hendricks was mildly taken aback when Mr. Oni came on the line with a crisp British accent: "Oni he-ah." They had agreed that Mr. Oni would be met in Macon by the two Mercer staff members.

A slow autumn rain was falling and the weather was unusually cool for early September. The train was late. As the two men stood under the shed they made nervous jokes about how they would recognize the student they were there to meet. Their playful mode was enhanced by the presence of the president of Wesleyan College, the oldest chartered college for women in the United States. Wesleyan numbered among its graduates such people as Madame Chiang Kai-shek, but had never had a black student. The president was waiting for a freshman arriving from New England, daughter of an illustrious alumna, he told them. Finding that they were there on similar missions the three men agreed that they should introduce the two students, perhaps arrange for them to lunch together to get them acquainted. When the Wesleyan president saw the deep mahogany of the student Hendricks and Mitchell were there to meet, he made a hasty retreat to his waiting car, the very blonde and spiffy young woman in tight rein.

A smiling Sam Oni greeted the two men, then led the way to the baggage area, ignoring the racial designations. He seemed at ease, totally in charge of the situation.

After the short drive to the Hendricks home Mrs. Betty Hendricks served the three a light lunch. Sam Oni playfully teased the Hendricks children, appearing comfortable.

"Well, let's go meet your roommate," Joe Hendricks said, shouldering Oni's heavy trunk and moving down and across Adams Street to Sherwood Hall, a dormitory named for a Mercer founder and early professor. Students shot furtive glances as Dean Hendricks and the black man came on campus, some sullen, but all quiet. It was as if they were seeing something they were not supposed to see, like stumbling by mistake into the wrong bathroom. Dean Hendricks called each one by name, casually yet deliberately, not slowing his pace. Dean Hendricks was a man to be challenged at one's own peril. That was his reputation. As he escorted the first black student ever enrolled at Mercer University onto the campus, the white bearing the black man's trunk in the spirit of Harris Mobley's words to the chapel audience, no one tested him.

Don Baxter greeted them in the first-floor corridor and led the way to their room. Still Dean Hendricks hovered, like a mother hen not quite ready to trust her brood. When the two students had agreed on the choice of beds, desks, and closets, they turned to minor housekeeping.

With the chores done, Dean Hendricks suggested they go to the snack bar. He was not through for the day. There were other waters to be tested. Ten years earlier Professor G. McLeod Bryan had entertained some visitors, one of them a Negro, along with several students. When an irate parent, also a trustee, called the president to complain, the president felt compelled to make inquiry of the young professor. Upon being told that it was just a stand-around picnic the relieved president responded, "A picnic? Then nobody sat down! That's all I need to know." The angry parent could be assured that Southern mores had not been violated. The principle of "vertical integration," made famous by Harry Golden and his *Carolina Israelite*, was acceptable.

But on this day Dean Hendricks would defy the sacred custom. He would sit, eat, and drink in the most public and popular place on campus with a very black man and his white roommate.

The same hostile stares followed them as they entered the snack bar and sat down. Dean Hendricks got the orders at the counter for all three and returned to the table. There was hushed chatter, eyes waiting, no one acknowledging their presence, Joe Hendricks not missing any of it.

Out of the crowd that had gathered in the hallway leading to the eating area a tall figure emerged and headed for their table. Dean Hendricks watched him as he moved. It was Tommy Day Wilcox, cocaptain, along with Don Baxter, of the popular Mercer Bears. He sat down, was introduced to the new student and shook hands. Like an old friend, he began taking bites of food from the tray of first one and then another.

Only then did Dean Hendricks leave them. Bread had been broken, as had the tension. The fledglings were ready to fly.

The dean moved through the crowd, pausing along the way to chat about the most ordinary things—summer vacations, parents back home, registration, upcoming events.

No repeat of the Tuscaloosa, Oxford, or Athens riots would be visited upon the progeny of Jesse Mercer.

Sam Oni was in school.

□

Chapter 12

Maybe because you're taller . . .

What were the antecedents of what happened at Mercer University in 1963? Nothing is spontaneous. Even parthenogenesis has a prior component. Lightning that strikes the mountaintop had its genesis in electrically charged water droplets, and the charges and droplets each had their own origins.

One cannot speak of the actors in the drama of 1963 without allusion to those who hoed the rows before them. Certainly Rufus Harris deserves a lot of credit for the changes made during his administration. But what embrocations moistened the scales on the eyes of those who rallied in support of the president and his resolve to do the right thing? They were all sons and daughters of the segregated South. Granted, many of them were motivated by expediency. But expediency was then timid in the face of pandemic racism. From whence their grit?

When questioned, their former students' answers varied. Some earlier, some gone on teachers have already been mentioned. Das Kelly Barnett, Marguerite Woodruff, G. McLeod Bryan. And Carl Steed, teacher of English, who roused many students from the deep sleep of apathy when the century was young, students who, in 1963 were old men, but still remembering that certain class in 1911 when "Baldy" Steed would jump from Charles Dickens to the streets of Macon, Georgia with a stirring discourse on racial injustice. Or his successor, Welcome Talmage Smalley, who often paraphrased Booker T. Washington: "If you put the Negro on his back you have to stay on your face to keep him there." Many who came between 1923 and 1955 had unforgettable, life-shaping moments at his feet. He was so tough his classes were often avoided.

The responses of some former students as to who had started them on their trek to freedom were surprising to others. Not every tool is tempered by the same tongs and forge. Spencer B. King, professor of history, though sometimes blatantly "Old South" in his thinking and certainly not notorious for social radicalism, was listed for telling his students in 1945 of hearing a conversation on a streetcar between two pregnant Negro women, nearing delivery, who could not afford to see a doctor and would bear their young in their hovels. Those former students say they had never before heard anyone suggest that such things were wrong. Truth, even when set loose in innocence, can return to turn one's world upside down.

Hugh Brim, Theron Price, Hansford Johnson, Howard McClain—a roll of honor, sort of. And there was Arthur Anthony, a Marxist economist who made fun of Little Orphan Annie and talked for twelve years of a just society, beginning in 1946. All scattered in the back decades, men and women who had ignited sparks that glowed anew in 1963 when reason was indicated to prevail over bigotry.

Later Kenneth Cauthen, Ray Brewster, Tom Trimble, James Holloway, Theodore Nordenhaug, Robert Otto, Mary Wilder, Louise Gossett, Harold McManus, Jean Hendricks. And Professor Willis Glover, a Mississippi-bred Republican who taught that history was not mythology. Two years before Oni's arrival Glover had made a memorable address to the student body explaining that desegregation was inescapable and that it was nothing to fear.

There were, of course, many others. Men and women who never rose to prominence in the world of education, never introduced a new philosophy, nor decided the fate of their post, but who, on some unsuspecting day, uttered something that snapped the fetters of intolerance in a farm or milltown boy or girl, opening their minds forever. It is often the whistle-stops that get the train of wisdom to its destination on time. And the best teaching is sometimes subliminal—values caught, not taught.

So who is to say what influence brought the thirteen men who voted to end the Mercer years of racial elitism to their feet that day? Or what neglected clock fixed the leaning of the eight who did not? And the hundreds who never forgave Harris and the Mercer trustees for taking their inevitable step?

There is another question as well. What force of soul prompted Bennie Stevens, Cecil Dewberry, and soon hundreds of other young black Americans to forego the security of Morehouse, Spelman, or Fort Valley State to enter the uncertain world of a heretofore all-white bastion of exclusion? Why did Sam Oni book passage and quit a country and continent in development to seek tutelage in a country in certain moral decline? Perhaps even they could not answer. Maybe it was instinctive grace: we must save white people from themselves. Whatever the explanation, those whites who stood in schoolhouse doors, boycotted, jeered, stoned, and insulted or simply ignored the black students will be eternally in the debt of those who, for whatever reasons, ran the blockade. All of the black students did what they did voluntarily. Despite the influences cited, we who are white, including the Mercer University community—let it now be voiced—did it because the sands of history's time had run out. And we had no choice. We can claim morality, that it was the right, the Christian thing to do. And we have some affidavits to buttress our assertion. But let us now, for one brief moment in this chronicling, think truth: *law and economics, not grace, made us do it.* Having thus thought, we are free to move on.

When Dean Joseph Hendricks left the seated, integrated breaking of bread in the snack bar, assured that Sam Jerry Oni was in school, he was right. Oni was *in*. But not yet *of*.

When nineteen-year-old Don Baxter agreed to room with Sam Jerry Oni he naively gave little thought to where they would attend church services. Going to church on Sunday morning was as routine with Baptist-raised boys as brushing their teeth. It was not something they had to decide or even think about. With Baxter the habit was disturbed from a strange quarter.

Normally, when a new session is about to begin there is active contention on the part of local ministers to get the students to affiliate with their congregations. Don Baxter was informed that the pastor of Tattnall Square Baptist Church, the Reverend Clifton Forester, wished to see him. If Baxter gave it any thought at all it was that the pastor wished to invite him to continue his association with Tattnall Square. He had been a member there since he entered Mercer two years earlier, and had preached there as a student preacher. However, when he stood facing his pastor outside Sherwood Hall that fall day he realized that Reverend Forester was there on a hostile mission, probably with a mandate from his board of deacons.

As Donald E. Baxter, M.D., professor of orthopedic surgery and world-famous sports physician, remembers the conversation today, he was told that his black roommate would not be welcome at Tattnall Square Baptist Church, that if he approached it, he would not be allowed to enter, and if he tried to force his way in, he would be arrested. It must have been dispiriting tidings to a lad who had been nurtured in the church, who had been touched to enter the ministry under the preaching of the renowned Dr. Louie Newton, and who had believed them when they sang:

Red and yellow, black and white,
They are precious in His sight.

"I went back to my room," the doctor says. He speaks of it somewhat dolefully, even after all these years. That brief conversation with his pastor may have been the beginning of organized religion's loss of a brilliant mind. Don Baxter had planned to be a minister of the Gospel. He changed his major that semester. I suppose Mark McGwire, Mary Decker-Sladey, Steve Sax, Carl Lewis, Chuck Fenley, Travis Mays, Joaquin Cruz, and many other sports figures and ballet dancers are glad he did; his skills as a surgeon have served them well. One must wonder, however, how many great preachers, poets, prophets, or painters have been stillborn by some gutless parson's trespass?

An added stain of the Tattnall Square rebuff was that the building was on the Mercer campus and had been organized in 1891 for the students and faculty of the university. Though not legally under the control of Mercer—there was the historic autonomy of the local congregation—Tattnall had always been under Mercer's sway. The church house was built to conform to the architecture of the campus and most students assumed it was the church of the campus as much as dormitories and the administration building were of the campus.

Finding a church home for himself and Sam Jerry Oni weighed heavily on the mind of the young Don Baxter. It was then unthinkable that the two of them would simply sleep late on Sunday. Both were deeply religious and wanted to be in church on Sunday mornings. And they wanted to be there together. Young Mr. Oni was a passionate Christian, a consumptive Baptist, still overflowing with missionary zeal. Going to the church house was reflex.

Although Oni would later seek admission to Tattnall Square, he would go alone. And he would again be turned back. As for the six-feet-seven-inch basketball center Don Baxter, the conversation with Pastor Forester was the end of his affiliation with the Tattnall Square Baptist Church.

Walter Moore, pastor of the Vineville Baptist Church, had been chairman of the special committee that had recommended the admission of Mr. Oni. Pastor Moore felt a special responsibility for the young man's spiritual well-being. In addition, he had long been burdened by the fact that as a minister in America he preached to an all-white congregation while as a missionary in Cuba his parishioners were of various hues. He

sent word to Baxter and Oni that they would be welcomed at Vineville
Baptist Church. Lamentably, he was not speaking for the membership,
although the deacons had voted to support him in that bid.

Joining a Southern Baptist church is normally a most effortless procedure. There is no catechism in which to be drilled, no confirmation
classes to attend, no creed prescribed. In more urbane circles the preacher
simply announces, following the sermon, "The doors of the church are
now open for membership in any of the ways we receive members."
While the congregation and choir sing the hymn of invitation anyone who
wishes to join comes forward. The minister may inquire as to whether
they come by profession of faith, in which case he asks if they are truly
sorry for all their sins and desire to follow the Lord in baptism. Of
course, the answer is always in the affirmative. At that point a vote is
taken which is always—*almost* always—unanimous. The person joining
is then a candidate for baptism, stands in front, and is given the "right
hand of Christian fellowship." Following baptism at a later time, the ones
baptized are given the "right hand of church fellowship," somehow not
the same as Christian fellowship, and is a full-fledged member, entitled
to vote at any church conference and to receive the elements during the
ordinance—not sacrament—of the Lord's Supper.

In more evangelistic settings the hymn of invitation is accompanied
by various pleadings, promises, and proddings to get the unrepentant sinner—generally understood to be those not already baptized—to the altar.

Other ways of joining the church are by "promise of letter," by
watchcare, or by statement. "By letter" means the person joining is
already a member of some other Baptist church and the clerk of that
church will send a letter so stating.

Watchcare, common among college students, is for transients. In that
case the person is simply stating that he or she wishes to participate in
the services of that congregation but their membership remains back
home.

By statement is a bit more tricky. That person states that he was once
a Baptist, joined some other denomination because of marriage, or whatever reason, but now wishes to reunite with a Baptist church. That is to
guard against receiving one of "alien baptism," one not baptized by total
immersion.

When the two Mercer roommates entered the sanctuary of the Vineville Baptist Church on the fourth Sunday in September 1963, their intention was to join by transfer of letter in the routine way.

As the hymn of invitation was sung following Walter Moore's sermon a number of students came down the aisle and presented themselves for membership. Sam Oni and Donald Baxter were among them. In the usual manner, all the names, except Oni, were called. The usual motion was made, and quickly seconded, that they be received. The vote was unanimous.

Pastor Moore moved to one side as the new members took their seats on the front row. As he began to speak, most in the congregation leaned forward to hear his words. "I am presenting the next person separately because he is special," he said, without sounding sanctimonious or tense. "He is special because he is a product of our foreign mission program. And he is special because he is an African." After telling some of the story of how Mr. Oni came to be in America and at Mercer—most of the story already known by the congregation—Mr. Moore presented Oni for membership.

Just as Jesus asked no questions of tax collectors, harlots, or soldiers who chose to follow him, Baptist congregations invariably accept new members without deliberation. Emphasis has already been placed on repentance. Nothing further is needed. But Sam Oni was, as the pastor said, special. The most notorious sinner in Bibb County, usurer, highwayman, or junkie, would have been received with rejoicing. But not if he was black.

I interviewed nine persons who were present at Vineville Baptist Church on that morning. Their recollections vary. Some recall a lengthy discussion and at times acrimonious debate. Others remember serious deliberation but subdued in tone. One person reported the conflict as dividing neighbors, friends, and families: burning utterances, consumptive passions, and prolonged harangues straying far from the spirit of the lowly Galilean. But all agreed that the prudent parson let all have their say, waiting, neither challenging illogic nor scolding impiety. Never before had anyone present heard debate on the admission of a soul to a Baptist church.

Sam Oni, one week in America, sat calmly through it all, thinking such thoughts as only he could reveal.

Two of those present insist that the vote was not taken until the following Sunday. The others remember no delay.

Near the end of the discussion a man prominent in the Macon business community and in the life of his church walked to the front and approached his preacher. With tears rolling down his cheeks, dropping onto his worsted vest, he stood in whispered conversation with Dr. Moore. After a time the two men stood locked in a prolonged embrace. As the man returned to his seat, humiliated perhaps that one of his age and station had wept openly over something no more grievous than voting on a prospective member, Dr. Moore explained that the brother was concerned that some were affirming that a segregationist would not go to heaven when he died. In his usual pastoral manner he explained that he expected to be in heaven with many segregationist friends and kin.

Most believe the vote was taken at that point, and that Sam Oni was accepted by a margin of two to one.

No one disputes that the issue was one of immense controversy. What had not been said on the inside was voiced in scattered talk in the parking lot. Men and women whose regal manners had been established in their breeding were exuding the most debasing incivility, speaking words they would not later recognize as their own.

One woman explained that Vineville Church that morning was the city of Macon in microcosm. "We were in turmoil over it," she said. "The entire city was in turmoil. We were all fearful."

"Fearful of what?"

"Sometimes we didn't know of what. With us, I suppose, we were fearful that if that young man was allowed to attend our church, there would be an unstoppable influx of local Negroes."

"But that didn't happen?"

"No. It didn't happen. And we should have known it wouldn't. . . . But we didn't."

So the church withstood the whirlwind. Unlike their sister church on the Mercer campus, Vineville kept its preacher and generally maintained its stated mission. Walter Moore, as chairman of the special committee that recommended Sam Jerry Oni's admission to Mercer University, had now succeeded in bringing him into his own fold. Esteem for this man tall of stature and refined of spirit remains high among those who were there and remember.

Still, there is a haunting, unanswered question: What if the congregation's worst fear had come to pass, a rapid influx of Georgia Negroes? Is not evangelism high on the agenda of Georgia Baptist churches? And is not church growth the dipstick of institutional success? Sam Oni was admitted because, after all, he was special.

But, do not even the Publicans the same?

Few remember the aftermath of the conflict inside the sanctuary and the heated exchanges outside. But one thirty-seven-year-old woman, a little girl at the time, still has the event stamped indelibly on her mind. As she sat at Sunday table in what she describes now as uncharacteristic quiet, pushing her food around on the plate, her mother coaxed her to eat her dinner. "Mama," the little girl stammered, "I saw my Sunbeam teacher vote against Mr. Oni." (Sunbeams—today, Mission Friends—was the Baptist organization to teach small children about home and foreign missions.) Thirty years later she recalls running to her room in tears, refusing to let her parents in to comfort her, although they had not voted with the woman who had cast her vote to keep the little girl's new friend, Mr. Oni, out of church, the same woman who told her stories about Jesus in Sunbeams. For a long time the little girl wondered if the stories were true.

Donald Baxter, M.D., now fifty-one, remembers also. He recalls a long and clumsy silence as the two new members of Vineville Baptist Church drove back to the campus. It was their wit that brought them closer than they had been since each entered the life of the other.

"Why did it take them so much longer to vote you in than for me?" Don Baxter joshed as they moved down Adams Street and parked near Sherwood Hall.

"Maybe because you're taller than I," Sam chuckled to the towering hoopster.

The two young men knew their friendship was secure.

❒

Chapter 13

Don't let them see you cry . . .

In tragicomical fashion Negroes had previously attended classes at Mercer University. At the time the story of Sam Oni's application for admission was in the newspapers Harris Mobley received a letter from a pharmacist in Columbus, Georgia. Citing as proof the records of the Veterans Administration, he stated that in 1947, following his military service in World War II, he attended Mercer University in a counseling program for wounded veterans. He lived, he said, in the Douglas Hotel, then a hotel for Negroes. At the time of his letter he said he was a registered pharmacist, practicing in Columbus and Phenix City, Alabama. His purpose in writing, he stated, was neither to encourage nor hinder the admission of Mr. Oni but to point out that the issue of integration of Mercer was moot, for the school had been desegregated by him in 1947. His assertion was never confirmed.

Another Negro attended classes briefly in the 1950s. A paraplegic student had a Negro attendant who cared for him. The attendant would wheel the student into the classroom, then stand outside until time to take him to the next class, to the library, or back to his room. During Mercer's early years, in the era of slavery, it was not uncommon for young men to be accompanied to school by slaves who served as valets, cared for their personal needs, and carried their books to class, then sat in the back of the classroom during lectures. Many slaves had received fine educations that way.

Dr. G. McLeod Bryan, noticing the handicapped student's attendant in the corridor, told him there were plenty of empty seats in the classroom and invited him in. This continued for a few weeks and Professor Bryan recalls that the attendant paid closer attention to the lectures than most of the registered students. But Professor Bryan's tentative bid to have an interracial class was short-lived. President Connell communicated to the professor that only those properly enrolled were allowed to sit in the classroom, adding that Mercer's constituency would disapprove.

The presence of Sam Oni, Bennie Stevens, and Cecil Dewberry did not engender the tumult other campuses experienced in the 1960s. Since Oni was the only one of the three living on campus he was the most visible. He was also the most active and outspoken.

Cecil Dewberry transferred to Mercer from Fort Valley State College, an all-black college twenty-five miles southwest of Macon. A quiet, unassuming young man, Mr. Dewberry lived in Macon with his grandmother and commuted to Fort Valley. Attending Mercer would do away with the driving and give him more time for study. In addition, Mercer had a better academic reputation in his biology and history majors. When he heard that Mercer was considering black applicants, he decided it was what he wanted to do.

During the early part of World War II, Cecil Dewberry's parents had joined the mass migration of rural Southern Negroes moving to industrial areas in search of a better life. Jobs in war-related factories were plentiful but in the South the better ones were generally not open to Negroes. The Dewberrys moved to Cincinnati when Cecil was two years old. His uncle had attended Fort Valley State and for financial reasons Cecil returned to Georgia for college.

Having grown up in Ohio Cecil was not a stranger to integrated situations. Nor was he a stranger to racial discrimination. At Mercer he found both. Mr. Dewberry is a gentle man and does not dwell on unpleasant experiences on the Mercer campus. When asked about his relationship to white students he responds, "Not too bad . . . overall, pretty well." Then he volunteers that he found Florida students more bigoted than those from Alabama, with Georgia whites somewhere in between. When pressed about particular faculty members of the 1960s he laughs cautiously, clears his throat, grunts good naturedly, shakes his head and says, "My, my." Then he moves the conversation along, talking about his work in quality control with Seagram's Distillery in Indiana.

Mr. Dewberry graduated in the class of 1965, the first African-American or black person of any nation to be awarded a Mercer degree. He recalls no special ado marking that distinction.

Bennie Stephens grew up in Macon and knew well Georgia ways. He was an exceptionally bright lad, well mannered, and with an impeccable record at the Peter George Appling High School, the Negro high school in Macon. Even as late as the 1960s the school was neglected where appropriations were concerned. Often several classes met simultaneously in the gymnasium, laboratory equipment was inadequate, and textbooks were generally those used in previous years by the white schools. Yet most of the teachers were well trained and dedicated. Teaching school was one of the few jobs available to Negro men and women with advanced degrees.

Young Stephens wanted to attend the U.S. Air Force Academy and was encouraged and aided in the long and tedious application process by his guidance counselor, Mr. Jack Sheftall. Mr. Stephens was convinced then, and still believes, that with his personal, physical, and academic record, had he been white, he would have received the Academy appointment. But he didn't.

In his junior year at Peter George Appling he was offered a full, four-year scholarship to Morehouse. He chose to remain in high school for the final year, despite the fact that his parents were not financially able to support him in college.

Mr. Sheftall continued as Stephens's advocate, though personally thinking his prized student should have accepted the Morehouse offer, fearing that otherwise he would not be able to go to college at all.

In the spring of 1963, following the admission of Sam Oni, Dean Joseph Hendricks, on his own, called and asked if Mr. Sheftall had a student he would recommend to Mercer. Stephens was the perfect candidate.

Stephens had often used the Mercer campus as a shortcut to the swimming pool. In that he had been comfortable. The thought of walking across the campus as a student was different. Years of conditioning gave him pause as to whether he could make it in the white man's world. A visit with Dean Joseph Hendricks convinced him he could. In the fall he would register along with Sam Oni and Cecil Dewberry as the first Negro students at Mercer University.

It was not easy for Stephens. Not because he was ill prepared but because he had an early morning paper route that sapped his energy during all four years. Detesting physical education classes, he enrolled in ROTC in which he excelled as a cadet. That resulted in a career in the U.S. Army, from which he retired with the rank of Lieutenant Colonel.

The disappointment of not getting an Air Force Academy appointment paved the way for a scholarship offer at Morehouse. Declining that left him as Mr. Sheftall's choice for the historic journey at Mercer. Distaste for physical education courses landed him in ROTC. That led to a successful career.

"I suppose history is made of fortuitous events," he says today.

Perhaps so. But those fortuitous events leave many victims in their wake. Bennie Stephens had risen to the top at Peter George Appling High School and was admitted to Mercer University on that basis. Sam Oni was the favorite of American missionaries to break the color barrier. Cecil Dewberry had demonstrated that he could make it in higher education. They were the top, the cream of the crop. What of the blue john underneath the heavy cream waiting to be churned into butter? What of the "average" and "below average" African-American students who, for whatever forces of birth and history, did not score well on the tests of academe and who were truncated by admissions committees and left to drop even further behind? "Best qualified" was the measuring rod in 1963; it continues to be so. Of what can we now boast to historically African-American colleges and universities? That we took their finest candidates as our own?

I was once privy to a discussion between a black high school principal and his white county superintendent of education. The school system was about to be tokenly desegregated at the faculty level by placing black teachers in the previously all-white high school. There had been a vigorous resistance among white parents to having blacks teaching their children. The white superintendent was enthusiastic and optimistic. He told the black principal that he welcomed the challenge and knew he could make it work. "Mr. Johnson," the white man said, "I want you to make me a list of eight or ten of the very finest teachers you have. I'll assign them to the white school and we'll show what good teaching Negroes can do."

The black principal, not surprised and no doubt amused at the irony of the order from his superintendent, replied that he would supply the list. He then inquired if the superintendent intended to ask the white principal for a list of his finest teachers to be assigned to the black school. That query was met with silence.

Perhaps it was too much to ask those questions of university administrators in 1963. The ergots of segregation and inequality had diseased the body politic for too long for perfection to be hoped for. A toehold, not equity, was the mission.

There were those, however, who would press on. It is impossible today to describe the emotional intensity of matters of race in 1963. The storm had raged since the U.S. Supreme Court had ruled against public school segregation in 1954, almost ten years. We can write that people were angry. But the manner in which they expressed their rage defies capture with words. One can hear Governor Herman Talmadge's diatribe against the Court and his vow that the people of Georgia would "map a program to insure continued and permanent segregation of the races." Or Governor Wallace's blatant outcry, "Segregation now! Segregation tomorrow! Segregation forever!" But that does not convey the feeling of Autherine Lucy as she pressed through a mob in Tuscaloosa, her car rocked and almost turned over, the curses, the threats, only to reach the registrar's office and be handed a telegram suspending her from the University of Alabama.

We can listen to the racist rhetoric of John Kasper, of New York City and Washington, as he talks of "outside agitators" in Clinton, Tennessee. But that is not the same as being the black youngsters who, once inside the school, faced jeering students wearing Confederate flags, throwing rocks, and shouting, "Nigger bitches" and "Dirty nigger whores," while having ink poured over their textbooks.

Mrs. Rosa Parks refuses to give up her bus seat to a white passenger in Montgomery and is arrested. There is a year-long struggle, people walking to work, jailings, beatings, a young preacher named Martin Luther King, Jr. rising to international prominence—we know that history. But our bodies and psyches do not bear, much less really feel, the scars.

We read of riots in Little Rock in 1957 when nine Negro children were denied admission at the end of the governor's bayonets and our spines tingle with surface empathy. But we cannot feel what that fifteen-year-old girl, Elizabeth Eckford, felt, sitting on a bench outside the school surrounded by a mob screaming, "Kill the nigger." A New York journalist whispered, "Don't let them see you cry." What was she feeling?

Four little girls, murdered at their prayers in Birmingham in 1963, a few months before Oni, Dewberry, and Stephens came to Mercer, lie rotting in their graves. Our pulse flutters as we read of it, and we deplore it. But we are not the mothers and fathers who grieve for their babies each time they pass their empty rooms.

Likewise, after thirty years, we cannot fathom precisely what Sam Oni felt that first night when he turned off the light in unlocked Sherwood Hall.

❐

Chapter 14

Yankee money
and good-hearted sheriffs . . .

Race was not the only controversy plaguing the Mercer campus in 1963. But it was in that atmosphere of contention that a small cadre of Mercer staff people resolved not to stop with the admission of three Negro students. It was that resolve, and that alone, that made Mercer different from virtually all other colleges and universities in the South during those years.

There were reasons beyond morality that brought Mercer desegregation. But it was morality that made them go further. On most campuses, when one or a few Negro students were admitted there was a collective sigh of relief. "Thank God! That's done and over with. Now we can get back to business as usual."

Some observers and actors in the drama believe President Rufus Harris would have been content to let Mercer rest on her laurels once the three Negro students were safely enrolled, that he did not plan and did not anticipate what the next several years would bring. For a time, with no court order, there were three times more black students registered at Mercer than at the University of Georgia, and Georgia had five times the total enrollment of Mercer and was desegregated by mandate of Judge Bootle's Court.

That did not happen by accident. If one looks at numbers alone during the two years following the trustees' decision to open all of Mercer's schools, there is not much to report. The same snail's pace taken by other schools was traveled by Mercer as well. But the seeming suspended animation was deceptive. Like the storm petrel, appearing to come from no shore and headed for no landing-place, there was undetected motion.

The social scientist studying progress in race relations at the small Baptist college in Georgia would find little to quantify. There was more calibration than expansion. But stars that seem fixed in place to the naked eye are moving more than a hundred thousand miles an hour, and the seemingly anchored moon is racing fifty-four thousand miles each human-measured day.

One reason for the leaden gait was test scores. When Chief Justice Warren read the momentous words "Separate educational facilities are inherently unequal," the Supreme Court displayed its great power, but it did not decree a retroactive antidote. This led to an impasse. Minority students who had attended unequal schools must compete for college admission with the millstone of inequity weighing heavily. Unless that could be corrected all the work that had gone before would be no more than a fugacious whim of the zealots.

John F. Kennedy, when campaigning for the presidency in 1960 frequently reminded the nation that the black baby born in America, regardless of the section of the country, had about one-half as much chance of completing high school as a white baby born in the same place on the same day, one-third as much chance of completing college, one-third as much chance of becoming a professional person, twice as much chance of becoming unemployed, about one-seventh as much chance of earning as much as $10,000 a year, and a life expectancy seven years shorter. When he became president, Kennedy pledged himself to work for programs to correct that disparity. Already whites were asking what more blacks wanted.

One thing they could ask for was that it be acknowledged that there were unfair cultural biases in the tests. Admissions officers were slow to buy that. The concept of affirmative action lay far in the future. Everyone, they thought, should be weighed on the same scales. But students who throughout the primary and secondary levels had been schooled with inadequate libraries, outdated textbooks, overcrowded classrooms, and in laboratories furnished with Bunsen burners while others used the most modern equipment, could not be expected to score as well on tests designed for those with the advantage that better facilities offered. Climbing irons were needed to scale the unfamiliar academic pole.

A few at Mercer were aware of all that. Dean of Men Joseph Hendricks was one of them. But he was a pragmatist. In his unabated yearning for Mercer to do better than others, he knew that Mercer was not going to admit black students in large numbers who could not compete in the context of the status quo. If higher test scores would lead to a greater number of black students on the Mercer campus, very well. That would be the next step. There must be a shorter route to balancing the scores than waiting the decades it would take for the public schools to do it.

Hendricks, in concert with his friend William Randall, felt a program of tutorials would help. Their aim was twofold. By tutoring black high school freshmen, sophomores, and juniors they were preparing them to succeed in previously all-white high schools, soon to be desegregated. That, in turn, would better prepare them for higher test scores and give them a better shot at being accepted by universities such as Mercer.

Together and at night Hendricks and Randall canvassed the black neighborhoods, asking parents if they would agree to let their son or daughter come to the Mercer campus for remedial reading, English, and mathematics. From the beginning it was a vague and unattached undertaking, under the aegis of no one. There was no budget, no sponsor, with neither grades nor credits offered. Those who came were there because they wanted to learn.

The university administration knew nothing of what was going on. It was not that Dean Hendricks felt there was anything improper in what he was doing, just that if they didn't know, well, there was nothing to explain when criticism came. He was, however, aware that chairs and chalk not his own were being used in his Mark Hopkins endeavor. Columbus Posey, Mercer's registrar at the time, remembers providing assistance. "Well, what I did was steal," the jovial Posey, now registrar at the University of Mississippi, remembers. "I arranged for all their mimeographing, xeroxing, telephoning, all kinds of supplies. I furnished whatever they needed. I was in a position to do it, and I did it. What it was was stealing. I robbed my own office."

The first group had seventeen students, all carefully selected by Hendricks and Randall.

In 1964 Negro students in the twelfth grade would be assigned to the previously all-white Miller High School for girls and Lanier High School for boys. Historically, white boys and girls had attended separate high schools. The two high schools for Negroes were coed.

The Negro students transferring to the white schools must be ready. The summer tutoring would help. Mr. Hendricks did some of the tutoring himself, knowing, he admits, nothing about teaching English and mathematics at the secondary level. Mary Wilder, a popular and brilliant professor of English, came to his rescue. Along the way he recruited others, often college students, to assist them, sometimes commandeering someone as he crossed the campus on his way to the classrooms. "Come on. I want you to do something for me." Hurrying on with his unsuspecting captive in tow Hendricks would tell them they were about to teach some kids about gerunds and participles while he taught some others about hypotenuses and pi-r-square. "Then I'll take your class and you take mine."

Throughout the summer of 1964 Mr. Randall would go from door to door each weekday night and deliver the students to the Mercer campus. For two hours Hendricks and his clumsy pedagogues polished the rough diamonds. It was a small bud that was destined to blossom, one whose fruit continues to ripen.

Samaria "Cookie" Mitcham was one of the gemstones. The second of ten children, she was of a proud, hardworking family. Her father was the senior cook at one of Macon's most fashionable restaurants. Later, when all the children were grown, Mrs. Mitcham returned to school and graduated from nearby Wesleyan College.

When Samaria was a junior at Appling High School, Mr. Randall visited the principal and asked if there were students who would apply to enter the senior class at Miller and Lanier. When the announcement came over the public address system, Samaria was one of the first to volunteer. She was an A student, active in the chorus and band, in drama, and in other extracurricular activities. She did not want to leave all that. But she did not feel challenged where she was. Today she says, "I wanted to see if I was really as smart as they said I was."

As one of the original seventeen in the unnamed—and so far as Mercer was concerned, nonexistent—tutorial program, she flourished. Still she was aware that all the students were black.

At the new high school she was one of very few nonwhite pupils. Still she was confident, even cocky, she remembers today. She felt she should be in the college preparatory curriculum. She was not placed there. Consequently her courses were senior arithmetic instead of algebra or geometry, civics instead of chemistry. No physics nor advanced English. She is still convinced that she would have done well in those subjects. And would have done better in college if she had had that undergirding.

When testing time came, Samaria did poorly. It confirmed what had been suspected: minority students were not doing as well on the tests, not because they were dumb, but because the test questions were not as nearly in the realm they had experienced as they were for whites. Academically, as well as culturally. Again, the culturally oriented test would be a handicap.

Samaria's guidance counselor would recommend her to Fort Valley State but not to Mercer. "You couldn't make it there." Samaria was disappointed but did not despair. Instead, when Dan Bradley, who had befriended Sam Oni, came to Miller High School on a recruiting mission Samaria sought him out. When Bradley reported to Dean Hendricks that one of his tutorial students had been advised not to try to make it at Mercer, Hendricks took it as a personal affront. He knew Samaria Mitcham to be a good and intelligent young woman. "You tell Cookie not to worry," Hendricks told his friend Bradley. "She'll get in and she'll do just fine."

Hendricks was dean of men, not in the academic domain. But his sphere of influence had been expanding since he arrived in 1959 as director of religious activities. While a later title, dean of students, carried a bit more weight than dean of men, he still had no authority in policy and decision making. Officially. His position was not a tenured one; the office itself not one that in the past begot controversy. But his network was intact. And still growing. His friend Cookie Mitcham was admitted.

Today she owns her own company, Med-Tech Services. She employs forty to fifty people, supplying nurses, technicians, and other health-care providers throughout the area. Ninety percent of those she employs are white. "I was never a separatist," she says. "I was never a black militant. I just always wanted to get the job done."

So far she has.

The tutorial volunteers were displeased that their effort had not brought the SAT and ACT scores up as high as they had hoped. At least, not with one of their first prized pupils. Knowing they could not hope to correct the cultural biases they saw in the tests, they reckoned that they must reach farther back and get the students as sophomores, even freshmen.

They argued among themselves. "Are we trying to deprive Negro young people of their culture by deeming them 'culturally deprived'? No one is culturally deprived. What right have we to try to infuse white 'education,' or 'culture,' into Negro minds?"

Even terminology was changing. "Black," not "Negro," had become the new appellative. They learned to use it. They were trying. Mercer as a facility was all they had to offer. If believing that a degree from Mercer would help a young minority man or woman enter America's mainstream was elitist and chauvinistic, then they would be elitist and chauvinist. The tutorials would continue—still without budget or standing in either the Macon or Mercer community.

In the second year of desegregation at the university black enrollment doubled. From three to six. Not enough for those who were determined that Mercer would move from token desegregation to authentic integration.

Things did not go well for some in the second and third years of desegregation. Samaria Mitcham, who came during the third year, had never made a bad grade in her life. An F in Chemistry her first quarter was a trauma she had never suffered before. "I was in a class, the only black and the only female, with students who had had one, two years of high school chemistry. I had had none."

In addition, the professor had to force someone to be her lab partner. She heard early that Reverend James Waters and the Mabel White Baptist Church would no longer have baccalaureate services at the church because soon there would be black graduates to sit in the front pews.

She remembers some kind students, among them Tommy Day Wilcox, the first white student to eat with Baxter and Oni, who went out of his way to be cordial. Most, however, never made eye contact, ignored her. "I wasn't even there," she says.

She remembers friendly faculty: Dr. Robert Otto, Dr. Paul Cousins in English who liked her writing, and Dr. Doris Raymond, under whom she made an A in Latin. Most, though, treated her as a nonentity. "Maybe they didn't know how to respond," she says. "Didn't want to single me out, make me special or different. But it hurt."

"Why didn't you just quit?"

"I've never been a quitter. And later things got better. A tall, red-headed fellow came the next year. Ed Bacon. He sang our songs, knew how to dance and cut up with us. We'd go over to Dean Hendricks's house on Sunday nights. I'd play the piano and we'd sing songs right out of the black experience. We had retreats. Some things brought us closer together. Some of us."

In the summer of 1965, while only six black students had been admitted to the university the previous fall, the ambitious tutorial program attracted almost 100 students, some being ferried in from as far away as Warner Robins, a distance of twenty miles, by Constance Curry and Winnifred Greene, white women who worked for the American Friends Service Committee. Hendricks and Wilder had enlisted other faculty, college students, and townspeople to help with the teaching and administering the program. The applicants would be ready when the admissions office was ready.

Some unanticipated help came from a group of UCLA students who were in Macon in the summer of 1965 to work with the Southern Christian Leadership Conference in voter registration. Dr. King had spoken on their campus and some student activists raised money to go South. Because Los Angeles was a media center, SCLC was anxious to have a student cluster in one of the South's hot spots. Calling themselves SCOPE (Student Committee on Political Education), they were soon under the watchcare of Mr. William Randall. Joel Segal, now film critic for ABC's "Good Morning America" program, was among the leaders. At first, some of the California students were ambiguous about Randall, seeing him as little more than a black Boss Tweed. Segal remembers thinking that here they were, far from home, risking their lives for a hack politician, a ward heeler. They early learned they were wrong. Mr. Randall was an astute politician all right. But he was far more. He was a leader in the community they could trust and learn from.

Whether attending Klan rallies or knocking on doors in black neighborhoods with their urgent messages of black suffrage, the Los Angeles students discovered that their presence was being felt. They learned fast of the ways of this distant and strange land they had come to redeem with education and the ballot, a land they saw as the benighted South. They made friends with some Mercer students, among them Tommy Darby, now a professor of political philosophy in Canada, and Sidney Moore, today an Atlanta lawyer. From them they learned there was a successful tutoring program in place on the Mercer campus. They volunteered to help and proved to be worthy allies and excellent teachers.

Soon they learned something of their own city. During an evening classroom break they watched the television and saw the Watts area of Los Angeles in flames. Molotov cocktails were spreading the fires over a 150-block area—like the napalm bombs raining from their country's airships on Vietnamese jungles they saw on the same telecast. Everywhere fire, a scorching testimony of anger and frustration the visiting tutors in far-off Macon, Georgia had not known to exist in their community. Sirens screamed, police raced impotently about, all no match for the pent-up equipage of wrath.

Less than a week later they heard the score. Thirty-four of their fellow citizens were dead. From seven to ten thousand had taken to the streets. Three thousand Negroes had been arrested, 864 injured. Looting and arson had resulted in $200 million of damage, all unorganized.

When the last of the weekend soldiers stacked their rifles, the last of the police holstered their weapons, the few remaining canisters of tear gas were stored, and the scroll of carnage unrolled, the California scholars heard the reasons for the tumult. The causes for the riots were listed as brazen unfairness by police to Negroes, poverty, de facto school segregation, political inequity. These were the things they had left the security of home to combat.

The UCLA acolytes of Mercer's tutorials were learning what they had not come South to learn. They faced it with exceptional maturity. Joel Segal discusses it from his New York ABC studio with candor.

> At first there was a degree of fear. We were living in homes of black Maconites. And we were white. Despite what had happened in our home town we found no cooling of the welcome and hospitality we had known in Macon. Then we were very sad about what had happened back home. We had not expected it, of course. This was followed by a period of defensiveness, trying to explain that we had never said Los Angeles was perfect.

Despite the fear, sadness, and defensiveness, they continued their mission with increased dedication and effectiveness. They were there to teach. And now, to learn. Mr. Segal remembers that summer as one of the most meaningful periods of his life. He talks in the manner of reviewing the latest film, with genuine frankness, with neither toadying nor patronage, of what they concluded from the experience.

> We learned that integration was going to be easier in the South, that things were going to get better because people knew each other and had a lot in common. The cliches we had heard from Southerners had a kernel of truth. People really had grown up together. Watts proved it. People didn't know one another. And now the problem is worse. L.A. is still segregated. If you are poor and black you can go ten miles and not see anyone who is not just like you.

Mr. Segal was editor of a humor magazine on his university campus. He did not lose his humor in Macon, Georgia, but he returned to California a wiser young man. And the contribution he and his little band of "outsiders" made to Mercer's tutorials is still remembered with deep gratitude.

As the broiling agonies of fire flickered into ash on Los Angeles streets, in Macon, Georgia, a hundred young Negroes were taking their burdens to an ad hoc classroom—yet hoping, still believing.

By then Joe Hendricks was president of the Georgia Council on Human Relations, the state arm of the Southern Regional Council. In that capacity, he, in his sylvan way, could inquire as to what others were doing, or not doing. And he could dream.

Since the coming of the first three black students in 1963 little had changed. The larger Mercer community had been shaken to the foundations during the ironfisted wrangling in 1963. The prize of a handful of nonwhite students did not seem to befit the price of broken friendships, severed collegiate ties, and loss of loyal alumni. Only six Negro students had been admitted in 1964. They were all fine students. It was the small number that troubled the spirits of those who had worked hard to bring Mercer beyond tokenism.

Something else was needed and Dean of Men Hendricks thought he knew what it was. No matter the SAT scores, no matter the social skills or how competitive they might have become in science, language, and mathematics through the tutoring experience, and no matter how many the university would be willing to admit, there was still the matter of money. How many minority students could afford to attend an expensive liberal arts college, particularly when, for a pittance, they could attend Fort Valley or one of the other black state-supported schools?

Thus the dream. At first it was to find philanthropy to fund a more extensive and professional compensatory education program than the limited tutorials had provided. But why not combine that with scholarship funds? Dean Hendricks would approach that with caution, like stalking game in his native Talbot County. He sent proposals to numerous New York foundations and quickly received numerous polite refusals.

Frances Pauley, executive director of the Georgia Council on Human Relations of which Hendricks was president, suggested he go to New York in person. He could do fund raising for the Georgia Council and test the waters for his own project. Arriving in New York in the wake of a snowstorm, he almost froze until a friend of a Mercer colleague, a professor at Union Theological Seminary, provided a heavy topcoat.

Those disbursing the trusts of Andrew Mellon and Marshall Field received him cordially but plighted no troth. Most of the foundations refused to see him at all. As evening approached, the discouraged, cold, and wearied country boy was ushered into an office that was becoming to an organization with unlimited resources, the Rockefeller Foundation. A formidable, Ivy League-appearing, middle-aged man, with gold-framed glasses and well dressed, introduced himself as Leland DeVinney.

Hendricks thought Dr. DeVinney was cautious, even a bit hard. But he listened attentively as Hendricks poured out his heart about the plight of Negro young people in his area, the impasse between legal rights and practical application, the limited tutorial program the Mercer coterie was operating, and their hope for expansion. He decided to mention the idea of scholarship funds only in an oblique fashion. "I just hope the students we prepare can afford the prize."

Through his thick glasses and tempered stare Hendricks saw an aroused moral interest. They talked for a long time; the tension eased. What Dean Hendricks did not know was that the moral interest of Leland DeVinney had a long history.

DeVinney's father, a Methodist preacher in Michigan, had sent his son to Albion College, a small denominational school similar in size and aspiration to Mercer. Albion had been founded in 1835, two years after Mercer. It is the same distance from Detroit as Mercer is from Atlanta. Seeds of caring planted at Albion did not leave the preacher's son when he moved into the professional world of higher education. Although Dr. DeVinney draws no straight line from a classroom at Albion College to sitting in an office in New York City with an awe-stricken lower echelon administrator from a small Georgia school, he agrees the nexus is there.

Dr. DeVinney, now eighty-eight years old and living in retirement in Pennsylvania, remembers the conversation with Hendricks as a propitious development in the thinking of the Rockefeller Foundation at the time. "It was precisely what we had been exploring," he says. "We were looking for ways to break down the barriers that had kept so many institutions in the South segregated, even after the legal partitions had been dismantled by the courts."

Hendricks' visit accomplished more than he had intended. By baiting a hook for his own school he helped the foundation formalize a program that would go on to assist a number of colleges and universities in the South to afford scholarship aid for minority students.

Mr. Hendricks, seeing through fresh eyes, returned to Georgia and called Leslie Dunbar, former executive director of the Southern Regional Council and by then head of the Field Foundation. Few things happened in the South of a liberal bent that Leslie Dunbar was not somehow involved in. Although the Council was financed largely by New York foundations, Dunbar was never known to stand in the way of others if he deemed their work worthy. Hendricks was sure DeVinney would contact Dunbar. He was right. Not only did he give Hendricks a favorable review, he put Dr. DeVinney in touch with Vernon Jordan, director of SRC's Voter Education Project. Jordan, a descendant of the same county as Joe Hendricks, and knowledgeable on the issues that concerned Hendricks, also spoke commendingly of what the Macon folk were about.

Several months went by with no word from the Rockefeller Foundation. By then Hendricks realized that he had to come clean with President Harris and the administration as to what had been going on behind their backs for more than a year. The tutorial program had no legal entity. Any foundation funds would have to be channeled through a recognized tax-exempt organization and Mercer University was the logical recipient.

President Harris listened as his dean of men tried diplomatically to explain his errant ways. He listened as a father might listen to a child confess that it was he who threw a baseball through the window. Finally, he turned in his chair, and with a knowing smile said, "Mr. Hendricks, it is difficult to conceal a hundred Negro teenagers on the Mercer campus."

Of course, as Dean Hendricks suspected, the president had known it all along.

In the fall Dr. DeVinney called to say he was coming to Macon to discuss the proposal. At first he said little about it. Instead he visited with the tutorial students, then talked at length about new programs being formed under President Johnson's War on Poverty. The recent establishment of the Office of Economic Opportunity already had several in place. Acronyms for some were becoming household words. JOBS (Job Opportunities in the Business Sector) was working to find employment for the chronically unemployed. VISTA (Volunteers in Service to America) was placing idealistic men and women of all ages in community improvement programs in depressed areas in the same way the Peace Corps was doing abroad. Head Start was providing preschool children from poor families with food, fun, and learning. CAP (Community Action Program) was organizing and coordinating local health, housing, and employment programs as well as free legal advice.

Mr. DeVinney reported the activities with hope and fervor, comparing what was happening under OEO to Franklin Roosevelt's opening the ears of spiritual deafness during the Great Depression.

Then DeVinney began talking about a pilot project of the Office of Economic Opportunity he was reviewing, one he found more exciting than all the others. He said the project sounded very much like the tutorials at Mercer. The idea was to take young people from disadvantaged homes and areas in their last two or three years of high school and provide supplementary teaching in the usual subjects as well as cultural exposure and experiences they might not otherwise have. Those who wanted to go on to college would be better prepared. Those who did not would stand a better chance in the marketplace where jobs previously closed to blacks were beginning to open up. Mr. DeVinney said the proposed name for the new medium of education was Upward Bound.

Hendricks had not heard of it. Hearing it now was somewhat disquieting. DeVinney encouraged Hendricks to be among the first applicants for the new Upward Bound. Hendricks feared that it was a polite but calculated dodge—Mr. DeVinney telling him that because the federal government was going to fund programs similar to the Mercer tutorials, Rockefeller would not.

Suddenly Mr. DeVinney made a statement that jarred Hendricks. DeVinney said he knew it would be some years before Upward Bound would impact previously all-white college enrollment. Knowing that, Rockefeller was considering funding scholarships for minority students.

Hendricks was ecstatic. The ostensibly powerless office of dean of students was unexpectedly empowered. If finance no longer stood between token desegregation and substantive integration, the last obstacle would fade. With a well-funded Upward Bound from the Office of Economic Opportunity to enable the timid tutorials, and scholarships from the Rockefeller Foundation to subsidize the cost of post-secondary education, the complexion of Mercer University could be changed in short order.

There was an initial grant from the Rockefeller Foundation of $60,000 for minority scholarships. Hendricks and Johnny Mitchell, director of admissions, took to the air in search of black students interested in attending Mercer University. Recruitment had previously been in all-white schools.

Mitchell owned an airplane and he and Hendricks covered Georgia and northern Florida in a few weeks. Many of the small towns did not have airports, nor car rental agencies or taxi service to take them to the black schools they were visiting. They landed on crop-duster runways, makeshift emergency strips, wherever they could. In an area where any white stranger might be taken for an outside agitator there was often suspicion of two white men landing an airplane, then asking for directions to the black school.

On one occasion Hendricks left Mitchell with the plane on a grass strip and was running down a country road in search of a public telephone to call the school and ask the prospective students to wait for them after school. They were behind schedule. As the out-of-breath dean of students neared a service station, a sheriff's patrol car pulled alongside and motioned him inside. The deputy sheriff was a prototype of central casting for a B-movie Hollywood set of an overstated Southland. With sideburns dropping to his jaws, one cheek swelled with chewing tobacco, scruffy uniform, and the voice of an exaggerated Jed Clampett, Hendricks feared the deputy meant trouble. In the back seat sat Johnny Mitchell, looking smug and pretentious, smoking a long cigar. Hendricks, well familiar with south Georgia sensibilities, and brother to a rural county sheriff himself, thought he knew what the deputy was thinking.

"The deputy is going to drive us to the school," Johnny Mitchell said with a gloating chuckle.

"What brings you fellows to our neck of the woods?" the deputy inquired as they rode on.

Hendricks nudged his colleague that he would do the talking. Trying to make the mission sound as unoffending as possible to the rural deputy Dean Hendricks sought to explain. "Well, Deputy, you know how it is in these days . . . all the government regulations and everything, we have to respond to every request for a visit. It's just routine . . . you know, but we have to stop by the colored school for a few minutes."

Speeding through the main part of town, passing colonial houses in well-to-do neighborhoods, the deputy, tight-lipped since Hendricks had stated their business, ran by the city limit sign and began turning down deserted dirt streets and back alleys, Hendricks sitting in uneasy silence, Mitchell grinning and waving at the people they passed. When the car finally stopped and they stepped out of the back door that could only be opened from the outside, the deputy cordially shook hands with them and said, "I hope you fellows can help some of our good students down heah. We need all the help we can get."

As the relieved Hendricks and still-beaming pilot and fellow recruiter walked away the deputy sheriff smiled and called after them. "Y'all lemme know if I can do anything else for you while you're in the county, ya heah."

Twenty-three black students were enrolled as a result of their journeys and the Rockefeller Foundation grant. Dr. DeVinney remembers the $60,000 grant, and a much larger one that would come later, as a wise and successful experiment for the foundation.

Those at Mercer wanting more than a pharisaic tip of the hat to integration felt that was a solid beginning. But only a beginning. Twenty-three was more than three, more than six, but still not enough.

❒

Chapter 15

What about me . . . ?

But whosoever shall offend one of these little ones who believe in me,
it were better for him that a millstone were hanged about his neck, and
that he were drowned in the depth of the sea.   —Matthew 18:6 KJV

The black class that entered Mercer University in the fall of 1966 has a
remarkable history. Joseph Hobbs, M.D. is at the Medical College of
Georgia as associate dean for Primary Care, vice chairman for academic
affairs, and director of student education. Carl Brown is a judge of the
Municipal Court in Augusta. Mary Alice Buckner is an attorney and
judge of Recorder's Court in Columbus. Her former law partner, Sanford
Bishop, is now a Democratic representative from Georgia's Second
Congressional District. James Norman, brother of Jessye Norman,
Metropolitan Opera star, has been assistant secretary of labor for the state
of Michigan. Jasmine Dawson-Ellis is an attorney for the U.S.
government. Renata Williams Boston operates a mortuary business. Gary
Johnson, who was editor of the *Mercer Cluster*, is now an official for the
Internal Revenue Service. Curtis Echols retired from a military career and
is now a minister. Jerry Boykin is an attorney in Atlanta. His twin
brother, James Boykin, has completed a successful military career.
Ernestine Poole Cole is an official with the DeKalb County Family and
Children Services. Arenilla Kennedy Bush is a mental health professional
in South Carolina. Yvonne Jackson Moore is a laboratory technologist in
Milledgeville, Georgia. Sherry Hicks is a teacher in Macon.

Not a one can be cataloged a failure.

Where would they be today without the efforts of a dean of men who
did not know enough to wear a coat to New York in the wintertime but
came away with the wherewithal for scores of youngsters to attend Mercer University? To that question we, of course, have no answer. They
were all bright and determined and probably would have succeeded somewhere. Again, perhaps the soul of Mercer needed their presence more
than the students needed to be there. Or perhaps each was a lamp on the
altar of the other, each casting a glow of hope on the dark pathway.

Pleased with what Mercer had accomplished, the Rockefeller Foundation made a new bequest of $200,000. Dean Hendricks and Johnny Mitchell were back in the air like swallows, barnstorming, following any faint trail that might lead to another recruit.

The entering class of 1968 was by far the most significant fruit from the Rockefeller money. More than fifty blacks registered that fall, bringing the total to more than a hundred. Mercer University could now claim to be more than tokenly desegregated. Oni, Stephens, and Dewberry had entered four years earlier, but only Oni lived in a dormitory. Likewise, of those who came the following three years, most also resided off campus. Now every resident hall would have black students.

The tension began when the black students realized that roommates had been assigned according to race. While most had no particular preference, the arbitrary assignments were a resurrection of the segregationist corpse they had hoped would be safely in the morgue of history when they enlisted in the Mercer experiment. The more perceptive saw it as gigantic dishonesty; a betrayal on the part of the recruiters who had said Mercer would be free of past indignities.

◻

Jasmine Dawson-Ellis remembers well her first night on campus. All freshmen girls were gathered for an orientation in the recreation room of the residence hall. Various people spoke. Although she and her roommate had already noted the room assignment pattern, things seemed to be going well at the gathering. Then the president of the Women's Association addressed them on proper behavior and lurking dangers. Early in her comments, as Mrs. Ellis recalls, the Woman's Association president told them they must be careful when walking on campus at night because of the "Niggers" who lived in the neighborhood next to the dormitory.

> My first inclination was to walk out of the meeting, but at the time I really didn't have the nerve. Later, after the meeting, all of the black girls gathered in my room. We were all hurt and angry. Somehow, in one sentence, this student had destroyed all of the careful plans that had been laid, all the assurances that we had been given, and all of the carefully structured welcomes we had received. For at that moment we knew what the average student thought about us. In our minds there was no way we could separate ourselves from those black people who live

in the communities. If she saw them as "Niggers" and a threat, then she saw us as the same.

It would have done no good at the time to tell the young black woman that the president of the Women's Association, with her conditioning since childhood, just didn't know any better, that she really didn't see the black students in the same light as she saw their brothers and sisters outside that dormitory. Actually that, though perhaps true, pointed to a deeper form of racism, or at least "racialism" (the notion that society should be arranged according to race in the same sense some believe it should be arranged according to class), than they had imagined. "Nigger" meant danger to the Women's Association president.

Mrs. Ellis has mixed feelings about her years at Mercer. "While the education I received was top notch, I still feel cheated by the absence of the memories of fellowship, camaraderie, and fun that I could have experienced if I had chosen to attend a predominantly black school."

She now sees Mercer as more of a mirror of the real world, and sees herself and her black classmates as "the chosen ones," setting the pace for those who came after them.

□

Maureen Walker was recruited from a high school in Augusta. Today she is M. Maureen Walker, Ph.D., and is staff psychologist for Harvard University's Graduate School of Business Administration. She remembers running to the bus stop to meet her mother, a domestic worker who in 1967 was not making minimum wage, telling her about the dean's visit, about being accepted at Mercer, and about the scholarship money, and hearing her mother utter, "Thank God."

Dr. Walker recalls her ambivalence when told by the housekeepers at Mercer not to use the titles Miss or Mrs. when addressing them in front of the white girls because the housekeepers needed the extra few dollars they got each week from doing personal ironing. They could not afford to be thought "uppity." She talks with tarrying hurt about learning, after she had held the candles, sung the songs, and drunk the punch at sorority parties to which she had been invited, only to learn afterward that she was excluded from ever being invited to join the sororities by charter and by custom. She talks with convincing candor about the bruises of rejection and hostility she encountered. She recalls a history professor extolling the virtues of slavery as a time of protection of black people. Another asserted his opinion that black people had brought homosexuality to Mercer, since he had not noticed it prior to their arrival. Someone carved a KKK inscription on her desk. An English professor asked her to attest to "the dearth of good Negro literature." She does not believe the pattern of insult and injury was ever addressed by Mercer during her years there. Yet she is not a bitter person. Dr. Walker remembers Dean Hendricks mediating most of those incidents. "I think we [the blacks] all believed he could fix anything."

While reliving a period of psychological assaults on the personhood of African-Americans, Dr. Walker also recounts with poetic tenderness the occasions when white faculty tried to protect them from hurt by opening their homes to the black students during periods of intrinsic rejection such as Greek week or the KA Confederate Ball weekend.

"I am forever grateful for my years at Mercer," she writes. "I gained a perspective on myself and the world that I can't imagine achieving in a different context. I left with enormous confidence and conviction about my place in the world."

No doubt the Graduate School of Business Administration at Harvard University is grateful for "the place in the world" she found.

❏

On Juanita Johnson Bailey's first day she was handed a schedule by her advisor who showed no interest in her preference of courses. When she asked why she had been assigned to remedial reading he responded that every student who scored under 1,000 on the SAT was required to take remedial reading. The presumption disturbed her. When she told him she had scored well over 1,000 he opened her file to check what she had said. Seeing the score he said, "Well, you're on scholarship, aren't you?" The inference was that if she wanted to keep the free ride she had to do as he said.

The sensitive little Catholic girl went to her room in tears. She was the proud recipient of a scholarship but she was not a charity ward. She received the scholarship because she was intelligent, had excelled in high school, and was a person of high moral character. Her years at Mercer would be far from a free ride. The Rockefeller scholarships were part of a package, sometimes supplemented by various work-study arrangements and sometimes by loans that generally took years for the student to repay.

At the second day of the remedial reading class Miss Johnson was told by the teacher that she need not return, that assigning her to remedial reading had been a mistake. But the hurt was deep. She vowed to do well and to finish as soon as possible. Three years later she graduated. With honors.

The callous advisor, however, had left his mark. Instead of going directly to graduate school as she had originally planned, it would be twenty years before she felt up to challenging academic life again to gain the doctorate in education.

Today she blames her immaturity and idealism for so internalizing that first-day event. She adds, "I do feel that the events at Mercer shaped my life. I have held this pain close in my heart for a long time. My dissertation topic focused on the struggles that African-American women experience in college."

❏

There were physical hardships too. In the first years of Mercer's desegregation there were no scholarships such as the Rockefeller grants offered. Betty Walker remembers it well. Entering Mercer one year after Sam Oni's arrival, she turned down a two-year scholarship to Spelman College in Atlanta. Mercer had been her dream since, as an eleven-year-old child, she had taken a shortcut to a Negro elementary school track meet. As she watched the students sitting on the beautiful Mercer campus, lolling in the sun, studying on park benches, she first had the dream. She did not even know the name of the college until she came back through on her way home. "Mercer University. This will be my college," she fancied.

Back home the little girl saw what she perceived as disapproval from her mother. In reality it was love, frustration, anger at a system, and protection. "Get that out of your head! You can't go to Mercer. That's a white school and you're a black child."

But the dream did not die. For a time the realization of it was more of a nightmare. She sat on one of the same benches studying but those who passed her by did not see her. "If I exist, but no one acknowledges my existence, do I really exist?"

It was the question of the noise or no noise of a falling tree in an uninhabited forest.

She was the only black student in all of her classes. She tried to sit where there would not be so many empty seats around her.

> The few black Mercerians, without planning it, soon began gathering in the Student Center during chapel break to prove each other's existence. We bound in a special way that required no words, no storytelling about prejudiced students or racial incidents. We knew the words, had lived the story, and just needed to be around someone who offered acceptance and understanding. These were special times for us.

Without question, they were special times. It was also the beginning and reason for what whites would later see as self-segregation and find difficult to understand.

But Miss Walker understood. At first she was hungry almost every day. "At the end of some days I would be so weak from lack of food I could barely rise from my desk to begin my two-mile walk home."

Then her brother joined the Air Force and sent her five dollars a month for food. At the co-op Miss Thelma, a black lady who was surrogate mother for many a student over the years, would put extra items on her tray and charge her for the least expensive. "God knew I was hungry and fed me through my brother and Miss Thelma."

Books. And the prescribed gym suit before credit would be given. A staff person authorized her to charge books on his account. Later he nonchalantly told her he intended for her to charge whatever she needed from the bookstore. Now she could buy a gym suit. Still later, a scholarship, work-study program, and National Defense Loan met her financial needs. "Someone is looking out for me. God has chosen Dean Hendricks to look out for me," the grateful young woman wrote in her journal.

Miss Walker singles out teachers for special commendation: Dr. Cousins and Dr. Waters in English, Dr. Flick in History, Mr. Posey in French, Dr. Jean Hendricks in Psychology, and Dr. Otto. "They all tried," she says. "Some just knew the best way to treat black students."

Knowing "the best way" was not always easy. Too little help was seen as raw bigotry. Soon, too much was seen as paternalism. They were difficult days, even for the righteous ones.

Miss Walker poignantly describes her years from seventeen to twenty-two:

> Everything moved rapidly. In 1964 I graduated from an all-black high school, on the heels of the March on Washington and the assassination of our president, to attend a predominantly white Southern Baptist uni-

versity that found it easier to admit an African student than a black American. The Civil Rights bill passed that year and white Americans felt blacks were being forced on them and that their rights were being snatched away. In 1965 I saw the Watts riots in L.A. and the signing of the Voting Rights Bill. Dogs, billy clubs, fire hoses, filled the airwaves. What next? God is dead . . . the colored want to be called black . . . we shall overcome . . . look at the churches on Sunday morning . . . burn, baby, burn . . . hippies and flower children . . . black power . . . nuns and a one-legged man march across a bridge in Alabama . . . riots on major college campuses . . . look out for snipers on tall buildings . . . Vietnam—where is it and why are so many boys being sent there to fight a war when there is one to fight at home? Let's have a Poor People's March (black and white) . . . but the Dreamer is dead . . . the president is dead and now they have killed his brother. Is this America? The 1968 National Democratic Convention? Where do we go from here? I hear the words to the song "In times like these we need a savior."

Betty Walker. The eleven-year-old child who had her dream of Mercer fulfilled but had not dreamed just what it would be like. She lived it all, and more. "Black and white together" was pivotal for her. When "the Movement" flirted with, and sometimes embraced, separatism and "Whitey has to go," she harbored transcendence. It was she, along with Ed Bacon, who led the Poor People's March through Macon, braving the most tumultuous day and night of that city's racial history.

Even so, she writes:

> Some stages of growth were skipped, interchanged, disguised . . . priorities changed without my consent . . . something else was supposed to happen during those years that didn't happen to me.

The little girl made it. With a degree in math she taught high school for ten years. After traveling in many parts of the world she began a career with Southern Bell as an engineer. She was voted one of the most outstanding young women in America. In 1980 she was listed in *Who's Who among Black Americans*. As an executive loaned to United Way for two years she received widespread recognition as a public speaker and for her success in persuading big business and industry to give generously.

As a single parent she has an abundant life with her nine-year-old-son whom she adopted at six months. Something did not happen to her when it was supposed to. But something did. She loves her son.

❐

Joe Cecil Williams is a physician in Sumter, South Carolina, certified in Internal Medicine and Geriatrics. His wife practices with him. By the time he entered Mercer he was already conversant with the writings of black writers considered militant—Baldwin, Cleaver, Malcolm X. He found allies in Jimmie Samuel, Robert Brown, Robert Mike, George Henderson, Gary Johnson, and others. He laments the chasm that would not let him be best pal with a white person he knew to be his friend and singles out Dean Hendricks as a case in point. He recalls standing and applauding when Willie Ricks ordered all whites, including the dean, from the concert hall before the Freedom Singers would perform.

"We were wrong!" he says today. "Please issue a twenty-five-year-late apology to the dean."

Though affluent now, Dr. Williams has forsaken neither his roots nor his ideals of the 1960s. Most of his practice is among the poor and elderly of his city. "No one in America should be without adequate housing, food, or health care," he writes.

He says his four years at Mercer were the easiest of his life and reinforced something that was already in him from his childhood in rural Harris County, Georgia.

❐

When Rebecca Copeland arrived on the Mercer campus in 1967 the first person she met was Oscar Chaplin. He was helping new students with their luggage. The impression each made on the other survived and deepened. A daughter and two sons are the issue. They look back with fond memories of their college years, and are a traditional American family with a business in Savannah.

❐

Ernestine Cole was a National Merit Scholar and the valedictorian of her high school class. Dan Bradley recruited her. She speaks freely of pleasant experiences like working in the alumni office with Frances Floyd, a woman she admired and still cherishes as a friend and mentor. And serving on the student union board under Jerry Stone.

But the negatives are etched and linger. Three white males met her on campus and one called out, "Nigger!" A white doctor in Macon said, "Girl, you've got the clap."

She had not had any sexual contact. A physician at home correctly diagnosed and treated a fallopian tube infection.

She remembers the near riot when black students sat in an area in the cafeteria designated for fraternities and sororities and credits Dean Hendricks and Dr. Jean Hendricks for preventing serious violence.

"Mercer was a very overt racist place during the '60s, Mrs. Cole says. "I saw few changes during my time there without a struggle."

Since leaving Mercer she has served on the executive board of the Alumni Association and has been placed on the ballot for trustee election twice.

Mrs. Cole is a successful social work professional, is married, and has two sons.

◻

Renata Williams Boston was recommended to Chi Omega Sorority by two prominent alumna. She was the perfect profile—beautiful, stylish, quintessentially middle class, bright, ambitious. But she was black. When interviewed, she did not mention that rejection. Instead, she talks proudly of the accomplishments of the fifteen blacks who graduated in her class in 1970. She speaks of the superficiality of black-white friendships initially but sees a genuineness about some that developed later. While she does not dwell on the postmortem of Mercer's racism in the 1960s, neither does she romanticize it. One leaves her with the feeling that for her at least, the verb in "We shall overcome" might be changed to past tense.

◻

Lydia Dumas Wysinger was one of the first black students to have a white roommate—after Sam Oni of course—an arrangement that did not last. While it did last, she was able to observe the pseudo-sophisticated white coeds at close range. "I was a not-too-smart streetwise girl from Columbus, Georgia," she volunteers. The invariant questions that arose in the late-night sessions she could not answer.

"How do black men make love?" *She didn't know.*

"How do black men kiss?" *Well-l-l.*

"Are black men more endowed than white men?" *The innocent little Columbus girl couldn't answer for either color.*

"Aren't all blacks sexually active by sixteen because they are over-sexed?" *No.*

"This one girl from a small rural county had watched me intently and finally admitted that it was after midnight and she had always heard that blacks grew tails after midnight."

"Surely you jest!"

"No. I swear it. She was serious."

"Then what?"

"Enough! I put my tail in her face and her butt out of my room."

In a different vein she tells of a biology professor, who, perhaps with the controversial Stanford University physicist William Shockley as his authority, told his class that blacks and whites had the same size skulls but blacks have a thicker skull, therefore whites have a larger brain. Shockley had argued that heredity and not environment accounted for lower test scores among some blacks. Although his notion was sternly denied by psychologists and geneticists, it attracted a following by many seeking scientific sanction of their bias. With that data, Mrs. Wysinger says, her professor concluded that a black student could make no higher than a D in his class. After regrading her exam, that was what she made.

□

Robert Mike, now a successful Florida attorney, was told the same thing, except stronger. "I don't know how you got in this class," the professor told him. "But I can tell you you're not going to pass. If you pass at all it will be with a D."

Mike had planned a career in science. He had made straight A's in high school but became discouraged when he heard that. Dean Hendricks steered him to Professor Nordenhaug's course called "Philosophy of Science." Robert Mike went on to major in philosophy and political science, and later graduated from Vanderbilt Law School.

□

Charles Roberts, who holds the Ph.D. degree from Michigan State University and directs the Mathematics Program of the Charles Drew Science Enrichment Laboratory at that university, has mainly positive memories of his years at Mercer. After graduating first in his class at Peter G. Appling High School he entered Mercer in 1965. Bennie Stephens and Betty Walker preceded him as valedictorians at Appling and also preceded him at Mercer. He would later work with Miss Walker as tutor-counselor and instructor in Upward Bound.

Dr. Roberts dismisses most incidents having to do with race as a part of his personal growth and the inevitable ebb and flow of a society in transition. He singles out Dr. William Palmer as being the chief influence in his academic development and sees him as the foundation of his career as a mathematics educator, a field in which he has few peers. His current passion is the training of teachers to teach mathematics and science among ethnic minority students. Upward Bound lives; a recent sighting was in East Lansing.

◻

Joseph Hobbs, M.D., now a leading administrator and teacher in the Medical College of Georgia was an exceedingly intelligent and ambitious student at T. W. Josey High School in Augusta. His youthful dream was an academic career in biology and chemistry. He remembers being sent by black teachers to Richmond Academy, the premier high school for white students, to pick up materials for important science experiments, materials secreted through the back door from the well-stocked laboratory by sympathetic white teachers. His caring parents had sheltered him from the harsh reality of segregation, and he believed there was something inherently fair about the system and that academic performance would sweep the stereotypes away. He was well familiar with the stereotypes but could not accept that they were directed at him. He knew he was not lazy or dumb and certainly knew he was not an underachiever. He assumed the white world would expect nothing further before opening wide the doors of academic opportunity.

He began to question his assumption even before reaching college. When he was in the tenth grade he and some friends began an ambitious scientific inquiry having to do with the psychophysiological effects of acceleration on albino Swiss mice. Such a formidable project would be more apt to be attempted as a graduate thesis or dissertation, not tackled by high school sophomores.

Even so, the project won awards at the local, state, and national levels and was the overall winner at a regional science fair the first year competition was open to black participants. At the International Science Fair in Dallas, young Mr. Hobbs, by then a senior, won a special award from the United States Patent Office for the most original project in biological sciences.

He supposed he was on his way. But to his dismay, when Dean Hendricks appeared at T. W. Josey High School to recruit students recommended by the guidance counselor, the name of Joseph Hobbs was not among them. Fearing that his last chance to get financial aid had passed him by and he would not be able to go to a reputable school at all, he confronted Dean Hendricks in the corridor and with uncharacteristic bravado asked, "What about me?"

When Dean Hendricks returned to Mercer and checked Hobbs's record of accomplishments, Hendricks was also incredulous that Hobbs had not been recommended. As in the case of Samaria Mitcham, it was the counselor's subjective judgment that Joseph Hobbs was not mature enough to succeed in a racially integrated setting. And, as in the case of Samaria Mitcham, she was wrong.

Returning to Augusta, Dean Hendricks gained a strong recommendation from the Josey High School principal who proudly reminded him that Hobbs was the school's International Science Fair winner in Dallas. With that and other support, Joseph Hobbs was admitted at Mercer.

Who does not remember the inaugural surge of loneliness when Mama and Daddy turn and begin the journey home, leaving their baby to face the world alone? Dr. Joseph Hobbs still feels the lump in his throat when he talks about it.

"Here, Son. We wish it could be more." His mother handed him sixteen dollars. "That's for your laundry and things."

And then they were gone. When they had arrived on campus he had never seen so many white faces in one place. And so few black ones. Initially he had taken comfort that Carl Brown, a friend from Augusta, was his roommate. That consolation dwindled when he discovered that all students, men and women, had been assigned roommates by color.

The lonely young man began to know what the next few years would bring. Black students, as different from each other as each white student was different from another, would be drawn together for survival. Not because they felt more comfortable with "those of their own kind" because they were as dissimilar in interest, background, personality, and character as their white counterparts. They would be drawn together by the sheer weight of white response to skin. His closest associates would be black, even if they were people of whom he did not approve and did not like.

Joseph Hobbs, surrounded by an ocean of whiteness, knew, without self-vaunting, that he was a superior student. But he was a superior student from T. W. Josey, a school that did the best it could and sometimes performed miracles but did not have the equipment, laboratories, libraries, and cultural events most of the white students had known. "I am well prepared for this," he remembers thinking. "They will be better prepared."

The exhilaration he had felt in midsummer when he got the news that he would receive full financial aid at Mercer was fast wilting. "Just what have I done? With all my striving and ambition, is this where I really want to be?"

Standing in his silent room, staring out the window as two people he had known for eighteen years as Mom and Dad eased down Adams Street in their well-used car, turned right on Coleman Avenue, and headed east, and clutching in his hand the sixteen dollars they had left him . . . for the first time since he was a small boy, he cried.

And in the moment of his weeping, Joseph Hobbs was a man. During the four years Mercer University would be his home, he would have to prove it time and time again. Health care in Georgia is the better for the proving.

❑

Judge Mary Alice Buckner has seen many changes since coming to Mercer in the fall of 1966. She says she was naive, knew little of the world into which she was moving, and had no expectations of that world except that it would give her the opportunity to study. It was not all fair weather. "But," she says, "it was the real world, the world I see in my courtroom every day."

She liked Mercer's size, liked the landscape and architecture, found the professors accessible, and unfriendly students irrelevant to her mission. Still, there is a sad commentary. When asked if the arbitrary designation of rooms by color bothered her, she replied, "No. If they didn't want me, I didn't want them."

Then with resignation the Judge adds, "Of course, it was clear from the outset that we weren't welcome. But we were there. We stayed. And we were prepared when we left."

◻

These are but a few of the African-American men and women who led the way in Mercer's passage to a new day.

Not one regrets the pilgrimage.

Yet few disagree that the grass and weeds and thorny growths from an overhanging past plagued the journey.

◻

Chapter 16

A new way of thinking . . .

Simultaneous with developments at the college level, the Upward Bound program was making steady progress. After the Office of Economic Opportunity's Upward Bound program had been approved by Congress, Mercer, with the advance tip-off by Mr. DeVinney of the Rockefeller Foundation, had been one of the first applicants. With the help of William Palmer, a mathematics professor, the Mercer enthusiasts had been at work writing a grant proposal appropriate for a government agency. One advantage was that they had a modest program in place, quite similar to what the Office of Economic Opportunity envisioned for the Upward Bound program. Another ace was their friendship with Leslie Dunbar and Vernon Jordan. Both were certain to be consulted. Within months Vernon Jordan called to tell Hendricks they would get the money for Upward Bound.

Not everyone at Mercer was happy with the fast-breaking developments. Some of the more conservative faculty who had not been for the admission of Negroes in the first place used the argument that academic standards would be lowered. Some staff persons felt that the presence of large numbers of black students would turn many whites away; that Mercer enrollment had been rising prior to 1963 precisely because of the exclusive policy. They could point to 1962 when the University of Georgia desegregated under court order and numerous white students sought to transfer to Mercer. A statement and telegram to the University of Georgia president signed by a good many of the Mercer faculty, however, said transfers to avoid integration would not be welcomed.

The zeal of those wanting Mercer to move forward would not be dampened. And President Harris was not backing away. At the same time Upward Bound was beginning, a reception for trustees and their guests was held at the home of the president. The wife of a prominent trustee approached Mr. Harris and asked why a program such as Upward Bound could not be held at a "nigra college" like Morehouse or Fort Valley

State. Rather than go into a lengthy accounting of the history of the program, the president tersely replied, "Because I invited them here."

Jean Zorn was selected as the first paid coordinator of Upward Bound. A white woman approaching middle age, with red hair, and not a slave of convention, she carried herself with no air of deception. Her sometimes-coarse language, punctuated by an ever-present cigarillo in a long holder, were seen as unladylike to the more prim. In a time when nonconformity was something the young were cultivating, she had no need to try. She had always been eccentric.

When a radio station reported that Mercer University was housing white and black and male and female students in the same dormitory and the university public relations office busied itself with denials, Jean Zorn responded with a sharp, "Who gives a damn!?"

Actually males were housed in Boone Hall and females in Dowell with Porter Hall standing between.

Zorn's brusque manner was an offense to some faculty and staff in the program and sometimes a scandal to pristine townspeople. But her militant pro-student stance made her popular with the high school youngsters who adored and respected her. To her, that was all that mattered.

The first Upward Bound session suffered many problems and setbacks. Dormitory counselors, mainly white Mercer students, often were not up to dealing with their noisy, sometimes mischievous, black charges. Some quit in frustration. Others did not know how to respond to the spirited Saturday night parties, unfamiliar with the nimble dances of a culture they had not experienced. Others would timidly move in, stand in the shadows, slip away.

There were exceptions. Ed Bacon, a slab-sided stripling from Wayne County, danced with abandon, laughed with exhilaration, sang with gusto, wept with those who wept, listened, and learned. The Upward Bounders loved him, as he loved them. Today the Very Reverend J. Edwin Bacon is dean of St. Andrews Cathedral in Jackson, Mississippi.

Dan Bradley. Though more reserved than Bacon, nothing preempted his concern for the students. Whether teaching them to drive in Central City Park, taking them on field trips to the nation's capital and to Florida and other places they had never been, assisting with college applications for the fall, or helping the few white students he had recruited from the orphanage where he grew up to adjust to an integrated setting, he was a friend none of them would forget.

And John Adams. Adams had just graduated from Mercer and was leaving in the fall to attend theological seminary. When asked to be a counselor during the summer of 1966, he saw it as his first ministry. Of his background he says, "I was reared in a Baptist home and sensitivity to the needs of others was a way of life. Today such sensitivity is called co-dependency; in 1966 it was a virtue."

That sensitivity would bring a new challenge to the congregation of Tattnall Square Baptist Church. Adams, along with his fiance Beth Adcock of West Palm Beach, Flordia, took two of his black charges, Dennis Groomes and Richard Clay, to the Tattnall Square church one Sunday morning. A white student accompanied them. Miss Adcock was a regular member of the church. Although they were seated and allowed to remain for the service, their presence threw the congregation into a turmoil from which it never recovered. Soon a vote was taken to ban black worshipers. Pastor Thomas Holmes and his wife Grace Holmes personally visited the black students with profound apologies, but they could not undo the damage. The incident disturbed John Adams and Beth Adcock for years to come, and was the catalyst that within a few weeks led to the dismissal of Pastor Holmes and his staff when Sam Oni tried to enter the sanctuary.

With Bill Palmer as academic director, teachers like Mary Wilder, counselors like Ed Bacon, Dan Bradley, and John Adams, and with Joe Hendricks evermore hovering nearby, Jean Zorn had a program of immeasurable excellence. At the end of the third summer, graduates scattered to colleges from Vassar to Portland State, always with some reserved for Mercer. Jean Zorn and those who succeeded her had ample reason to exult.

A few summers later Joe Hendricks discovered that Jean Zorn, who had resigned from Upward Bound, was sick. Hendricks, Bill Randall (the black businessman and patron of the early tutorials), and Herman Mathis (former student president of Upward Bound), visited her in an Atlanta hospital. They found her near death from cancer but still spunky. With no maudlin whimper she told them what they must do when she died.

The service would be in the chapel of Randall Mortuary, a place where obsequies for a white person had never before been said. Herman Mathis, the black president of Upward Bound, would preside, Joe Hendricks would give a brief homily. The music would be civil rights and folk songs popular with her groups. When the time came, her Upward Bounders filled the chapel.

Jean Zorn had further instructed that her ashes be strewn upon the grounds where the Upward Bound House once stood. Mr. Randall delivered the remains to the spot in his finest limousine. Dean Hendricks was waiting. Together they honored her request. In an earlier vesper service Dan Bradley had used a metaphor about roses by the tennis court to suggest what Upward Bound was about. Jean asked that a rose be planted there in her memory. That, too, was done. Thus was a beautiful and beloved lady laid to rest. Decently and in order.

Almost from the start of Upward Bound a young man was involved who would later nurture it to full-grown status. Under his leadership it would become an exceedingly important contribution in the life of Mercer University.

Jacob Beil came to Mercer two days after Sam Oni arrived. His Russian grandparents had escaped to Manchuria following the revolution of 1917. Jacob Beil was born in Manchuria in 1945. When he was six years old his family, finding that Jews with their views fared no better with the Communist takeover of China than in their native Russia, migrated to Phenix City, Alabama and later settled across the Chattahoochee River in Columbus, Georgia.

From a family of Conservative Jews, and a product of three cultures, young Jacob flourished as a brilliant and inquisitive American. It must have been disquieting to his parents when they delivered their son to the Mercer campus, twelve years after arriving in America, and found tight security because of the presence of an African. To add to their anxiety, as they approached the campus they heard that four little girls had died in the Sunday morning bombing of the Sixteenth Street Baptist Church in Birmingham. Well aware that Jews, Negroes, and "foreigners" were routine targets of the Ku Klux Klan, it was difficult for them to drive away and leave their son in what they surmised a hostile environment.

They need not have feared. As a diligent student, well-mannered, and gregarious, Jacob was soon a favorite on the Mercer scene.

Jacob Beil was not directly involved with Upward Bound during the summer of 1966, since he was at Yale for an Intensive Summer Studies Program. When he returned in the fall for his senior year he was touched by the stories he heard of what had taken place while he was away. When Professor Wilder asked him to help with the Saturday morning teaching that would continue through the fall, winter, and spring, he readily signed on. It was the beginning of a long and successful association with Upward Bound.

Mr. Beil graduated in 1967 and stayed on to teach an Upward Bound course called "Western Man." Embraced by the students, he was given the pet name of the course he taught. "Let's go talk with Western Man." His teaching assistant was Ed Bacon.

Mr. Beil, today a practicing attorney in Columbus, fondly remembers the Saturday night dances in the Student Center, Bacon's imitation of James Brown with howling approval of the students, ninety-five percent black, and the close, daily association with the tight-knit group. He also recalls an integrated party going to a popular Riverside Drive restaurant which, in 1967, was still a novel event in Macon, Georgia.

By the summer of 1968, having finished his first year of law school, Beil was responsible for all Upward Bound humanities academic activities as well as for teaching a course called "Twentieth Century Man." That was the year the pioneering class of 1966 graduated from their high schools and would soon graduate from Upward Bound. Almost 100 percent were on their way to college.

There had been sobering events in America during 1968. Though they were still exuberant and fun loving, their heroes were dying deaths of violence. On April 4 Dr. Martin Luther King, Jr., epitome of hope and prophet of nonviolence, lay dead in Memphis, victim of one shot from a scope-sighted 30.06 Remington rifle. From fifty to a hundred thousand marchers followed a farm wagon pulled by two mules carrying the body of their beloved warrior. Georgia's Governor Lester Maddox, who refused to close the schools and protested the lowering of the flag, was not among the marchers. Sam Oni was.

The Upward Bounders were also hearing new songs, new sounds. "We shall overcome!" was being foreshadowed by calls of "Get your guns!" The cries escalated soon after the Upward Bounders returned for the third summer of learning. On June 8 they watched again as another of their heroes was lowered into the ground. In a candlelight service in Arlington National Cemetery, Robert Kennedy, victim of an assassin's bullet, was buried.

Someone whispered, "Burn, baby, burn!" It was only a whisper. But it was also a sign, perhaps a premonition. Although Mercer had been spared the violence, partly by Southern religion, partly by outlets such as Upward Bound for the new idealists, the young were watching. They had been children when Berkeley's Free Speech Movement flowered. Now they were young men and women.

Already that year there had been more than 200 college demonstrations in every part of the country. Buildings had been burned and dynamited, college administrators had been physically abused, and obscenities unthinkable a few years earlier had been scribbled on dormitory walls, on placards, and on lapel pins. Most of it in protest of a war in Southeast Asia no one could comprehend. Daily body counts of men, women, and little children seemed the only promise of victory.

And yet at Mercer, Upward Bound was the nearest thing to disorder the administration had known. Still, there was the whisper. "Burn, baby, burn!"

In the midst of it all Upward Bound went on. With Jean Zorn gone and Jacob Beil, now a student in the law school at the helm, the program entered the fall of 1968 with vigor, reaching into every area of the lives of the students: intellectual, cultural, and physical. Beil had Mary Dieterich, an able teacher who had been at Lassiter High School in Macon to assist him. And LaConstance Taylor, who had been the secretary of the program since it began.

Jacob Beil remembers the dental care provided, and says it was astounding how many students had never been in a dentist's chair. He saw young people who had been embarrassed to smile now beaming, their pretty teeth on proud display. Others could see to read well for the first time. Physical infirmities of long plague were treated or corrected.

Upward Bound, at first a tenuous appendage to the university proper, suspect for some, detested by others who saw the esprit de corps of the students-not-really-students as infatuation, having little to do with the legitimate objective of a university, had become a significant part of the Mercer campus and moved into a new facility. It had come a long way since the stealthy days of Joe Hendricks and Mary Wilder slipping a few students into classrooms for remedials.

The new locale had a place for administrative staff, rooms where students could meet for study, counseling, activities, or just to hang out. Most of them had no such place at home. It was theirs, and they were always welcome. Jacob Beil recalls those years as the conjunction of "the highest and most positive union of the idealism of the 1960s, with a practical, realistic approach toward the resolution of the problems that idealism sought to eliminate."

Beil sees his participation as the most worthwhile and rewarding experience of his life.

For most of those involved in running the venture it was more a mission than a program. "None of us had any idea what we were doing," Mary Wilder reminisces over iced tea in her artistically decorated home in North Macon. "I went over there day after day, night after night, and taught English. But I never was sure exactly what it was we were trying to do."

Mary Wilder is a modest woman. She did far more than teach English. Drawing on her experiences with the tutorials of which she had been so vital a part, she assisted with the curriculum, interviewed and helped select staff and faculty, assigned classrooms, arbitrated differences, did public relations in the Macon community, participated in social events, and performed many chores to make Upward Bound a school within a school, a combination summer camp and college preparatory training center.

None of them had a body of experience from which to draw as they approached the job before them. Initially they thought they could help improve mathematics and literary skills, help disadvantaged young people get over the academic hump. That was their most ambitious aim. It is difficult to quantify their success. What can be said with certainty is that a special relationship developed, something called "community." A most amazing cultural interchange was taking place. In Georgia. Without intent. Without, as Mary Wilder said, anyone knowing what they were doing. Here was a boisterous, singing, playing, dancing, debating, bonding, studying, performing, uninhibited playhouse. With contagion it reached throughout the campus. College students who had been beyond high school for two or three years, drifted by to see what could be such apparent fun on this little-known, quotidian Baptist campus. The fun, they discovered, was black and white together, overcoming.

Young people who had been known as minorities, disadvantaged, culturally deprived, to be studied more than to study, pitied more often than accepted, suddenly were none of those things. Just young people. Coming to believe in themselves and in each other, believing they could do it, that they were ready to face the world. A hundred of them, sequestered in academe, a world of which they had dreamed but not expected to enter—learning, loving. Life.

Mercer had been invaded by more than the modest and clandestine tutorials had portended.

The "Upward Bound Family," as Jacob Beil calls it, is still extremely strong. It has now existed for twenty-eight years with no geriatric symptoms. Those in the early groups keep up with each other, exchange special greetings, visit when they can, name children after each other. Jacob Beil reflects:

> Upward Bounders have now, after all these years, taken their place in American life, as mothers, fathers, doctors, lawyers, professionals, and in all sorts of activities. Some Upward Bounders are no longer with us, but their memories will always be with us, as will the memories of everything that was done during those wonderful years. The mosaic of our individual lives has, in significant part, been filled out, in rich colors, by our experiences in Upward Bound.
>
> If we sometimes long for those days of yore, we long for them not out of mere nostalgia, but because of the feeling that what we were doing, in a common joint effort, was making a difference, and that we were serving a greater purpose than, perhaps, what we are now serving. It was, after all, a time when, perhaps, idealism was more in fashion, and fanaticism not so much in vogue, and when individuals felt that they could make a difference in their country and in their world, and did not suffer from that jaded pessimism and cynicism, which now seems to pervade so much of our national and political life. We were, after all, young and did not know any better.

The Office of Economic Opportunity spent a great deal of money on the Upward Bound programs in the mid- and late-1960s. It was a mere trifle compared to what was appropriated to put a man on the moon, or to send 500,000 of our finest to Southeast Asia in a cause today embalmed in our national conscience. What would the nation be if those funds had been diverted so that every two-year community college, every state college and private university in America—there are almost 4,000 of them—had brought in the likes of Jean Zorn, Jacob Beil, Mary Wilder, and others, working with the same zeal, engaged in a program commensurate with what happened at this little Georgia school?

We can envision it. No earthling yet on the moon. (What exactly, anyhow, was that "giant leap for mankind"?) No incredible Star Wars with its commodious budget. No haunting nightmare of Vietnam with daily weeping at the wall. Just, what if . . . none of that? Instead, 4,000 Upward Bounds all those years, with the "culturally deprived"—who could not avoid the draft and were being shipped to Vietnam like cattle— being educated.

Instead of the present obsession with building more prisons to solve the crime problem, how many prison cells would stand empty today?

How safer would be the streets of America's cities? How fewer home-less? How many more stable family households? We cannot say. We can say that of the more than 1,000 that have participated just in Mercer's Upward Bound, more than ninety percent went on to postsecondary train-ing and hold responsible jobs. We can say there is no known record of a single one of them being in prison. Or sleeping in cardboard boxes. If the fruit of 4,000 Upward Bound programs had advanced to the work-rooms of business, industry, and education, paying taxes instead of being a tax ward, just what prevenient would it have done to America's economy?

Since we will never know, we can look back with Jacob Beil as he says:

> Those were good days; those were rewarding days; those were successful days. And the memory of those days will live with us, until the end of our days. Perhaps, when we are called to a final account, the scales of what we have, or have not done with our lives will be tipped, in our favor, by what we did in Upward Bound.

Looking back with one who was a young dreamer twenty-five years ago, we can dream of a future with him, a time when the sons and daughters will dream anew to set right our ill-advised endorsements. We can also look forward with Mr. Sam Hart who now, as assistant dean and director of Student Support Services, provides laudable leadership for what is still called Mercer's Upward Bound.

□

The climate for what some called a "new way of thinking" about race can be tracked back to the tenure of President Spright Dowell. Under his leadership the Christianity Department, which had generally been staffed by Baptist traditionalist preachers, brought in young men with Ivy League credentials. Teachers earlier named—Harold McManus, George McLeod Bryan, Theron Price, Das Kelly Barnett, and Howard McClain—all influ-enced by their study of Theology and Social and Christian Ethics under Reinhold Niebuhr and H. Richard Niebuhr, bound to challenge the thinking of many students on the issue of race. The activists they left when they moved on—Hendricks, Holloway, Brewster, Otto—held aloft a flaming torch. Though it glowed with varying degrees of intensity, the frozen pond of rabid segregation was beginning to thaw.

At times the "new way of thinking" was not directly related to race. In 1962, a year when silence on tangential issues was encouraged so that the ongoing discussion of racial inclusiveness might be primary, fourteen members of the Mercer faculty involved themselves in a raging controversy regarding methods of biblical study. Professor Ralph Elliott of the Midwestern Baptist Seminary in Kansas City had written a book on Genesis in which he seemed to suggest that the creation story of Adam and Eve might have been allegorical. Broadman Press, the publishing arm of the Southern Baptist Convention, published the book, then removed it from circulation when there was a storm of contention. Subsequently, Elliott was dismissed from the seminary faculty. With the acrid pen of Dr. James Y. Holloway the fourteen Mercerians released a harsh censure of those who questioned the historic Baptist principle of the right of the individual to study, interpret, and teach the Scriptures.

Sometimes the bright, bold, and youthful faculty members would resort to serious frivolity, making fun of themselves and everything having to do with Mercer while at the same time driving home a discerning point.

On one occasion some of the same ones who had publicly challenged the Baptist hierarchy for censoring and firing Ralph Elliott wrote and widely circulated what they called, "The Complete 95 Theses." Martin Luther had posted his "Ninety-five Theses" on the Wittenberg Cathedral door in 1517. They sought to upgrade Luther with their own satirical grievances against established religion.

Most of them held advanced degrees from Yale University and Union Theological Seminary in New York. In their mischief the two became "Yailanunion."

"Some graduates of Yailanunion are Christians," thesis number 6 said.

"H. Richard Niebuhr is a sinner too," read number 18.

Number 26: "If the Apostle Paul could walk the earth again he would feel more at home in a Billy Graham meeting than in a Yailanunion seminar."

"Reinhold Niebuhr is right in thinking that many New York Jews are as Christian as he is."

Other slurs included: "C. S. Lewis has done more to advance the Kingdom of God in the world than H. Richard Niebuhr, and H. Richard Niebuhr has done more to advance Yale snobbery than C. S. Lewis."

"Paul Tillich could have learned to speak English if he had wanted to."

The Social Gospel, with several adherents on the faculty, did not escape their jest.

19. "Rauschenbusch was the last Christian in the Social Gospel movement."

20. "The Social Gospel movement dwindled away when the only poor people left were dirty."

21. "The Social Gospel movement was founded on the conviction that the Christian faith was only for the rich and that the poor ought to be content with things of this world."

Jokes about Yale and Union were funny to most of those receiving "The Complete 95 Theses." But when the jesters reached their hidden agenda, the lampooning of Mercer's Holy Mother Church, the Southern Baptist Convention, the laughter ceased. Especially when Duke McCall, executive secretary of the denomination at the time, received the first salvo: "Duke McCall is Antichrist."

Southern Baptist preachers followed: "The chief requirement for advancement in the Southern Baptist ministry is cultivated ignorance."

Though it did not make the slate of ninety-five, one of them had earlier said Mercer University was run by forces beyond control: "the law of anticipated reaction of the most devious, mugwump Baptists."

Thesis number 9: "Among the faults of the Southern Baptist Convention are: (1) It is too Southern. (2) It is too Baptist. (3) It is too conventional."

Other theses said: "The most significant ritual among Southern Baptist is counting each other."

"The Home Mission Board should stay at home."

"The Apostle Paul was not a Baptist."

"Tithing is a device by which rich pharisees prey on poor pharisees."

"Some tithers don't get rich."

And thesis 55 stated: "Propaganda techniques of the Southern Baptist Sunday School Board are more highly developed than those of the Kremlin."

Those were all sacred cows. Georgia politicians, revered by Mercer's majority constituency almost as much as Southern Baptists, were not immune either: "There have been at least three senators in American history who have accomplished less than Herman Talmadge," read number 90.

Obliquely there would also be mockery for those who opposed admitting Negroes to Mercer because they feared it would lead to miscegenation: "Most of the white people involved in racial mixing are segregationists."

To further aggravate the pietists, they wrote: "Negroes, being fully human, do not have souls either."

And number 92: "Southerners are the only white Americans who are afraid they would marry Negroes if the law did not prevent it."

Then finally: "Foolish virgins don't last."

It was designed to be funny. And to vandalize narrow minds in their world. Since no one knew the authors, and satire is always difficult to refute without making the brunt of the joke appear even more laughable, "The Complete 95 Theses" was covertly passed around the South for months, perhaps making more of an impact than the most analytical challenge of the status quo.

Those who published "The Complete 95 Theses" did not do it from a spirit of insolence. They were men deeply devoted to Mercer University and committed to saving her from dissembling obscurantists.

Despite such lapses, by 1968 Mercer and America had reached a point where little was funny. Brokenness was rapidly competing with and often overwhelming the sense of community that Mercer had seen and thought secure.

Some of those who provided the leadership were thinking that maybe they laughed too soon. On a fund-raising trip to New York, Dean Hendricks was seated next to a personable black woman who happened to be on the faculty of Howard University. When the conversation turned to programs on their respective campuses Hendricks talked for a long time about the successes they had known through the Upward Bound program, and the recruitment of minorities. Since he had played the pivotal position from the outset he did so gladly, and with an air of pride. After all, this was happening at a small, previously all-white, Baptist college in central Georgia, a region not notorious for its progressive efforts. It must have seemed reason enough to preen. But as the plane taxied to the gate the woman gave him a scolding look and said, "How could you!? How dare you think you have anything to teach black young people today?"

Not long after that one of Hendricks's favorite Upward Bounders, a bright, and previously lighthearted young woman, who had spent the summer in Colorado on a Martin Luther King, Jr. scholarship, took a seat in his office and after a perfunctory greeting exclaimed, "I know now that I have a responsibility to hate you."

On another occasion, when Dean Hendricks and two students were walking across the campus of Clark College in Atlanta, where he had driven them to enroll, some students along the walkway chanted, "Here comes the master and two of his slaves."

Now Joseph M. Hendricks the radical—the one who had joined William Randall in talking black ministers into challenging segregated city buses; who had, almost singlehandedly, integrated Macon's hospitals by getting on a committee to report the truth to the federal government; who had, with his machismo presence, walked the first black student onto the campus, defying any would-be challenger; and who, in his naivete, went to New York and Washington and came home with enough money to turn a little Southern Baptist college into the most integrated educational institution in Georgia with the successful Upward Bound program and aggressive college recruitment—was the conservative.

But he and the little army of reform were not quixotic do-gooders (or perhaps they were, to their everlasting credit). While some of Mercer's officialdom no doubt agreed to desegregate for expedient reasons—federal and foundation grants, loss of accreditation, even vainglory—that was not what propelled those who moved the process to a higher level. They saw the batteries of benightedness that had been unlimbered against all the influences for decency and common civility since the Brown decision of 1954 as a threat to their own humanity and as a heathen corpse, a contradiction of their Christian values. They saw the dark horizon and sought to blow a trumpet of warning to a people they loved and of whom they were very much a part—the South. Their motives might at times have been more Stoic than Christian. Still the new rejection was a painful awakening, a lesson Hendricks realized he should already have learned because, by 1968, there had been ample warning. In his busy-ness he had been tardy in discerning the signs of the times—the depth and legitimacy of the grievances African-Americans justly felt against his people.

It had been but four years since Martin Luther King, Jr. was awarded the Nobel Prize for peace for his nonviolent crusade. But even before that, parameters drawn by Dr. King for justice without chaos were beginning to erode.

By 1968 it had been three years since the bloody Sunday at the Edmund Pettus Bridge where 600 blacks and a sprinkling of whites were met by horsemen armed with guns, tear gas, bullwhips, and billy clubs that sent the marchers running, stumbling, and crawling back to the Brown's Chapel A.M.E. Church. And two years since Willie Ricks, a SNCC worker and familiar face in Macon, along with Stokely Carmichael, near the end of a march from Memphis to Jackson, Mississippi started by James Meredith who had been gunned down shortly after he had begun, stood on flatbed trucks in Greenwood and Yazoo City and began what became known as the "Black Power Movement."

"The Negro is going to take what he deserves from the white man," Carmichael had shouted.

"Black power!"

"What do you want?"

"Black power!"

"What do you want? Say it again!"

"Black power!"

Dean Hendricks would be forced to leave a lecture sponsored by black students but paid for by the university when Willie Ricks demanded that all whites leave the hall. "The sisters haven't come all the way down here to entertain white folks," Ricks said. Hendricks, who had arranged the funding of the program with the proviso that it be open to all students, was so angry on that occasion he went to the bank next morning to stop payment on the check. Willie Ricks had beat him there. In a heated confrontation in a remote section of the Science Building, Hendricks asked Ricks if his agenda meant teaching black students to break solemn agreements, as whites had done to blacks for centuries. Robert Mike, standing nearby, was certain Hendricks was going to attack Ricks.

So the little Mercer coterie had heard the rhetoric, understood that it was inevitable in the face of the past. Yet they had exulted in seeing old times pass away in their midst, supplanted by a brief spirit of *communitas* Mercer and the South had not known before. And one that most of the South still spurned. Now they were forced to acknowledge that a new day had dawned, a day when old-fashioned integrationists were in large measure passe.

Still, with the continuing enthusiasm and interest in Upward Bound among blacks, and some poor whites, in Macon and in the surrounding counties, and with a greater number of black students in college than any nonblack school in the state, public or private, they understood the difference between perplexity and despair. So they resolved to continue the journey as best they could through the troubled waters they knew lay ahead.

One way they met the new day was to take another look at their own goals. They began to see that the disadvantaged were not confined to one color. They would not be stampeded into what they saw as the feckless corner of separatism, no matter how fashionable it might become. In effect, they accepted their newly defined status as "old-fashioned integrationists," and began recruiting college students from unlikely places. "If integration is what we are about, well, let's be about it. It isn't going to end by turning Mercer into a primarily black university."

One outstanding example of this turnabout was a young white son of a hard-working but extremely poor mother. He was recommended by one of the most obstreperous Ku Klux Klan leaders in the South. A strange development indeed. And one the Rockefeller Foundation might have had trouble understanding, seeing it as taking their eleemosynary commitment too far.

The young man did not follow the path of his sponsor. However, for two years he was highly suspicious of Dean Hendricks, having been told repeatedly by the Klansman that Hendricks was under his and the Klan's control and that any violation of Old South ways could mean the end of his college education. The unsophisticated student was led to believe his fees were being paid by the Klan. Even so, he chose his own path. By the end of his sophomore year he had learned to sing, "We Shall Overcome," "The Answer Is Blowing in the Wind," and "Alice's Restaurant." He shook hands with the Movement grip, and adopted the beard, hairstyle, and dress code of his contemporaries. For a time he was torn between a feeling of disloyalty to the Klansman he thought responsible for his being there and leading his own life. He could not discuss it with anyone. While black students were dubious of white motives, this white student was bothered because the words he was hearing and the behavior he was seeing did not fit the mindset of those back home he had been told were his benefactors. Reconciliation had to be sought on three fronts. But out of his private hell he emerged as an excellent student and campus leader. In his third year he was a counselor for Upward Bound. Today he is a gracious citizen, husband, and father. He teaches his children of manners, fairness, generosity, equality, and nobility in general. He and a wife he courted at Mercer are active in church and civic affairs, are devoted alumni, and are engaged in a worthy vocation.

Dean Hendricks now admits that he should not have been shaken by the words, "Now I know I have a responsibility to hate you." But he was. And he dates those words as the beginning of learning to live with the label he had earlier worn in comfort: "White liberal." White liberal was becoming a mark of opprobrium in the minds of many he had thought he was rescuing.

Ah, Bob Dylan.

Come mothers and fathers,
Throughout the land,
And don't criticize
What you can't understand.
Your sons and your daughters
Are beyond your command . . .
For the times they are a-changin'.

Jacob Beil had said the days were good ones. And for those of whom he was speaking, they were. But not for everyone. Certainly not for the more than half a million who were in the uniform of their country, fighting and dying in Vietnam for something they knew not. Not for the thousands of innocent and uninvolved civilians who died as a result of daily shellings and bombings. Nor for the 567 old men, women, children, and babies slaughtered at My Lai on a March 1968 Saturday morning.

From the isolated village in Southeast Asia where that carnage, led by Lieutenant William Calley, took place, to a small city in one of America's original colonies where Jacob Beil, a gentle-hearted, though tough young Jew, with lineage stretching from Russia to China to Phenix City, Alabama, violated his Sabbath on that Saturday morning to teach the young at a Christian school to care, seems so paradoxical as to defy comparison. But Beil's Upward Bounders were listening. Not only to him but to the six o'clock news. And when they heard that General Westmoreland, when asked about victory by "body count" and if the large number of civilians being killed bothered him, replied, "Yes, but it does deprive the enemy of the population, doesn't it?" the course called "Twentieth Century Man," taught by one of the few white people ever to treat them as equals, took on new meaning.

Listening. And watching. Watching later as a heavy metal fence was built around the campus that would detour black children who had for years taken the time-saving shortcut to school, to the park, and to stores. Watched and saw a gate installed when the fence also caused inconvenience to white children who lived on college-owned property. Watched as Urban Renewal leveled block after block of slum-landlord houses adjacent to the campus, making way for future Mercer development.

On summer and weekend afternoons black youths lined the rock wall that was a dividing line between campus and community. Signs, regularly spaced, appeared: DO NOT SIT ON THIS WALL. They watched. And they knew what the sign meant. Florida parents out college shopping with their high schoolers might see so many idle black youths—to them potential muggers and rapists—so near the campus, and drive on to the next prospect farther up the highway.

A number of Mercer faculty vehemently protested the fence, knowing that it was enhancement of the wall of separation between those who were of the academy and those who were not intended to be, as well as buttressing the wall between white Americans and black Americans. One faculty member resigned over the issue. But those voices were not heard by the youngsters who could no longer walk across the campus nor sit on the wall watching the cars go by. Nor by the families whose houses were being razed in the name of Mercer's progress.

Even the Upward Bounders and black college students were getting mixed signals. "Are we, or are we not, welcome?"

As they listened, watched, and pondered, the earlier whisper, "Burn, baby, burn," grew a little more audible. Soon, even at what had been a drowsy, disengaged rampart of conservatism, the whisper would become the chill blast of protest and insurgence. . . . Where nothing slept.

For the times, they are a changin'.

❐

Chapter 17

Turn on, tune in, drop out . . .

All that most maddens and torments; all that stirs up the lees of things; all truth with malice in it; all that cracks the sinews and cakes the brain; all the subtle demonisms of life and thought; all evil, to crazy Ahab, were visibly personified, and made practically assailable in Moby Dick. He piled upon the whale's white hump the sum of all the general rage and hate felt by his whole race from Adam down; and then, as if his chest had been a mortar, he burst his hot heart's shell upon it.
—Melville, *Moby Dick*, chap. 41

And then again the rage!

To understand Mercer University in the mid- and late-1960s it is necessary to consider Macon, Georgia. Rufus Harris had written President Nathan Pusey of Harvard that Macon, being on a line with Montgomery, Alabama, and Jackson, Mississippi, had not known outside influences. Those words might have mustered sympathy and support in Cambridge but would not have been recognized as being entirely accurate by many Mercer students.

Far from being the backwoods little Southern city Harris described, with conservative politics and racial bigotry being the major components, by 1967 Macon was alive with limousined rock musicians, a robust drug trade and rollicking good times. Although the pristine set of Macon remained much the same, The Allman Brothers Band, Otis Redding, and Little Richard were changing the city's image. Southern Rock was big business. Their producer and abettor Phil Walden was a graduate and friend of Mercer. Former students remember Otis Redding performing for fraternity parties for fifty dollars a night, even when dancing was not officially permitted on campus. And before Negroes were allowed as students.

That was but part of Macon. And but part of Mercer. The many churches, civic clubs, garden parties, patriotic organizations, and conservative politics remained. The same was true of the University community.

But the counterculture was emerging and gaining ground. Neither town nor gown was exempt. Neither was ready for it.

To many, Capricorn Records was a thorn in the flesh. To others, it was liberation from cultural captivity.

In late 1967 Otis Redding was killed in a plane crash on frozen Lake Monona, a few miles from the University of Wisconsin. A few years later Duane Allman died in a motorcycle accident not many blocks from the Capricorn recording studio. A year after that Berry Oakley, the Allman Brothers bassist, met an identical fate near the same spot. Allman and Oakley are buried side by side in a ravine in Macon's historic Rose Hill Cemetery. After all these years a steady stream of middle-aging fans come by to sit at the sepulcher of their near-gods, play their old cassettes, and leave faded "Eat a Peach" album covers, flowers, guitar picks, wine bottles, and paraphernalia.

(As Duane Allman was dying he kept muttering, "Eat a Peach." The band was halfway through cutting an album at the time. The material he had already recorded was used on the album. The album was named "Eat a Peach.")

The headstones bear the telling psychedelic mushroom logo.

Greg Allman survived, went West, and married Cher. Little Richard turned to preaching, then back to his first love, and still insists that he is the godfather of Macon's Southern Rock era.

It was a brief and, for many, a tragic epoch. But in the while it left an unforgettable marking on many who came of age during its reign. The influence of Macon's Southern Rock swept the nation and lives on. Mercer students were not many blocks from the axis of it all and some of them drank deeply from the wellspring of one of music's unique regimes. They were a minority, but a garrulous one.

The subculture that caught fire like kingfishers in the 1960s was late coming to the Mercer scene. Most had remained content with Baptist Student Union retreats, grades, beauty contests, social fraternities, and routine campus activities. When drugs did come, it was as a prairie fire in a winter snow.

◻

"Are you all right?" one of the boys asked the sophomore girl who was lying on her back with her arms outstretched, almost like a cross. The girl wore ice blue shorts with a red, man's-style shirt. The shirt ends were tied tightly around her waist, accentuating her hips and bust. It was a balmy fall afternoon in 1967. Two hours earlier, right after lunch, a group of students, all white, had loaded into a rickety Volkswagen bus with a Florida license plate. When they couldn't pull another one in, three others followed in a car. They had driven west on state highway 74, then turned north onto a county road after they crossed the Tobesofkee Creek and finally up a wagon road left by timber cutters. They stopped in a clearing where the creek did a dogleg bend.

"Like, what county is this?" one of the boys asked the driver, a girl, when they stopped.

"Just so it ain't Talbot," another one said.

"On account of Dean Hendricks's brother is the high-h-h-h ole sheriff in that county," said someone else."

"Like, man, he ain't no higher than I'm fixing to be," added another, pulling a small package tucked underneath his shirt and passing it around.

The girl lying on the ground had been one of the more frolicsome ones since they arrived, wading in the water, making mud pies, making up limericks. When she fell she was struggling to form her body into a triskelion. When she grabbed her second leg, and there was no third one to grab, she fell.

"She must be a philosophy major," someone said. Everyone laughed. "One of Trimble's philosophy majors."

"Or Nordenhaug. He knows about three-legged people," someone else said.

As the girl fell she did a sort of cheerleader split before going down completely. With a fading grin she sang, "I was sinking deep in sin . . . whee-e-e!"

After she rolled over on her back she began clapping her hands above her upturned face, singing in sarcastic fashion:

Jesus loves me, this I know,
For the Bible tells me so.
Little ones to Him belong,
They are weak but He is strong.

Her voice was shrill and sometimes she lost the words. The others, seeing that she wasn't hurt, formed a circle around her, joining hands and skipping around her like children playing "Ring Around the Rosie," everyone falling down on cue. When she finished the verse they all joined in the chorus, singing in soft contrast to her loudness. With a hush.

Yes, Jesus loves me. Yes, Jesus loves me. Yes, Jesus loves me.
The Bible tells me so.

In close harmony.

The sound of their bare feet on the dry leaves was the only accompaniment to their singing.

Earlier they had laughed and teased each other as they sang bawdy songs they had learned from a record made by a Harvard mathematics professor whose name none of them could remember. "Tom something or other," one of them said.

Now they had turned serious. Just dancing around the prone figure who didn't get up.

The girl didn't proceed to another verse of the song, instead, repeating over and over what she could remember of the first one. "Jesus loves me . . . Bible tells me . . . Little ones . . . He is strong." Slurring now.

When she fell silent, another girl, outside the circle of dancers, began another song, but in a regular voice.

Jesus loves the little children,
All the children of the world.
Red and yellow . . . Whoops! . . . and white,
They are precious in His sight.
Jesus loves the little children of the world.

When the girl exclaimed "Whoops!" in her song, instead of "black," those in the circle giggled and formed a new circle around her, leaving the other one on the ground. Each time the singer reached "Whoops!" in the lyrics one or another of the students would yell out the name of one of their black schoolmates. "Red and yellow . . . Gary! . . . and white, they are precious in His sight. Red and yellow . . . Sam Oni! . . . and white, they are precious in His sight."

Sam Oni, of course, was no longer a part of the Mercer scene by the fall of 1967. At least not physically. He had already graduated and was in California, having vowed never to set foot on Georgia soil again. Some of the students on the outing that day had never met him. But the name of the first black person to break the color barrier would be a part of Mercer lore for a long time.

When they ran out of names of well-known black students they milled around the area, some pairing off and drifting into the dense undergrowth. "Don't forget your hygiene," one of the girls called to another as a couple disappeared.

"Are you all right?" the boy who had been leaning over the girl on the ground kept asking.

"Where's Captain Trips?" another of the girls asked, clearly alarmed.

"Captain Trips" was a code word for someone who knew how to bring someone down who had had too much of a drug. Sometimes he was a dealer, sometimes an older student, but always one experienced in recognizing when someone was going out.

"Captain Trips didn't come," someone said. "He has two finals tomorrow." The students who were still in the immediate area gathered around the girl on the ground, concerned now.

"My god!" one of the boys yelled, almost crying. "Is she flipping out? I've never done this before! Is she going to die?" Earlier he had been as playful as the others, chasing oak, maple, and sweet gum leaves as they drifted down from trees preparing for their winter's rest. When a marijuana cigarette was passed to him, he would take a long pull, holding the alien smoke deep in his lungs until he choked and burst with laughter. After each draw he would say, "Cool. Man, that's cool. Far out. Out of sight."

All the hip words he knew. When he said "Cool," it sounded halfway between *cull* and *cool*. One of the girls said he sounded like a Yankee talking. That seemed to please him.

Now he was turning round and round, scattering a pile of leaves he had called a snowman. He grabbed one of the girls by the hand, the one who had driven the Volkswagen, and through a muffled sob exclaimed, "Take me home! I want to get out of here! Please! Please! Where is Captain Trips? Who is Captain Trips, anyhow?"

"Captain Trips is our friend," the girl replied, trying to calm him.

The sun had gone down and a light fog was settling over the swampy area where they were. An older student, one who had not engaged in much of the frivolity, moved from where he had been watching. He was wearing heavily scuffed combat boots, faded dungarees and an Ike jacket with corporal chevrons on one sleeve, an outline of where stripes had been torn off on the opposite sleeve. Underneath the unbuttoned jacket he wore a dingy white T-shirt with a washed-out logo. His stringy red hair fell almost to his shoulders, framing a short black beard.

"I'm Captain Trips," he said softly.

No one challenged him as he addressed the sniveling boy who was much larger than he. The boy was neatly dressed, smooth-faced, as if he hadn't yet started shaving. He looked about seventeen.

"Everything's cool, man," the older one said, trying to pronounce "cool" the way the boy had.

The terrified boy pushed him away, screaming. "You don't know what you're doing. Get away! Get away! She's going to die and I'm going to be in a lot of trouble! Oh God! Oh, my God!"

He was spinning round and round again. "Mama!!" he yelled, his hysteria seeming to mock the easy sound of crows cawing in the distance.

The older student, now Captain Trips, turned to the girl who seemed to be the big boy's date. "Walk him around. Talk to him. Hug him. Keep talking. He's in worse shape than she is," he said, motioning to the girl on the ground as he moved toward her. "Just don't panic. Let him hold onto you. But watch him. Don't let him get off on his own." Then, under his breath, "Christ, I might as well be back in Nam."

Quickly now he nudged aside the boy leaning over the girl. He sat on the damp leaves and nestled her head in his lap. At first he didn't say anything at all, just sat very still, watching her, making very sure she was breathing. He began stroking her hair, mumbling something as he did. Occasionally he would lift her head to his cheek, whispering something, sometimes kissing her gently on the forehead. Humming at first, then singing, he began the last words she had sung, in a sort of cooing way. "Lit-tle-ones-to-Him-belong, they-are-weak-but-He-is-strong."

As he sang he hugged her loosely, still stroking her hair and sometimes whispering something between lines of the song.

All the others had pulled back, no one making a sound, everyone coming down, their party over.

Gradually the girl's body began to stir. As it did, the man who said he was Captain Trips held her closer, still humming, singing, whispering.

Suddenly she jerked herself into a stiff sitting position, clearly afraid. She grabbed his beard with her fingers, then pinched her own cheeks. "Am I breathing? I forgot to breathe, didn't I?"

She was kicking her heels in the ground, her whole body trembling vigorously. In her drug-fog she kept repeating that she wasn't breathing. Picking her hand up by the forearm the man let her hand fall onto her heaving breast, pressing her hand down lightly with his own hand. He held her hand there for several minutes, letting her feel herself alive.

Gradually she began relaxing, talking back to him, answering his questions.

Finally he said, "We'll go in a minute. "We'll be back by supper-time."

The story is a composite of many such trips. The characters are real, unnamed because most of them made their way through those fierce days. And because they are forty-five now. Some older. With children, housenotes, and orthodontist bills.

Back at Mercer, as the chimes struck eight o'clock, Ed Bacon, president of the Student Government Association, was closing a meeting. The agenda had explored upcoming campus lectures by William Stringfellow, Alex Haley, and Dick Gregory, and student participation in the SCLC Poor People's March that was scheduled to pass through Macon. Bacon reminded the group of a scheduled concert by the Beach Boys.

Students, in pairs and small groups, were in unused classrooms studying for tomorrow. Laboratories were still seeing last-minute, midterm experiments.

The Ministerial Association had convened to have the annual group picture taken by Joe Cook. "This will go all over Georgia," one of the senior students, the president of the Ministerial Association, said. Then he gave the closing prayer.

> Holy Father, we just ask You to bless us as we go from this place, and Holy Father, we just ask that You bless Your ministers all over the world, and Father especially do we pray for the missionaries on the home and the foreign fields, and dear God we just pray that if there be any unsaved on this campus You will just use us to lead them to give their hearts to Christ before it is too late, and Holy Father just lead, guide, and direct our faculty that they lead us in the paths of righteousness, for it is in the name of Your precious Son we pray. Amen.

All the ministerial students joined the Amen. Some of them told the association president that was a pretty prayer. It was a time warp Jesse Mercer would have applauded, the ongoing dream of Penfield.

Julian Gordy, who had arrived at Mercer an inveterate racist but soon changed through his friendship with James Norman and Gary Johnson, was preparing a speech he intended to give in chapel claiming government at the highest level was spreading drugs on college campuses to subvert antiwar demonstrations. Gordy became a Lutheran and is now a pastor in Ocean Springs, Mississippi.

Sandra Rich, a popular cheerleader, was being escorted across the campus by John Ellington, later to be her husband and a medical doctor. Miss Rich had recently been crowned Miss Mercer in the campus beauty pageant attended by Judy Ford, Miss America that year.

The *Cluster* staff was locking galleys on the next edition. Gary Johnson, the first nonwhite editor, had completed assignments for the following week. Larry Finkelstein, now a rabbi in Texas, would do his column on "Integration Leads to Civilization." Joseph Hobbs was doing the last revision on his column. Called "Blacks Face Search for Concealed Identity," it was at once an upbraiding of whites who saw integration as letting high-achieving blacks become honorary whites, and a challenge to the black students to take pride in who they were, learn of their heritage, and stand tall. He saw the recently organized Black Student Alliance as a significant first step. Editor Gary Johnson had written a stinging, satirical piece on white fraternities as seen in the black context and was relinquishing his space for the rabid response that was crowding his desk.

Sallie Carter and Dr. Jean Hendricks were driving in from Milledgeville.

As the young woman with the blue shorts moved down the walkway to her dormitory, a girl on either side, they met Ed Bacon. "What's happening, Baby Chile," he called.

"Not much, Sweetie," she answered, trying to be nonchalant but not stopping to talk.

Across the green the bearded veteran, still in his half-uniform, was standing in the shadows of the Student Center Building. From a darkened side door a lone figure moved toward him. Broad shouldered, moderately barrel-chested but otherwise of medium build, the man was neither a student nor an outsider. It was clear this was his turf. When a campus security guard walked by and hesitated, the man motioned for the guard to move on. It was Dean Hendricks.

"How'd it go?" the dean asked, obviously troubled.

"Not good, not bad."

"Handled all right?"

"Handled all right."

"What they was, my man?" The dean could be just about as hip of tongue as the most jivey student.

"Pretty much guessing," the man said. "Ludes, I think. On top of a bottle of cough syrup. God, that Robitussin. Codeine. Bad mix when they don't know what they're doing." He shook his head, then went on with his report. "Other one, grass. Mostly weed I think. He's just a kid. Scared hell out of him though. Lord, I'm not one to talk. But they're getting strong stuff around here now."

"Come by my office tomorrow," the dean said. "I'll talk to you then."

"Think there's gonna be a bust?" the bearded man asked before walking away.

"No bust. Not if I can help it."

When the self-announced Captain Trips made his way up the stairs and entered Dean Hendricks's office early next morning, well before any of the staff had arrived, he was dressed the same as before.

"You want some coffee, my man?" Hendricks asked.

"Yesir," the man said, combing his hair and sitting down.

Hendricks moved from behind the desk, poured the coffee, then sat in a chair facing the man directly.

"Do you know what you're doing, Bud?" the dean asked, blowing the steam rising from his cup.

"I must have brought a hundred down in Vietnam," he answered.

He sounded confident but not cocky. He spoke with halting, deliberate words. His bearded face was without revealing expression of anything he was thinking or feeling. "When I wasn't on a wild roar myself."

For what seemed a long time neither man spoke. Then, "What did you have over there?" the dean asked.

"Same as here. We had it all. Speed to kill with. Pot and hash to forget it. Acid in between to figure out what the hell it was all about."

Except for the guttural sounds coming from the dean's troubled spirit, there was more silence. When he spoke again the words were out of character for someone who seemed ever in command. "Tell me about dope. I'm grazing an alien pasture here."

"Afraid it's not a pasture, Dean," the man said, putting his coffee on the floor and ambling about the room. "More like running a spring-toothed harrow through new ground."

"I know what that's like," the dean said. "You're going along all right, you think. Then a harrow tooth hangs in a root, the mule keeps going and the handlebar kicks you smack in the belly."

"Something like that," the man said.

"Where're you from anyhow?" Dean Hendricks asked him. "To know about new ground and springtoothed cultivators?"

"Terrell County."

"Then you know."

"Yesir. I know."

The man poured more coffee and sat in another chair, farther across the room. "Where you want me to start? About dope, I mean?"

"I'm in kindergarten, Friend. You're talking to a cat who's never had a glass of wine. I just know dope is dangerous. That it'll kill you."

A man who had a reputation for turning jeremiads into doxologies was pitifully asking for help. Then, as if to regain ascendancy, asked, "Are you clean? I mean now?"

The student across the room sat staring out the window, clenching his right hand, holding the coffee cup with the other one. "Does now mean today?" he asked, nervously inhaling the pale steam rising from the coffee cup, holding it in his lungs as if smoking marijuana. "Today, yes. But I told you I would shoot straight with you. I've done a lot of drugs, Dean. I'm not saying I'll never do it again. I take it one day at a time, plowing through the tangled roots and rotting stumps. I never know when the cultivator will kick me in the belly."

"You know we lost a student to drugs two weeks ago, don't you?" the dean said. "One of our finest kids."

"Yesir. He was my pal. I was just outside the room when he died."

Dean Hendricks thought the student was going to cry but he didn't. Instead he went on. "Senseless. Plain damn stupid. The boy started into the emergency room five times. Turned back. Scared of the consequences. When we got him to the hospital it was too late."

The veteran was pacing the floor now. Suddenly he whirled and faced the dean directly, moving closer. "Goddamit, Doctor! Y'all send us halfway around the world and tell us not to be afraid of bombs and mortars and bayonets and bullets and strange-looking people and ask us to be proud of how many gooks we slaughtered. We come home to a sweet little Christian college that has the frigging U.S. Army training kids for the next echelon, teaching them how to kill your God's babies, and we're afraid to tell you we smoke dope."

He was almost screaming now, and using language that in earlier Mercer days would have led to a reprimand or disciplinary action. Now the dean heard it without a blink.

"If he hadn't been scared of y'all, he'd still be alive. Can't you, for Christ's sake, understand that?!"

The dean stepped to the outer office and sent the secretary who had just come in on some unnecessary errand.

Back inside he found the man sitting on the far side of the room with his face in his hands, sobbing deeply. For a minute the dean stood watching him, saying nothing, letting his pupil-teacher express the hurt of an era neither had chosen but into which both had been born. Expressing it the way humans finally must. Just . . . weeping.

When the man composed himself he pulled a blue bandana from his pocket, fiercely blew his nose and, without apology, spoke again. His voice was almost a whisper now and he seemed calm for the first time.

"You say dope is dangerous. You say it'll kill. You say we lost one of our finest to it two weeks ago. Okay, Doc. Let me tell you something. He wasn't sent home in a body bag. And then let me ask you something. How many of our finest have we lost in this goddam war?"

The dean didn't answer. But he knew the answer. He knew all the dead by name. And where they were buried.

The student, still calm, moved behind the oak desk and sat down in the dean's big chair. The teacher had asked the student to teach him. He was ready to teach him. Dean Hendricks sat facing him, notepad in hand, their roles reversed.

"I wasn't making excuses, Dean," Captain Trips began anew, his voice stronger. "You say you're in kindergarten. Well, I reckon I'm in graduate school. I did it all. In Nam, I mean."

He named all the drugs that were readily available in Vietnam, how common each one was on the Mercer campus, and the pharmacology of each. The dean asked him how all the drugs got to the middle of a war. The veteran's answer seemed ready, like he was waiting to be asked. "If you don't have morale, if you don't have patriotism, you don't have fighting soldiers. So. You bootleg. Drugs in Vietnam are counterfeit esprit de corps. So where do you think the drugs come from?"

The dean didn't answer, so the man went on.

"But I guess you're wanting to know about the hippies. And I reckon I'm an old hippie. I'm twenty-seven years old and still a sophomore. I spent almost two years here, three years in your glorious army, and two years running around half crazy."

"But now you're back," the dean said. "And I'm asking for your help."

"Let's get something straight," the student-turned-instructor said. "I'm not a narc. I will never, ever give you the name of who is doing what.

Not who's dealing, who's tripping, nothing. You said you're asking me to help Mercer University. I don't give a rat's ass about this institution. I haven't been back long but when I was here before it stunk. Seems to me it still does."

"I said I'm asking you to help," the dean said. "And I'm not asking you to squeal. But I'm in over my head. Maybe we stink but we're not expelling kids, sending them home with every infraction of the rules, not calling the cops to the dormitories or sending students to the slammer. We're trying, some of us anyhow, to do a piece of educating here, not create criminals."

"Let me finish," the man said. "By the way though, we're already criminals. Everybody under thirty in this rotten country has already been criminalized."

The dean didn't respond so the student continued.

"I told you I would come on board. But I'm not coming on any damn institution's board. Not even on yours, even though I think you're on the level. I know what dope will do. I see these pimply faced kids—I saw a sweet girl out there yesterday. Just a puppy, lying there stoned out of her gourd. And a little boy. An overgrown, little bitty boy! We can't let this happen to them."

Hendricks thought the man was going to cry again but he quickly regained his composure.

"That's all I'm asking you to do," the dean said, reaching across the desk and giving the man a firm handshake.

"All right. So you want a lesson in drug management."

"The management will be your part," Hendricks said. "I just want a lesson in nomenclature."

"Don't bullshit me, Dean. There hasn't been anything to hit this campus in twenty years that you didn't manage. Or try to."

The dean ducked his head with a modest smile.

"Do you know what a joint is?" the teacher began.

"Marijuana cigarette."

"Right." The man laughed and digressed. "We learned a lot of things before we got to Nam. Back here we would get the grass and then have to clean it. Stems, seeds. Most of the guys in my Stateside unit were city dudes. Kept asking, 'Where'd all these seeds come from?' Finally I figured it out. Seeds come from the bud, the start of the flower. Those damn Mexicans were sending us the culled stuff. Keeping the buds, the power. Then we figured out those seeds would come up. So. When we shipped out we took seeds with us. They'd flat grow in those jungles. We wouldn't be there for the harvest but somebody would. And maybe we'd find a harvest at the next bivouac. Seldom did though. Most of our smokes were prerolled joints we bought from little ole Vietnamese women trying to feed their young."

The dean wasn't commenting, so Captain Trips went on with the lesson.

"You know what a roach is? That's the butt, when you've held it with a roach clip—usually a hemostat night-requisitioned from the medics—until the last crumb was burning your lips. But don't call it marijuana. Weed. Pot. Mary Jane. Tea. Grass. Reefer. Joint. Hemp. All the same. Not hash, though. That's tougher."

He went over the names of drugs that were common. Psilocybin mushrooms, Pot, L.S.D., S.T.P, quaaludes, P.C.P., the amphetamines, barbiturates, heroin, cocaine.

"Not any heroin here. Never seen a needle. Not here. God, but I saw plenty of them in Vietnam. It was nothing to send a soldier home with a five-hundred-dollar-a-day heroin habit. Now that's a certified junkie. Not here though. Not much alcohol either. Only the jocks do alcohol. Hippies laugh at them. Very little coke. Too expensive. Few rich kids. 'Bout all."

The dean was scribbling rapidly, the man talking with only an occasional breath.

"The big ones are speed and acid. Easy to come by. The big campus dealers go to Atlanta—Piedmont Park. And Emory-at-Oxford. Lots of it there. Little ones hang around Le Carousal—you know, colored juke joint. They don't sell it but there are always some dealers hanging around."

They sat for more than an hour talking. The man explained the dangerous combinations. "Acid won't kill you but it can make you kill yourself. P.C.P.—angel dust—mean stuff. Cheap. Easy to make. You can make a barrel of it for a few hundred dollars. Kids love it. Very psychedelic. Makes colors more colorful. One hell of a trip. Distorts time."

He said the danger was that it mimicked LSD.

"Take somebody to the emergency room and they'll think it's a bad acid trip. Fill 'em full of thorozine. Does no good. Their whole nervous system is fried. I've seen 'em run smack through a barbed wire entanglement and wonder next day where they got so cut up."

He told the dean there were two classes of hippies on campus. Some, primarily those on psychedelics, were trying to find a better life; reacting against the values of their middle-class parents and communities.

"Cut the umbilical cord! Whack it clean off! Expands your mind, Man. I read *The Critique of Pure Reason* and three other books without ever going to sleep. Almost a hundred hours."

He said others were taking drugs just trying to get wasted. To have a good time or get away from a bad time. Some of it, he said, like "shroom"—mushrooms—opens the doors of perception, brings things out in the open and you have to deal with it.

"That's the spiritual side of it. Ever wonder why you have so many more philosophy majors after drugs hit the campus? We're looking for answers, Man. We're looking for truth, something worth holding on to."

The dean asked him about communes. A few were springing up near the campus. The man laughed.

"They won't last. And I'll tell you why. The women in them, well, you know, Southern women. Their mamas have taught them how to cook, clean up, sew, things like that. The men, like, their daddies sat in offices all day. The boys don't know how to do anything but sit around and let the women wait on them. It won't last. So don't worry about it."

The man jumped from one subject to another as things came to him. He told the dean about a fellow bringing 200 tabs of L.S.D. to the dormitory. "That's a lot of hits!"

"What's a hit?"

"You tear a tab off a perforated sheet that's been impregnated with acid. Generally they had logos stamped on each little square. Mr. Natural. Mickey Mouse. That's a hit. Far out!"

Dean Hendricks was making a good student. He was beginning to grasp the romance of it all and it bothered him. The man was slowing down, almost as if he feared he had told his pupil too much in one lesson.

But he went on. As if he might never have this chance again. "The biggest one around here is speed—white crosses, black cadillacs, gradmets. These mostly aren't for fun. That's to get you through college. That's what kept me awake for four days. I thought I could put my foot on the neck of a cyclone."

It was what his teacher told him last that frightened the dean the most.

"You have to understand. It—I mean things like acid—there's a social aspect to it. I'm telling you now. I hear words like, well, 'community,' bandied about a lot on this campus. Well, that's what a lot of the drugging is about. There's a real, a sure-enough bonding to a lot of what's taking place now. Like, you've been through something together and you're friends for life. Both of you have been to the same foreign country—the same forbidden foreign country—and you thumb your nose at folks who haven't been there too. Then you quit thumbing your nose and become evangelistic. Missionaries. You want to take everyone around you to that forbidden country."

The man had told Hendricks earlier that a big difference between the beatniks of the 1950s and the hippies of the 1960s was that with the beatniks, hard drugs became a whole culture. A way of life. Down-and-outers. One junkie would rip off another one for a fix. Or to satisfy some drug-crazed mood. Hendricks had pretty much put everyone who took drugs in one camp. Now he was hearing words like "bonding," "community," "evangelistic," "missionary" and "truth." His words. Mercer's words, what it claimed as its vocation. He was beginning to understand "flower children." And the understanding made his job more difficult.

At the end they discussed what it was Dean Hendricks was asking Captain Trips to do. Discourage drug use among students when he could. Bring them safely down when he couldn't. Together they would try to keep kids alive and in school. And the police off the campus.

It was the Mercer way.

The afternoon found Hendricks in the president's office. The dean explained in detail the plan. "You'll have to give me a little rope on this one, Cap'm."

The president told his dean he trusted him. And that he loved him.

Rufus Harris was a man trained in law and had been dean of two law schools and president of two universities, a man whose days were numbered, who had given his life to traditional education, who had walked with kings, yet now was able to perceive, to appropriate, and to see that neither law nor the classical academy held the key to these precarious times. They would act out of an aroused moral sentiment. And do the best they could.

The afternoon also found the girl who had been brought down by the combination of quaaludes and codeine the day before in the office of Professor Jean Hendricks. The girl had come for healing.

To say drug parties dominated the Mercer scene would be a caricature of reality. But to suggest that the use of drugs on this little Baptist campus was not common during the late 1960s would be a distortion of that same reality.

More than Dean Hendricks and Captain Trips, the most effective conservator of peace on the drug front was a young man named Jerry Stone. He had grown up on the Mercer campus where his father was a business manager. From junior high school through his college years he worked for the Macon YMCA. He knew every lawyer, doctor, and policeman in the city. When he became director of student activities at the university he needed no orientation. His military service as an army ranger, plus his years with the YMCA, had afforded him an active, indefatigable body and a fleet wit. He was a valuable ally to Hendricks. Against the two, few would tread.

Stone's philosophy was that students were adults, a university is not a prison, and the campus should handle its own problems. What students did off campus was their business. If they got in trouble with the law off-campus it was between them and the law. What they did on campus was the business of the university. Sometimes it was difficult to separate the two. But Stone, as a ranger lieutenant, had been trained to fight behind the lines. Ideologically he was to the right of Joe Hendricks. But his military background had prepared him to keep his politics out of his work. He expected his superiors to do the same.

Mercer had a speakers series they called Insight. Insight sought to bring outside speakers representing every view. This led to intense controversy during the Vietnam War. Sometimes there was contention within.

David Schoenbrun, American correspondent who had covered the Vietnamese conflict from the French Vietminh negotiations through the Geneva Conferences of 1954 and 1962, was invited as an Insight lecturer. He was one of the few Western journalists who had been received in Hanoi after America's involvement. His book *Vietnam: How We Got In, How to Get Out* had advocated military de-escalation and a negotiated settlement. According to Stone, the CIA contacted President Harris and said Schoenbrun was an unreliable crackpot, inappropriate for an academic platform. When Harris told Stone that Schoenbrun should not be invited and Stone said the invitation had already been extended, Harris curtly advised that the invitation should be withdrawn.

"Who else, Dr. Harris, can present that side?" Stone says he asked. Dr. Harris replied that Eugene Patterson, editor of the *Atlanta Constitution*, had been to Vietnam and could make a fair assessment of the situation. Stone somehow learned Patterson's schedule and invited him on a day he would be out of the country.

"Dammit!" the president exploded. "You tricked me."

"But he didn't pout," Stone says.

When criticism of Schoenbrun's appearance poured in, Rufus Harris took his usual protective stance, replying that Mercer students were mature and capable of hearing all sides of an issue and making up their own minds.

"We're educators. We want our students to hear all sides of every issue."

Other Insight speakers included Saul Alinsky, Dick Gregory, James Kilpatrick, Bernadette Devlin.

The clamor surrounding the appearance of Jane Fonda was the most fierce of all. Jerry Stone says he told President Harris that Mayor Thompson had indicated that in the interest of protecting the students from treasonous talk, he would have Jane Fonda arrested if she appeared in Macon. Stone was not a fan of Fonda's, felt she did not know anything about Vietnam and was an intellectual lightweight, a view not shared by Stone's colleagues. Still, as director of student activities, it was his duty to host her.

"I can tell you this, Jerry," President Harris said. "I'm a lawyer. And if she comes, she'll speak. And no one had better arrest her on my campus."

When Jane Fonda arrived, accompanied by the head of Veterans against the War, a black man, the campus and Macon were as tense as anyone can remember. The foyer of Williamham Chapel was packed with Air Force wives from Warner Robbins Air Force Base, protesting Fonda's appearance, chanting, "Hanoi Jane, Hanoi Jane." The students were about evenly divided between those who did not want her to speak and those who wanted to hear her. For forty-five minutes she calmly discussed the issues. Even some of the detractors remember it today as a brilliant performance. Interrupted often by catcalls and applause of affirmation, she never flinched, stating in full what she had come to say.

A white waitress in a fast-food restaurant remembers asking Jane for her autograph for the waitress's little girl. "What's your daughter's name?" the waitress remembers Miss Fonda asked her.

Instead of signing the menu with her own name Jane Fonda wrote the little girl's name. In parenthesis she wrote, "Your name is just as important as mine."

"That little girl is a school principal now. She still shows that to her own children."

Jane Fonda left deep tracks in Macon, Georgia. Committee X, a special committee appointed by President Harris to handle disturbances, breathed a hefty sigh when she was safely out of town.

"Dupont Cheney was my main man when it came to handling drugs," Stone says. Cheney was a law student and an ex-police detective with eight years experience. To capitalize on his expertise Stone employed Cheney as director of men's housing. That gave him access to dormitory rooms. If they had reason to believe a student was dealing or using drugs Cheney knew how to search. On one occasion they were sure a student had a cache of drugs but the student sat in the big oak chair at his desk, saying nothing as Cheney and Stone explored rugs, tennis balls, pillows, the ceiling, desk drawers, clothes pockets, everything. The student sat there smiling. "Look all you want to. You won't find anything in my room."

Conferring in the hallway, about to give up, it struck them both at once. "Why didn't he ever stand up?"

Back inside the room they found four big hollow chair legs, filled with amphetamines.

"Those into heavy drug use trusted us," Stone says. "They knew if they dealt with us the worst thing that could happen to them was to be expelled. If they dealt with the police they knew the penalty was a lot more severe."

Tommy Michaels was a bright, creative young man Tom Trimble admitted to Mercer right out of reform school. Michaels was artistic, funny, and popular. As an actor he had no campus peers. But he made no secret of his drug habit. Again, it was Mercer's position that what he did off campus was his business. So he talked often with Stone about what was going on. In part, it was to keep informed himself. The code they had was to ask about the weather.

"What's the weather forecast?" Michaels would ask.

"Fair to partly cloudy."

That meant Stone and Cheney were looking for something. If Stone replied, "I hear there's going to be one hell of a storm," Michaels knew there was going to be a bust.

"When Jerry Stone said a bad storm was coming I knew the level of the Ocmulgee River would rise two feet by morning from johns being flushed," Michael said. He would put the word out and everyone got rid of their drugs. That was fine with Jerry Stone. That was all he wanted.

A student owed a drug dealer a lot of money and the dealer had come to the dormitory to collect. Tommy Michaels told Stone the dealer was upstairs with a forty-five, threatening to kill the boy. Stone bounded up the stairs, accosted the man and said, "Can I help you?"

"No," the man said. "Just a little something between me and this dude."

"Are you a student?" Mr. Stone asked.

When the man said he wasn't, the ex-ranger said, "Well, you'd better get your ass off this campus before I throw you through that window."

Through another student Stone and Cheney learned that the man was scheduled to bring a big haul of drugs from Atlanta that very night. A stakeout resulted in the biggest drug seizure the Macon police had known. "The cops got their pictures in the paper. The dealer went to prison. The student lived on and everybody was happy," Jerry Stone says. "Except the dealer," he adds, laughing.

"Yeah, we played hardball sometimes," Stone says. "Dupont knew how to operate a lie detector. We'd take a student downtown, if we knew he was dealing, hook him up, ask him questions. Get the truth. The damn thing wasn't even plugged in," Stone laughs. "We made it through those days, Mercer did. Better than most I think."

Mercer, with only intramural football, had fierce competition on the playing field. Especially between fraternities. Black students, with a sprinkling of whites, fielded a team. Calling themselves the Panthers they soon became the most powerful on campus. Race was a dominant factor in the competition. Dean Hendricks and Jerry Stone found it necessary to patrol the games, and on numerous occasions the two men had to go onto the field and break up fights before they reached riot proportion.

Mercer missed most of the beatnik era, that period when its adherents sought to destroy the fabrics of society and replace it with a new way. But these were not the beatnik junkies of the fifties. The hippies had arrived. More and more, whatever was deemed proper was anathema. While they could identify those not of their order by the way they dressed, talked, and wore their hair, first the beatniks and then the hippies proclaimed their values with shabbiness and exaggerated disregard for the status quo. That is not to say there was not ample reason for their defiance. And logic in much of their stance. Likewise, it was erroneous to classify those who were burning ROTC buildings, taking over university campuses, and disrupting National Democratic Conventions as irresponsible addicts and dismiss their protests as acts of crazed junkies. As the ranks of antiwar sentiment and activism swelled with campus student intellectuals, professors, priests, nuns, and men and women from every walk, drugs were not what egged them on. But it was an important factor with the young.

By the time the drug culture came to Mercer the beatnik era was winding down. Hippies resented being confused with beatnik junkies. Heroin, as Captain Trips told Dean Hendricks, was not their thing.

By 1968, though Upward Bound was in its heyday and Mercer was pursuing its aggressive recruitment of minority students with abounding success, the walls were crumbling. What Students for a Democratic Society was calling "a people's army to fight a people's war" was recruiting on this heretofore scrupulously orthodox Baptist college.

Andy Warhol gave them art and told them, "In the future everyone will be world famous for fifteen minutes."

Fifteen minutes would be long enough for these fragile warriors playing Russian roulette with their lives.

Timothy Leary was their prophet and counseled them to "Turn on, tune in, and drop out."

Jimi Hendrix, Bob Dylan, and Janis Joplin—until overdoses claimed Hendrix and Joplin— sang to them and they cheered.

Allen Ginsberg was their poet and they followed his bells and iambic chants.

As early as 1964, before being prevented from addressing the University of California's students and faculty, Mark Savio, the Berkeley leader, had seen the Achilles' heel of the Free Speech Movement when he said, "If they let me speak, we're dead."

Some heeded Savio, among them Joseph Hendricks and Rufus Harris. They let the students speak. At times, though, it was a delicately finessed and orchestrated performance when the free speech they allowed was expressed.

That, too, was the Mercer way.

❏

Chapter 18

You have kept your secret long enough . . .

In large measure Sam Oni's effort to enter the Tattnall Square Baptist Church in the fall of 1966, and the rebuff he experienced, marked the beginning of Mercer's radicalism.

Sam Oni's arrival in the fall of 1963 had but slightly aroused the Mercer students from the slumberous 1950s. The furor of opposition among alumni and trustees had little effect inside the compound. The liberal arts faculty had gone on record as willing to teach students of any race long before the trustee meeting made it official. That happened despite the fact that a poll showed sixty-one percent of the students rejected any integration at all. Seventy-three percent responded that they did not think racial segregation at Mercer was unchristian. But when desegregation came, although individual black students felt the sting of Old South views in the air, overt protests were kept to a minimum. Under the eagle eyes and disciplined exertion of those charged with keeping order, there had not been much to fear when Sam Oni, Bennie Stephens, and Cecil Dewberry came.

What is meant here is that there was little the institution had to fear. The institution knew that it could keep things quiet.

There was much the black students had to fear. But in the beginning they feared in silence.

Much had happened since the fall of 1963. For one thing, the African student who came to central Georgia as one who had heard the Christian gospel from white lips and believed had come face to face with daily denials of that Gospel. Children were murdered at their prayers, citizens gunned down for no reason other than their color, guard dogs growling and snapping at those who took "these truths to be self-evident" seriously, civil rights workers murdered and buried in a red-clay dam. And the war raging in Southeast Asia that further aroused their passions.

So by September 1966, when Sam Oni faced the Tattnall Square deacons who turned him away, he was angry. He had made many friends in the Civil Rights Movement, had been an activist even before he arrived. Since coming to America he had participated in activities with SNCC, SCLC, and the NAACP. Malcolm X had visited Nigeria, and Oni was deeply distressed at Malcolm X's assassination.

So when Mr. Oni left his room in Sherwood Hall and headed for the showdown with the deacons, he intended that the world know of his anger. And the world did. Adams Street was teeming with television camera crews and newspaper reporters that morning. When accused of doing what he did for publicity reasons, he did not deny it.

"You have kept your secret long enough."

By evening the news was being seen and read in cities around the world, including Kumasi, Ghana, where Oni had been expelled from Sadler Baptist Secondary School for challenging inept teaching methods, and it was heard in Lagos, Nigeria, the site of Oni's birth.

"Let the word go forth . . . to friend and foe alike," John F. Kennedy had said at his inaugural. President Kennedy was killed two months after the young African arrived in the land in which those words were spoken. Now, in Oni's wrath, he would let the news go forth. To friend and foe alike. "This is what is happening." Those who said he was an angry young man were correct. And many whites were angry in return. He had seen that their emperor had no clothes, always an enraging revelation.

Tattnall Square Baptist Church was not an integral part of Mercer University. Still, there was the historical connection. Official Mercer was extremely embarrassed by what happened and never reestablished the relationship it once had with the church.

By the time Sam Oni, beginning his senior year, made his stand at the historic church, the black students were no longer a timid, cowed minority on the Mercer Campus. The militancy that had loomed on the horizon since the beginning of the Civil Rights Movement, but kept under wraps by the rhetoric and long-suffering of Dr. Martin Luther King, Jr., had grown with each new act of violence against the black community.

As the decade neared its end the militancy was flowering and bearing fruit. The once unqualified nonviolence of the Student Nonviolent Coordinating Committee, under the chaste leadership of John Lewis, had yielded to the declamations of Stokely Carmichael and the Black Panther political party.

"Black power!"

"What do you want?"

"Black power!"

As the shouts echoed from the cellars of poverty, rebounding on the rough places of tarrying intolerance, many formerly sympathetic whites saw it as a litany of hate, fragmenting the nonviolent commitment Dr. King had exacted from his followers. Jaded with white promises, many black people in all sectors were renouncing the "beloved community" and turning to what they believed more productive means. As that was happening, more and more liberals in the white community were turning away. In addition, the antiwar movement was siphoning allies from civil rights activities. Financial and moral support was waning. Patience was no longer a virtue, particularly with young blacks. Nowhere was this more true than on college campuses.

The black students on the Mercer campus, greater in number than in the other formerly all-white schools in the South, had been carefully recruited and were all of outstanding intellect and ambition. While other schools waited for black students to apply, then often screened out as many as they could, Joseph Hendricks and Johnny Mitchell were on the roads and in the air actively recruiting. All that was no secret to the guidance counselors in the black high schools and they skillfully steered their best students to Mercer, a school that was not only anxious to enroll them but was offering attractive scholarships. Thus the black students at Mercer were well prepared to organize and to act.

Many had plunged into campus politics and were in positions of leadership. Gary Johnson was editor of the influential campus newspaper. Joseph Hobbs was a regular columnist. Sam Oni was a fiery contributor.

The administration was lengthening the leash as it was pressed to do so. Jacob Beil and some of his industrious friends needed longer hours in the library. On an arranged occasion they simply refused to leave when the library closed. The hours were quickly and quietly extended. Money for the library had been donated by the widow of Eugene Stetson, Mercer graduate and a New York banking tycoon. Fearing that Mrs. Stetson would be offended by the controversy, William Haywood felt she should hear it from the university. "What a wonderful thing to protest," she responded. Later she called to say if additional funds were needed to employ more staff for the longer hours she was prepared to contribute.

Some of the women students were smarting under the dormitory curfew imposed on them but not on men students. Dori Ripley, a sprightly and untamed young woman who wanted her flirtation with the wild edges to result in something positive saw the one-sided curfew rule as a cause.

This was a time when many saw being a student leader as a sellout. Yet many were trying to figure out how to be antiestablishment but at the same time responsible. It was a tight rope to walk.

On a balmy evening, under the leadership of Dori Ripley, most of the women dressed for bed, took pillows and blankets outside the dormitory, and when eleven o'clock came ignored the dean of women's command to move inside. Although university rules required the matter to go before the discipline committee, their challenge ended curfew hours for women students.

Dancing was still seen as sinful on most Baptist campuses of the South in the 1960s and was not allowed. The prohibition was embarrassing to many Mercer students who had grown up in communities where dancing was as acceptable as shaking hands. They were particularly humiliated by jokes that abounded about Mercer's narrowness.

"Why can't Mercer students make love standing up?"

"Because the dean of women might think they're dancing."

That and variations of it was a favorite, always sure to get a chuckle unless one was a Mercer student in a sophisticated setting.

The issue had become a cause celebre on the Mercer campus. Apparently the Baptist ban was annoying to the urbane Rufus Harris as well, although he had declined to deal with it.

On one occasion Tommy Day Wilcox, president of the student body, told Dr. Harris that feelings were running high and serious disruption was certain if the matter was not resolved.

Dr. Harris chose an oblique approach. "Tommy Day, when you go to other campuses for a basketball game isn't there usually a reception following the game?" the president asked. Wilcox answered that there was.

"Do the students ever dance on those occasions?" Again the answer was in the affirmative.

"Well," President Harris continued, "don't you think it discourteous if we don't reciprocate with a reception for teams when they visit our campus?" When the student body president agreed, Dr. Harris said, "I think you're right. We should have an appropriate reception for our guests, don't you know. So why don't you arrange to have music to go along with the punch and cookies? And if some of the young people should choose to dance during the reception, well, surely it would be rude to tell them they couldn't."

President Harris quickly added, "Of course, if it should be reported that I authorized dancing on the Mercer campus, I would have to deny it."

The student body president knew that a major grievance among Mercer students had been resolved without conflict.

From then on, when a dance was announced on campus the code word was "reception."

Required chapel, a seasonal snarl that seemed to sprout with the coming of spring, somehow faded away as well.

All over America college students were challenging the traditional curricula. Mercer was no exception. Changes were made, some considered too radical by the purists. A program called "Wonderful Wednesday" was established. There were no scheduled classes on Wednesdays. Instead, students were free to pursue their own notion of what an education should be. Out of that program came the Experimental Freshman Program, later called Alternate Freshman Program, that went far in letting first-year students prescribe their own course of study. The merit of it was the intimate relationship resourceful faculty could establish with a few students. A dozen or so students, with a faculty leader, formed a sort of collegial family, deciding on their own what mind-expanding experience they wanted to chase. Some planted and cultivated gardens with mule-drawn equipment. Back to survival on the land. Some learned to cook. Others who were not poets dabbled in original poetry. Self expression. Running the rapids of the Flint River or rappelling its banks. Sleeping on the ground, exploring nocturnal mysteries. In reality, it was seen by the administration as an escape valve for student activism. At the same time, the more creative faculty did some of their best teaching. By stealth.

But it was not such things as curricula changes, dormitory curfews, and library hours claiming the energy of the radical element of Mercer students in the late 1960s. It was race and war, with race paramount with blacks, war with whites.

If one considers the word "radical" in the historic Christian sense, the most revolutionary person on the Mercer campus during the 1960s was a woman never identified as a social or political activist—Jean Hendricks.

Doctor Jean, or Sister Jean as some called her, was said by most students interviewed to have been the most influential teacher they had. A student and advocate of B. F. Skinner and behavioral psychology, she has taught a lot of laboratory rats to ring bells and climb ladders. But her true vocation was healing young minds with tough love and ascendant understanding of the human condition. It is no wonder the young girl who overdosed on the banks of the Tobesofkee Creek sought her out. Many did.

In unbending professional circles she would have been seen as a pietist, a label that would not have offended her because she was not concerned with labels. Whether in the classroom, at the frequent prayer meetings in her apartment, or at 2:00 a.m. counseling sessions, her message was the same: every human life is important; everyone has the potential to make a significant difference in the lives of others; we all make a contribution for good or for bad in our own little circles, so we are all powerful; we can choose what kind of difference we will make; whether Christian or not-Christian we can make the world a better place.

More with works than words Dr. Jean communicated her message. Her methodology in the area of integration was to put black and white students together in a classroom or on a common task where color was not a factor. When race became a factor it was met head-on. Sometimes a Social Psychology class would turn into what appeared to be a group therapy session: black students screaming at whites and vice versa, drug users railing at middle-class values, straights passing summary judgment on homosexuals. Dr. Jean backed away from nothing. Students flocked to her classes and sometimes could be found in her presence at all hours of the night. Wounded birds were her specialty.

Typical of those deeply influenced by Dr. Jean was Sallie Carter, a spirited and gangly seventeen-year-old white student from Columbus who skipped the twelfth grade to enter college to prepare for a career in medicine. She writes graphically of the academic, but especially the extracurricular impact Jean Hendricks made on her life:

> The summer after my freshman year, Jean went to Harvard and left eight of us in full-time residence at the Central State Psychiatric Hospital at Milledgeville to toilet train and table train children and adults. When I started with a ward of about sixty adult severely retarded and behaviorally disturbed women from fifteen to sixty years of age, they spent their days in a ward thirty by sixty feet. It had no furniture save a few chairs for aides to sit on because several of the women were so violent and destructive the others had to be protected from thrown and broken furniture. There were two toilets, but no toileting routine for these adults, many of whom had never been toilet trained. This was be-

fore disposable diapers, and there was always stool and urine on the floor.

There was no air conditioning in the building, nor were there fans, and the windows faced the afternoon sun. Many of the women would not wear clothes. Some ate rags. Several ate feces. When it was mealtime, the food was brought in on big carts on individual trays, which the stronger and faster women slung to the floor so they could get plenty of their favored food. The others got the leftovers. They all ate off the floor amid feces and urine with unwashed hands. After mealtime, the women and the floors were hosed down and the food fragments, rags, and excrement washed down the drain.

Sallie Carter, at eighteen, almost died that summer. She and the other students worked fourteen- to eighteen-hour days. Sallie ruptured a disc lifting a patient. She was nearly raped by a security guard who laced her Kool-Aid with LSD. She had a severe strep throat and went into anaphylactic shock in reaction to the medication. It was a tough learning assignment Dr. Jean had left her young charges. Today Sallie Carter speaks of that experience in the same fashion Jacob Beil talks of his involvement with Upward Bound:

> I still recall that as the most important work I have ever done. We toilet trained all those women and by the end of the summer they were going to the dining hall in a line to sit down to table for meals. We made a tremendous, tangible difference in the lives of those patients, aides, and the institution. We proved that these humans didn't have to live like wild animals; they were capable of learning skills that would make them acceptable in supportive home-like settings.

Despite, or, perhaps, because of, the sway of Dr. Jean, Sallie Carter was also a militant activist. When she and some other Mercer students were pictured by the campus newspaper at a silent prayer vigil for Vietnam War dead and wounded, along with the headline "Mercer Radicals Plot Burning of White House," the FBI launched a heady investigation that gravely embarrassed and intimidated her Georgia kin. But not Sallie.

After three years at Yale Divinity School and a stint as chaplain of Sweet Briar College in Virginia, Sallie Carter returned to her original goal—the study of medicine. In her activist years at Mercer she had turned to philosophy and the social sciences, neglecting the prerequisite courses for medical school. For those prerequisites she enrolled at the University of Virginia. While there she was pastor to the historic Preddy's Creek Baptist Church near Charlottesville, the oldest Baptist church in Albemarle County. Today she is a pediatrician in Anderson, South Carolina where her patients are mainly from poor families. She is a single adoptive mother of two children.

"If I die today," she says, "I know that my life has made a difference. Dr. Jean communicated that important message to me."

Sallie Carter, M.D. is but one fruit borne of the tree known by many as Sister Jean in the years that were the 1960s.

Radical? What did it mean at Mercer University in the 1960s? Who would have picked Robert Otto as being among them? A shy, scholarly, spiritually knowing and eminently decent individual, he saw his job as dean of the chapel and professor of philosophy as a vocation to people heaven with lucid saints. From his pulpit in the chapel he railed against the forces of darkness. And when he prayed, it was as if he reached and took hold of the highest pinnacle of heaven. Why would so many Georgia Baptists say him nay? For whatever reason, in the decade of the 1960s he seemed a lightening rod for pharisaic fury.

Otto early made friends with Sam Oni and anyone else facing rejection. When his own congregation refused to admit black students, Otto and his family moved their membership to a church that would. When Sam Oni came to the funeral of an elderly white woman who had befriended him, and Otto, seated between two prominent and wealthy Macon citizens, heard one of the men whisper to the other "He looks like a monkey," Otto stood up and moved to join Sam Oni for the remainder of the service.

It was Bob Otto who gave the news to Sam Oni that his mother had died, and shared his tears. When Otto joined the Poor People's March that formed in the parking lot of the Vineville Baptist Church he was loudly cursed by a leading member of the congregation. And when he and a colleague served as observers of the first sit-in at a Macon lunch counter they were told by their barber that if ever they came to his shop again, they would find out what a razor was made for.

That threat was followed by a call received by Mr. Otto's eight-year-old daughter that if her father ever preached at First Baptist Church again the Otto home would be burned to the ground. The FBI later identified the caller as the same one making similar warnings to President Rufus Harris regarding the admission of Sam Oni.

None of that held a candle compared to the controversy of a single homily in Willingham Chapel. The Reverend Dr. Otto meant his sermon to be no more offensive than the singing of the doxology. His intent was to instill in his young charges a consistency of faith and respect for language. It might have come from the Epistle of James, those pages that so often admonish us toward purity of tongue. His subject was "Are You Saved?" His point was that we talk one way in church and another way on weekdays.

So that all could understand his message, Dr. Otto told of words he had heard from a student the night before. "My wife and I had walked out on our front porch. From across Adams Street, the direction of Sherwood Hall, we heard a male voice yell: 'F--- you!!!'"

The remainder of the sermon dealt with the dishonor the student who spoke the vile language did to himself, the university, and the Almighty. And to his subject for the morning, "Are you Saved?"

Never mind that. A campaign to have Dr. Otto fired was immediately mounted by one of Macon's most powerful preachers who was also a Mercer trustee. This pastor arranged with a local radio station to have a statement about Otto's chapel vulgarity read every hour on the hour from 5:00 a.m. until 5:00 p.m. the following day. The same trustee sent telegrams to all Georgia Baptist associations requesting resolution of "the Otto matter." Another radio station began having an engineer tape all of Otto's sermons for the determined trustee to monitor.

It was widely accepted by the Mercer community that the campaign to get rid of the Dean of Chapel did not have to do with defilement of the sanctuary but with Otto's views on race, war, and economics.

Although Bob Otto had no litigious intent, a local attorney advised him that he had an eight-count bill of particulars for slander and libel. The attorney cautioned, however, that a Georgia jury would have to be convinced. That, in the climate of the time, was an unlikely issue out of his affliction. Reverend Otto had no intention of taking a brother, no matter how erring, to a court of law.

President Harris, in his sometimes manner of handling a serious matter with wit, said to his dean of the chapel, "Doctor Otto, I know that you follow the leading of the Lord in all you do and say. And I know you followed His guidance that chapel morning. But I must say, I think you made a mistake following Him on that occasion."

That was the end of the matter so far as Rufus C. Harris was concerned.

There were times when the delicate balance between the Mercer mode of preserving order, and allowing free speech among the students did not dovetail. This was particularly true when more and more white

students became enraged over the Vietnam War. Perhaps it was paternalism, perhaps white cognizance that black students had an authentic reason
for anger and protest. For whatever reason, administrative endurance of
white assertion of grievances was conspicuously shortfused.

Leaving the campus on Thursday evening, driving to Washington,
D.C. to demonstrate against the Vietnam War, then back to school by
Monday morning became almost ritualistic with a number of students. On
one occasion the passions of the group were further singed when President Nixon came down at 5:00 in the morning and tried to impress the
demonstrating throng by talking about football. A number of Mercer students were among them. When they returned to Mercer it was ROTC
Day. An army general, the local commandant, President Harris, and other
dignitaries were on the reviewing stand for the outdoor ceremony of
speeches and commissioning.

Steve Bell, Sallie Carter, Jinx Schwenke, and Steve Thomas, along
with about thirty others, had gathered on the east end of the drill field,
prepared to disrupt the proceedings. Dean Hendricks, sensing that a storm
he could not allay was brewing, was quickly in their midst.

"We're going to lie down in front of the cadets when they march,"
one of the students told him.

"No, we're not, Dean," Jinx Schwenke said. "We are going to wave
placards and banners expressing our anger at having a military presence
on a Christian campus."

Schwenke, a true radical from a conservative Florida family, was trying to offer a buffer zone between the dean and the more militant protesters. She would later become a lawyer, then finally marry a born-again
Christian, Vietnam veteran, and potter, and live on a mountain in Tennessee. Her effort to keep peace on the drill field was short-lived.

"We're going to burn the ROTC Building to the ground and take the
consequences," said another student.

Some of them had already moved down to the drill field, ready to
throw their bodies in the path of the oncoming cadets.

Dean Hendricks was not sure of his strategy. He knew the students
were weary from the long ride from Washington. He also knew that he
was seeing more rage than he had seen in them before, with abundant
resolve to make their point. His first strategy was to try to capitalize on
the uncertainty and disagreement in the ranks of the students. He tried to
reason with them, explaining that their interruption of the ceremony
would almost certainly result in cancellation of federal loans and grants

to many poor students, black and white, who could not afford the loss, and that neither he nor they could rectify such damage. Not sure of his ground he sought to bargain. "Don't disrupt the ceremony and I'll sit with you. Together we'll carry the day."

Without waiting for an answer he turned his back on the protesters, walked halfway up the bank and sat down. Although he had been uncertain when he made his move, the tense dean suddenly realized he was surrounded by the trusting students. Still he never stopped talking, stalling, promising.

His respite was short-lived. Phil Bell had returned from Washington with a ring in his nose larger than a silver dollar, suggestive of ownership and oppression. At the moment the visiting general began to speak Hendricks noted Bell's rapid breathing, his wrath rising, and edged over beside him. Just as the dean reached him Bell bolted from his prone position and screamed, "Bullshit! Bullshit!! Bullshit!!!"

All eyes from the dais were fixed on them, Hendricks particularly noting the stony glare of President Harris. The dean engaged Bell in conversation: President Nixon, the Washington protest, anything to harness Bell's anger. Hendricks would not break his pledge by leaving the other students who continued to sit in silence.

What Hendricks did not note was the snapping of a *Macon News* photographer's camera. When he reached his home at the end of the harrying day, spent and needing to get away from it all, the afternoon paper greeted him. Underneath a three-column picture of him seated with the protesting students on the bank was the caption: "Dean Hendricks Sits with Demonstrators."

A few restless minutes went by and then the inevitable telephone calls began. The first one was from Colonel Jones, ROTC commandant. Without waiting for Hendricks to explain that he was with the students to parry a disruption in the ceremony the piqued colonel said, "Dean, I know that you sat with the protesters." His intonation made it clear that he equated protest with sedition. "But what I want to know, Sir, did you rise when the national anthem was played?"

The frustration and anger escalated by the week and the manifestation and direction of both were unpredictable. There was, however, one occasion when trouble could be anticipated. The annual Old South Week celebrated by the Kappa Alpha Fraternity was a blatant reliving of the imagined power and pretended triumphs of the Confederacy. And it was an affront to black students whose indignities must again be borne as the pretenders basked in simulated glory. Battles that were lost a hundred years earlier were now won with two light field cannons and a basket of minié balls. Slaves were auctioned and Cotton was King again. Bills of secession were passed and proud soldiers waved goodbyes to their sweethearts, vowing to defend their honor.

In May 1967 it was Old South once more on Adams Street. The previous few years had not been good ones for the Kappa chapter of KA at Mercer. Wearing the name "Kappa," the tenth letter in the Greek alphabet, meant the Mercer chapter was the tenth one in the country to be given a charter. It was a source of pride, and trouble within the ranks of such a prestigious chapter was frowned upon by the national office in Lexington, Virginia. Defection or other apostasy by members was especially disturbing.

Over the years the Kappa chapter had claimed such luminaries as Dr. Ferrol Sams, Jr. In the 1960s two prominent members had voluntarily dropped out. One, Ed Bacon, on good terms, the other in an acrimonious clash.

In 1968 Ed Bacon was president of the student body. He had also become active in civil rights and antiwar activities and was appealing to his draft board for a conscientious objector status. Sitting in the fraternity house one evening, watching the events surrounding the death of Martin Luther King, Jr., it struck him that he had strayed far from the commitment of most of his brothers. He had already been told that he should spend more time in the KA house and in fraternity activities. Although ill feelings were minimal, with tears and hugging all around, he severed his relationship with the fraternity, leaving behind as much of the residue of the mystical ritual of Kappa Alpha as he could.

With Tom Darby the exodus from the Order of Kappa Alpha was a more perilous trek. He grew up a Georgia establishment family, was cared for by the traditional "mammy" of the aristocracy, a black woman whom he loved in that strange and schizophrenic fashion not even those who have experienced it can explain. He really did feel deeply for his black mammy. Yet he was possessed by all the entrenched negrophobia of the generations.

Darby's reactionary views on race and his love for the woman who nurtured him bothered some of those close to him, but he saw no conflict. Only with the coming of Sam Oni did it begin to dawn on him that the contradiction between his love and his politics was a paroxysm gnawing at his being. He had nestled at a black woman's breast but had never shaken a black man's hand. He began to see that his allegiance to his beloved Kappa Alpha, of which he was president, was but the unrolling of the scroll of carnage they celebrated. What he had seen as divine equipage of a region, honor against dishonor, courage against cowardice, a righteous cause against an evil empire, became a Babel tower, a human tragedy that should not have been.

In many ways Tommy Darby was as gentle a young man as Ed Bacon. But in his new awareness he was consumed by frustration and ire. In his rage he stomped his fraternity pin on the lodge floor and walked into the night, a night that would at times be as wintry for him as the one he was leaving. By way of retribution the playful ex-brothers pushed their fallen leader's car into a creek. He, in turn, taunted his former confederates with leftist articles in the literary magazine he published, with loud, interracial parties, and with other acts of betrayal.

One occasion saw a melding of militancy, conservatism, and good humor. The KA brothers, dressed in Confederate gray, bedecked with various emblems of rank and gallantry, and with the sure cold steel of valor fixed on their sides, were ready to call for their ladies waiting in Mary Erin Porter Hall, the oldest women's residence on campus. When they reached the walkway they formed two lines, arched their swords and when the double doors were swung open a brother and his date, dressed in the mode of 1860, were introduced. "Colonel Jeb Stuart and his lady Flora."

The protocol is for the next couple to follow immediately. On this occasion, though, a black couple jumped between the first couple and the one to follow.

"Mr. Rastus Jones and his lady, Mandy," a voice called out in the fashion of a blackfaced minstrel interlocutor.

The man was Gary Johnson, popular enough to have been elected editor of the campus newspaper, controversial enough to be roundly hated by a sizeable number of white students. Gary Johnson was wearing a miserly Confederate cap, the kind tourists buy for their children at Stuckey's when they stop for boiled peanuts, hotdogs, and Coca-Cola. His date was wearing a red bandana on her head and a skirt stereotypical of house servants of the Old South.

Dean Hendricks was watching. It was another situation where to do anything at all was a gamble. So he continued to watch. Another KA couple made their appearance. "General Lee and his lady, Mary Ann."

They proceeded underneath the tense, but still arched, swords. Propriety survived, though anger was mounting.

"Mr. Bones and his lady, Minerva," the interlocutor called as another black couple interrupted the ritual.

Dean Hendricks saw violence as inescapable. "Any dean that would let this happen is a goddamed communist," an irate fraternity brother standing near him said. He meant for the dean to hear him.

"Sam Jerry never gave us this much trouble," said another student.

The last couple strolled down the walkway and the Confederates broke ranks. Everyone, black and white, drifted away. The relieved dean returned to his office when the last ones were out of sight.

Soon his phone was ringing. It was the president of Wesleyan College. His voice was trembling as he told Hendricks a riot was about to occur on his campus and, "What, Sir, are you going to do about it?" It was the same man who had been at the train station when Sam Oni arrived.

Once more, Dean Hendricks had missed a fold in the blanket. He had not known that the KA entourage would proceed to the Wesleyan campus to repeat the ceremony for Mercer boys dating Wesleyan girls. The black students had followed the KAs. The Wesleyan president saw the presence of Kappa Alphas in Confederate uniforms, escorting young ladies in hoop skirts, trailed by black Mercerians wearing counterfeit rebel caps, as a rendezvous cloven of trouble, an imperilment to his lily-white cloister of John Wesley's daughters. He was calling for help.

What Hendricks found was a bevy of enraged KAs, facing several jocular black students who were about to burn a Confederate flag. It was just a tiny flag, bought at the same souvenir shop, the kind seen tied to auto antennas or waved at football games. Nevertheless, it was the revered standard of the brotherhood.

The fraternity brothers not involved in the ceremony were gesturing threateningly at the black students not fifty feet away. Other white students from Mercer had joined the procession to the Wesleyan campus and were in league with the KAs. There was no time for negotiation. The crossed-sword ceremony was about to begin. The dean knew this situation was more geared for serious violence than what had happened on the Mercer campus. For the moment he was stymied.

Suddenly Hendricks sensed confusion among the black students. They were talking excitedly among themselves, rushing about, searching their own and one another's pockets and book sacks.

No one had a match.

A lone KA, seeing their quandary, stepped from the hostile ranks and moved toward the black students. Other white students moved solidly behind the fraternity man. Dean Hendricks knew it was time to make his move.

He strolled quickly and deliberately, meaning to do whatever was necessary to interrupt the impending encounter. He quickened his pace when the advancing KA reached in his hip pocket. The object he withdrew glistened in the bright spring sunlight. The troubled dean, now close by, heard a sharp click, like the sound of a switchblade knife.

He stopped abruptly, realizing the shiny object was a Zippo lighter. The KA had flicked it to full flame and was offering the flabbergasted flag-burner a light.

"It's a piece of cloth," the KA said to his confederates who gathered around, stunned by this deed of their impulsive brother. Then, a white member of a fraternity actively committed to preserving the ethos of the Old South, soberly aided a baffled black man in burning what to one was an emblem of past glory, to the other a reminder of grievous wrongs.

A somewhat dazed, though now amused, assemblage of American young men, of disparate lineage, stood watching the icon of the Lost Cause cringe, curl, char, and for that supernal moment, disappear, under the unsullied heat of a bilateral pyre.

The awestruck dean stood with the others, beholding a scene that would forever eclipse his own expertise in conflict resolution.

A scene he would not forget.

Good humor prevailed: collegiate mayhem interdicted by the flick of a Kappa Alpha cigarette lighter.

❐

Chapter 19

All a part of the zeitgeist . . .

"Some of their own students called Sam Jerry Oni their 'Gonorrhean'," former mayor Ronnie Thompson tells a visitor. "Get it? He came here from Ghana. . . . I never did that. They were harder on him than the townspeople."

Ronnie Thompson is remembered by many Mercerians of the 1960s as being the most vehement racist mayor in Macon's history. He remembers himself as a progressive, a populist who did much to advance the cause of Macon's black citizens, and poor people in general. Sitting in the office of a Macon mortuary where he is night manager, not far from another mortuary owned by William Randall, he states his case.

The former Republican mayor has a colorful past. He had been something of a folk hero as a television gospel music personality, a prize-fighter, jeweler, and newspaper columnist. A dark-haired, handsome, well-proportioned man who looks considerably younger than his years, he pulls from his pocket a faded newspaper clipping and hands it to his guest. It is a column about a black man he says was a dear friend.

"That column you're holding is about Bullfrog Milhous Eisenhower Nixon," Ronnie Thompson says. "That's what they called him. 'Bullfrog.' His real name was Archie Campbell."

Mr. Thompson launches into a lengthy monologue about this poor, mentally retarded little man who stood approximately five-feet-four and weighed less than 110 pounds. Today he would be called a street person. Sometimes, during the day, he would sleep in a stockroom of Mr. Thompson's jewelry store, and at night he slept in cardboard boxes behind a local drugstore or sometimes find an unlocked Greyhound or Trailways bus.

As a prank, two men from the White Citizens Council told Bullfrog they would give him a free ticket to Detroit. It was not an unusual practical joke in the 1960s for a defenseless black person to be put on a bus and sent to a Northern city in what they called a "one-way freedom ride."

A telegram to the mayor usually preceeded the arrival of the new citizen. In this case Mayor Jerome Cavanaugh received the wire.

> Of course, he was like a little child. Happy as he could be. They bought him a one-way ticket, gave him a five-dollar bill, and put him on the bus. There he was, sitting in the back of the Greyhound bus, wearing a brightly colored clown's hat with a long feather in it and emblazoned across the hat's front in carnival type embroidery were the words "The New Frontier." It was 1961, Kennedy's first year in office. Bullfrog left there just grinning and waving back at them as the bus pulled off. Thanking them, you know. They told Mayor Cavanaugh, who already had 60,000 unemployed black citizens, that since folks in Detroit loved colored people so much they were sending him one. One way. Told the mayor what bus Bullfrog would be on. Said the mayor might want to meet him personally.

Ronnie Thompson indicates his outrage.

> I was in my first year in the jewelry business and didn't have a lot of money. Twenty-six years old. But when Bullfrog called and told me where he was I arranged to get him back to Macon. Nothing racial about it. He was my friend. And I was his friend. It wasn't a racial thing with me. It was a human thing.

Ronnie Thompson talks about how he got Bullfrog committed to the state hospital in Milledgeville. The judge appointed Thompson as Bullfrog's guardian.

> I drove him over there. When we got there they had our names reversed and wanted to keep me. Probably that same crowd that had sent him to Detroit in the first place. Of course, I had the keys, Bullfrog dressed wildly, and they soon got it cleared up.

As Mr. Thompson talked, some family mourners came into the mortuary to view a body that was to be cremated. A young woman complained that the deceased does not look natural. "His mouth isn't shaped right."

The former mayor tells them he will have the mortician fix it before the body is cremated. When they are gone, Mr. Thompson smiles knowingly, shakes his head but doesn't comment.

> Bullfrog came back here and lived in a nursing home until 1974. When he died I was the Republican candidate for governor. Field of sixteen. Busby, Maddox, Bert Lance. During Watergate. Anyway, I went to his

funeral. Not more than five people there. In a little black church in Old Macon.

The phone rings and Ronnie Thompson is courteous and precise. When he finishes he runs his fingers through his wavy hair, smiles faintly and says, "I was at Bullfrog's funeral. And they called me a racist. Where were all the liberals?"

In 1963, the year Sam Oni, Cecil Dewberry, and Bennie Stevens were admitted to Mercer, Ronnie Thompson was elected to the city council. He talks proudly of his accomplishments as chairman of the library committee.

> Black people couldn't use the main library back then. Had a little no-count colored library. Very quietly we closed it and everyone used the main library. Not a word was said about it. We just did it. No big to-do. No press releases to enflame folks. And we started putting branch libraries in different neighborhoods. Nothing racial about it.

Mr. Thompson boasts of his accomplishments as mayor from 1967 to 1975.

> Otis Redding provided my first office as a candidate. Good man. Killed in a plane crash. I told Otis I could help black people by bringing industry in. This town was controlled by cotton mills and railroads. My strength was in South Macon. Same as Wallace. Goldwater too. Eisenhower endorsed me. Saw my TV show in Augusta and pinned my campaign button on his lapel. I got 1,500 black votes too. Should have got more. Race wasn't an issue until my opponent brought it in. My administration built three new hospitals. Jet airport, firehouses, integrated the police department, had black personnel in every department. We went eight years without a tax increase or bond issue. I had a bi-racial committee that met every month. Just little things to white people, but not so little to blacks. Things like doctor's offices. Black patients had to go in a back door. We got it stopped. And the newspapers had a different edition for black subscribers. My committee talked to them, and they stopped it. You know who got the maddest when they started putting white news and black news on the same page? A Mercer professor. And that's the truth.

None of what he said fit the reputation he had among Mercerians as "Machine Gun Ronnie." When asked about Mercer directly his mood changed. Sizing up the interviewer to see where he was coming from, he jabbed, feigned, and dodged like the boxer he was.

I went to Mercer when I was fifteen years old. To sell them news-papers. They didn't like the way I ran the city. I wouldn't give Jane Fonda the key to the city. Then when some Chinese journalist came, I didn't treat him—a communist—like royalty. When the Black Libera-tion Front came down. Wasn't going to have it. The guy who headed it was a heroin addict. And a deserter from the army. Came to city hall every day. The American flag was a doormat. Made threats against me and my family. Interfered with business, blocked commerce. Gave me an ultimatum. Unless we gave them five million in money, said they were going to burn the city down. I talked to black and white leadership alike. So-called leadership. Said they didn't want to get involved. I issued an executive order: "Shoot to kill." Anyone engaging in anarchy must be stopped. So, shoot to kill. Had it on billboards all over town. Shoot to kill. With a picture of a machine gun. That made national news. They called me "Machine Gun Ronnie," but that stopped the Black Liberation Front.

With that the former mayor shifted back to the posture he had taken in the beginning, that of a Southern populist.

You know the real reason Mercer didn't like me? Why Mary Wilder and some of them took potshots at me every day? I'll tell you the truth. Didn't have anything to do with race. Of course, I didn't like Sam Jerry Oni. Big mouth. I didn't know him except to speak. Any meeting, oh, he'd take it over with his big talk. Lots of folks didn't like him.

Now it's true I had some things to say about Otto. And the streak-ers. Things like that. And they didn't like it because I spoke up for Lieu-tenant William Calley. Visited him in the Fort Benning stockade. But that wasn't the real reason they didn't like Ronnie Thompson.

When the phone rings again he continues to look his visitor straight in the eyes, as if he is still talking to him, which he is when his phone conversation is over.

One day Rufus Harris invited me and some councilmen to the campus. They were trying to expand the campus in a westward direction. To do it they had to condemn a large residential area. Of black and poor-white's houses. And small merchants. Harris had all these charts and graphs in the trustee dining room. Big luncheon for us. When he un-veiled the charts, there it was.

One of my closest advisors was a Mercer trustee. I think he had told Harris I would go along with taking the property. Eminent domain. I said, "No way. I'm not going to go for that."

Harris made the presentation like he was giving me instructions. Harris was the liberal. He wanted to seize poor people's houses. I was the conservative who wasn't going to have it. Later he said Mercer was going to move. I said, "I'll call U-Haul."

A trustee came and told me if I would agree he was sure Mercer would give me a doctor's degree. Now what the hell would I do with a doctor's degree? I was just pro-private enterprise. Let them negotiate if they wanted somebody's private property. That's the American way. I wasn't going to sit by and watch church and state team up to run over some little people. So. They didn't like me. But I won two terms. And the Republican Party has been getting stronger in the South ever since.

Whether racist demagogue or bona fide populist, or a combination of both, who is to say? What is certain is that Ronnie Thompson presided over Macon in perilous times. Mercer University was one of his problems. And he was one of theirs.

Mercer was changing too fast for Macon, Georgia. Sometimes the changes were anticipated and, in part, orchestrated by Mercer. Sometimes they were mandated by the black students who were becoming increasingly militant. The repressed anger of the earlier black students was gone. By 1968, with more than 100 black students, the rage was apparent to all who had eyes to see or ears to hear.

The black students initially had an informal association under the influence of the relatively mild-spoken, but deep-thinking Joseph Hobbs. Called the Black Student Executive Council, in the beginning it was little more than a forum for black students to confer with each other. Today Dr. Hobbs says, "We sought to collect data and identify problems facing black students and articulate those concerns to the administration."

Students entering later, like Robert Brown, Jimmie Samuel, and Robert Mike were more vocal and formalized the association as the Black Student Alliance. It was more confrontational, as students throughout America were more confrontational. Even so, Samuel, Brown, and Mike were pragmatists. They understood that at times Dean Hendricks was representing the administration and that he could be pushed only so far. They also knew that university administrators all over America were fearful.

During a six-month period in 1968 there had been 221 college and university demonstrations involving some 40,000 students. Many of them had been violent confrontations. The most notorious one, even overshadowing the Berkeley uprising four years earlier, was at Columbia University under the leadership of Mark Rudd, president of the Columbia chapter of Students for a Democratic Society. What had been the catalyst on the Morningside Heights campus was Columbia's ownership of slum property and the university's plan to build an $11.6 million gymnasium on land leased from Morningside Heights Park.

Samuel saw Mercer's westward expansion by eminent domain as analogous to the Columbia situation. With his rhetoric he sought to convince Hendricks that he had his troops on the verge of revolutionary tactics that would make the takeover of Columbia University seem as tame as a Baptist Student Union retreat. What he said to his troops was more conciliatory. Not wanting a showdown he felt they might lose, Samuel cautioned, "We're trying to make history, not the six o'clock news."

On the other hand, when he thought he had a trump card he was ready to sit at the table. Such an occasion came when Judge G. Harrold Carswell, an alumnus of Mercer who had been turned down by the U.S. Senate for a place on the Supreme Court, was scheduled to speak at Mercer. Carswell had the reputation as being a rigid white supremist. The Black Student Alliance let it be known that they intended to make a statement by disrupting the event. Rufus Harris saw it as a public relations havoc. For both external and internal reasons he wished to protect the university from the embarrassment a confrontation would bring.

At one o'clock in the morning Dean Hendricks was still negotiating. Joseph Hobbs was present, but was saying little. Although it was not known outside the organization the leadership of the BSA was in a period of transition. Jimmie Samuel had not been openly challenged, but Robert Mike was becomming more and more influential. Robert Brown, previous BSA president, was still an established factor. As was Joe Cecil Williams. Hendricks had worked with them all and knew that to side in the vying would serve no useful purpose. Almost all the black male students were in the room. One of the ironies of the civil rights movement was its chauvinism, and the BSA was no exception. The menfolk presumed to lead.

The BSA knew they were holding a card Dean Hendricks, bargaining for the administration, did not want them to play. Mr. Hendricks knew it as well. Someone had to fold. One of the grievances the students had emphatically stated was that there were no black faculty members. Instead of folding, Hendricks was ready to play a card he was not actually holding. If the students would call off the demonstration, he would assure them black faculty would be hired.

Shortly before two o'clock in the morning, Dean Hendricks telephoned President Harris. When Mrs. Harris answered Hendricks said, "Tell Cap'n to sleep well. It's all under control. But I have to see him early."

When morning came President Harris honored the commitment. "But Hendricks, just where are we going to find them? The truth is, every white school in the country is trying to find qualified black faculty."

It was an exposing adjective. White school. Implicit in the black student's bid was that Mercer University no longer be a "white school." That late-night bartering was a beginning. It was pragmatic politics in the lineage of Harry Truman and Lyndon Johnson.

After Carswell spoke, with the black students keeping their word, Hendricks drove to Fort Valley State to procure part-time black faculty. A deal was a deal.

But the deal was not as easily made when a call came that the black male students were refusing to leave the campus snack bar at closing time. With entire campuses being taken over around the country, students occupying presidents' offices, classroom work being disrupted, buildings burned, one can understand the jittery nerves at a small Georgia school that had tried hard to handle its own problems and keep police off the campus.

"Committee X," the group that had been appointed by President Harris to handle any disruption in normal campus activities, was on call twenty-four hours a day. It consisted of Dean of Students Joseph Hendricks; Jerry Stone; Thomas Trimble, assistant academic dean and a teacher in the Department of Philosophy; Liberal Arts Dean Garland Taylor; and William Haywood, college business manager and a man consummately committed to the wishes of Rufus Harris.

It was after eleven o'clock when they were summoned to the snack bar, actually a small cafe. What they found was just short of a mob, a hostile, teeming, taunting, baiting gathering of young men and women in no mood to negotiate. Hendricks, generally less obsequious and patronizing than most administrators, was worried, using courtesy titles for students half his age. Choosing not to call the police, as most universities were doing when a facility was taken over, he had instead brought along Terry Todd. Todd, a professor of education, was big. Weighing almost 300 pounds he was a physical phenomenon—a world-champion weight lifter, and an excellent tennis and Ping-Pong player. Despite his size, Todd was as agile as a gazelle. He was the only man at Mercer who boasted that he could whip Joe Hendricks in a fair fight. Fortunately their close friendship precluded any such eventuality. Hendricks knew that he, ex-ranger Jerry Stone, and the cyclopean Terry Todd could contain any physical encounter that might develop. It was a risk to take, but better, he reasoned, than to expose Mercer students to strong-arm police tactics.

Robert Mike, now a well-known attorney in Florida, looks back on the night with humor. But the members of Committee X were not laughing when they had to get dressed and report for duty to face as hostile a group as they had ever encountered.

Mr. Mike, a graduate of Vanderbilt's prestigious law school, recalls the incident as little more than the BSA's reaction to what was going on around the nation. Such historically temperate schools as Princeton, Oberlin, Duke, and Mills College had experienced disruptive violence. Closer to the hearts of the black Mercerians was Tuskegee, in nearby Alabama. "Man, we thought we were supposed to do something. Else we would be seen as a bunch of out-of-step little black Sambos down South, too scared to breathe. So we decided to take over the snack bar."

In retrospect, given the tenor of the times, with buildings in flames and police and national guardsmen being called to restore order, taking over the snack bar, so far as the university was concerned, was about the most innocuous thing they could have done.

"Mr. Haywood did the talking at first," Mr. Mike says. "He said, 'What are your demands?'"

Attorney Mike, after twenty-six years, roars with laughter. "Demands?! We hadn't even thought about demands. We were just going to take over the snack bar."

Jimmie Samuel remembers it differently. He had been deeply affected by a statement Dick Gregory made when he was on campus as an Insight speaker. Gregory had looked out over his audience, many of them wearing ROTC uniforms, and proclaimed, "Any black student who wears that uniform is a nigger."

From the beginning of Mercer desegregation, a disproportionate number of black students had enlisted in the Corps because it offered financial advantages, and they would not be drafted and would graduate as commissioned officers. It was a way out of poverty and lowly status. Bennie Stephens, the first black graduate of Mercer, was already serving as a lieutenant. "Better to be saluted than to salute," many reasoned. Jimmie Samuel was well on his way to joining Lieutenant Stephens in this rung up the ladder. After hearing Gregory, and reflecting on the number of poor black draftees who were being killed in Vietnam, Samuel resigned from ROTC and participated more in campus activism.

Even today Mr. Samuel puts no halcyon spin on his years at Mercer.

> We were angry. And frustrated. Most of us did not have cars, had no place near the campus we were allowed to go. We were landlocked. We could go to the snack bar and play bid whist until closing time, then go to our rooms and shut the doors. That was it. White students could go to town, go to Atlanta, do anything they pleased.

Mr. Samuel remembers it as a Rosa Parks experience.

> We just weren't going to the back of the bus anymore.

> We were ready.

> And we were mad.

When Committee X arrived, Dean Hendricks felt that the Black Student Alliance did not have a good hand. The university was integrated, black faculty had been hired, and most of the black students were on premium scholarships. But to these angry black students those things were not items for discussion. To them Mercer was not *integrated*, but tokenly *desegregated*. Even a white spirit as sensitive and perceptive as Joe Hendricks could not feel the deep hurt black citizens daily endured. As for black faculty, that was minimal, with no one in a decision-making position of power. And as for the good scholarships, although they were grateful, and without exception more deeply appreciative now, at the time it was one more reminder of their beholden station—a condition of servitude.

One complaint they stated was that there were no black secretaries or clerical workers. Only cooks, maids, grass-cutters, janitors. Mr. Haywood quickly replied that he had hired a black secretary that very day. Monnie Brabham, a caricature of ferocity, a basketball player who was making no effort to conceal his hostility toward Haywood, countered that the black students didn't like the way Andy Anderson, the white superintendent of buildings and grounds, treated the workers, all of whom were black. They said he worked the men like a plantation overseer. Mr. Haywood said he would speak to Anderson about it.

(Later some of the black workers confronted the students and told them Andy Anderson was their best pal on campus, that they went fishing and hunting together, shared things from their lunch boxes, played cards, and asked them not to get him fired because his replacement was apt to be a mean and harsh "bossman" type.)

Tempers were at a pitch not seen before at Mercer. Everyone present remembers it as a night of wrath. All the appliances of hubris seemed to be showing on both sides. Hendricks slipped to the telephone and called Dean Garland Taylor, a member of the committee but not present, to apprise him of what was happening, that they were on the verge of the first serious violence Mercer had known. Dean Taylor's response is comical to recall. "Are things moderately sedate at the moment?" was his inquiry. "Please call me in the morning."

"We were on the edge of a volcanic eruption," Hendricks remembers, "and the academic dominion wants to handle it during office hours."

The white negotiators, Committee X, feeling at times that they were in Nebuchadnezzar's furnace, had no choice but to let the cannonading continue, hoping for an eventual cessation. William Haywood remembers that the encounter lasted all night. Joseph Hendricks, who usually heard the buzzing of bees as honey makes in the log, sat apprehensively with the others. When, toward daybreak, he sensed an opening, he moved in. "I'd like to put something on the table," he said. "Why don't we move on to something important? We just been floating down the Flint River here. Lots of rapids but nothing we can't handle."

There was a general stirring in the ranks. Boos, hisses. By then virtually every black student was present. Both men and women. This time the women were as vocal as the men.

They knew Hendricks to be their friend. But right now he was a white man, trying to stomp out a brush fire. They we're't ready to let him in the club. But he went on when the rustling died away.

"If you want longer hours in the snack bar, an all-night hangout, no big deal. That can be worked out by daylight."

Again there was the flurry of protest. Again Hendricks continued.

"Somebody mentioned getting black studies in the curriculum. Let's see if we can put a saddle on that horse."

With that the clamorous sit-in, that had begun with no clear focus, became substantive. As rays of sunshine began to peek through the narrow windows, another pact had been struck.

This time, however, the early morning adjournment of the snack bar skirmish did not end the matter. Unlike the assurance of Joe Hendricks that black faculty would be hired, an addition to the curriculum required committees and faculty approval. Sympathy for black studies was far

from unanimous in America's academic community. Many who enthusi-
astically supported total integration in all of society guarded scholastic
matters as sacred, immune to change. Some of Mercer's faculty argued
that not enough had been written on the subject to merit an academic
discipline. Black students saw that as chauvinistic evasion. Others felt the
idea itself was administrative invasion of academic terrain. Blacks saw
that as no problem of theirs. They simply wanted it done.

When the study committee made its recommendation to the College
of Liberal Arts faculty the black students showed up en masse. They
lined the corridor leading to the meeting room, sat in the stairwell, and
stood just outside the door. They were not disruptive, simply letting their
presence make their statement. When at last the debate of literary trivia
ended, courses in black studies were melded into the curriculum.

Again, Professor Terry Todd came upon the scene. Todd was a popular teacher in the Department of Education, completely committed to the
new wave in education. He brought in some of the leading educational
theorists for summer terms that gained a national reputation. Among them
were Edgar Friedenberg, Jim Herndon, John Holt, Miriam Wasserman,
Peter Marin, and Arpine Tateosian, and writers Julius Lester, Wendell
Berry, and Gary Shaw.

Despite Todd's successes in teaching education, however, there was
a problem inherent in his appointment to teach black studies. Terry Todd
was white. When a delegation of black students brought this to the attention of Joseph Hendricks, their leader saying "No white person is capable
of teaching anything about prejudice," Hendricks had an answer: "A deer
that has been run over in the road may not be the best one to talk about
trucks."

Hendricks was not sure his analogy held. But it gave Professor Todd
a crack in the door.

Notwithstanding his whiteness Terry Todd approached the task of
being Mercer's first director of Black Studies with the same aplomb as
he had competitively faced the bench press, and with the same dedication
as teaching future teachers how to teach. His method was exposure,
precept, and example. He remembers an early experience.

> I had a young woman in the first class by the name of Gwen Middleton,
> and she was a force. She was on the small side, but built like an athlete
> or a dancer, and she was filled with electricity and anger. She and some
> of the other students seemed to me in need of some sort of confronta-
> tion, and so I invited one of Mercer's senior professors in history, Dr.

Spencer King, to speak to our class one day. Dr. King was a courtly old man, white-haired, and I invited him because he had coauthored a history textbook that was used all over the state in public schools. The book contained a section on slavery that read in part: "The beauty of their voices and the richness of their singing made work seem light." It also discussed the kindness of the slaveowners, adding, without irony, that often the owners and the slaves were "even closer then friends."

Todd read from the book, including those passages, and then asked Dr. King to explain to the black students how he came to write them. Following his torturous endeavor to explain, Gwen Middleton and others told him how much they were hurt when they were required to read those words in junior high school.

As a counterpoint Todd brought in some of the more militant local civil rights activists to speak, then Arthur Ashe, the mild-mannered but highly respected tennis professional. There was learning.

Dr. Todd, now a professor in the Department of Kinesiology at the University of Texas, believes that the black students at Mercer really did need the Black Studies program, but that the need was more political than curricular. He also believes the director of Black Studies should have been black, but believes that more from political than pedagogical reasons.

They needed for us to do the thing more than they needed the thing itself. The demand was sweeping the country. Black Studies at Mercer was one of the programs that came, at least in part, from the wind that was everywhere blowing.

Mr. Todd adds something he probably learned in a course of which he was the teacher:

One of the things they learned by pushing the institution to implement the program was that sometimes it took pressure—real pressure and teamwork—to get what you wanted. They needed to feel the power.

Step by step. With the implementing of the Black Studies program the black students began feeling more secure. As Todd said, they recognized that they really did have some power. They had not reached the promised land. But they had established a lookout on the mountain from which to view it.

With more black students on this small campus than in any previously white college or university in the state, no matter the total enrollment, they were bolstered by their number. Having tasted victory with the administration, some of them felt it was time to challenge the white students who, they felt, still had not acknowledged their presence. It was not a simple matter. Some of the liberal white students felt they were being snubbed by the black students. Many whites reported that they had consciously gotten aquainted and, they thought, made friends with black classmates. "When I meet them on campus and speak they ignore me," several stated. The general black response to this claim was that white students were friendly on campus but when they saw them elsewhere with their white friends they were not as cordial. "If they are not my friend in town, they are not my friend on campus."

One irritant of long standing had been the routine seating arrangement in the cafeteria. For reasons of no consequence there were carpets around the perimeter of the dining area and a tile floor in the middle. Different fraternities and sororities had, over the years, established tables in the carpeted area as their place. Since fraternities and sororities did not accept black students the majority of those seated in the tiled area were black. Over time this led to the feeling that the black students were deliberately relegated to a certain area, segregated.

The word went out: "This evening all black students get through the cafeteria line early and sit in the carpeted space."

When the fraternity men came in and saw their usual tables had been occupied, and that the black students were in no hurry to depart, there was a near riot. Abusive language from both quarters filled the air. A black coed had food land on her back, sending the males into a fury. Joe Hendricks and Jerry Stone were attending a conference in Miami. When the ruckus continued, the campus police were called, further infuriating both sides. As other students came in, the battle lines were drawn. Tom Trimble, a member of Committee X, accompanied by Dr. Jean Hendricks, managed to negotiate to a point of no further violence that evening, but it was only a partial truce. Joe Hendricks flew in from Miami, too late for that day's clash but in time to admonish the fraternity men against further confrontation. His advice fell largely on deaf ears. For weeks Dean Hendricks was present at the evening meal in the university cafeteria. Once again serious racial strife was avoided.

But everything was motion. All a part of the zeitgeist. With the stem of Jesse resolved to endure.

❏

Chapter 20

Unless and until . . .

Four people were on the twenty-seventh floor of a downtown Atlanta hotel. Harris Mobley, sixty-four years old, was there to meet Don Baxter, now Donald Baxter, M.D., for the first time.

As Mobley entered the room, Don Baxter, without introduction, began reciting words from the sermon the young missionary, the Reverend Harris Mobley, had preached in Willingham Chapel thirty years earlier. He recites the words with authentic ministerial affect:

> Look at our houses. Where do we find a missionary? Perched pretentiously on some imposing hilltop, isolated from the African community, in colonial fashion, high above the tin roofs of the villages below, or out in the exclusive suburb for Europeans, or crowded together in an insulated island transplanted from the Southern United States and called a missionary compound. . . .

"Great Lord Almighty!" Mobley exclaimed. "I couldn't recite those words myself. How old were you when you heard them?"

"Nineteen," Don Baxter replied. "And now I'm fifty." He gave Mobley a vigorous handshake, then introduced his son who was sitting quietly against a far wall. The son is a handsome young man of twenty-two, a Phi Beta Kappa named James who was well on his way to a Ph.D. when he was struck down by an affliction that has already claimed his hearing and from which only a miracle can deliver him. The two men begin to reminisce. "I guess you did me a big favor when you sent me an African roommate," Dr. Baxter said. "Changed my life."

"I reckon it changed mine also," Harris Mobley said.

"How was that?" Dr. Baxter asked.

"Well, it got me bumped off the foreign mission circuit for one thing."

"I never forgot that sermon," Baxter said. "I never got it out of my head. You know, I started out to be a preacher."

"The big boys said the sermon was sophomoric," Harris Mobley laughed. "But looka here. You've done all right, don't you know."

"Well, I guess the IRS thinks so. Yes, I reckon I've done all right. For a little Georgia boy."

Don Baxter does not forget his son. He is taping the conversation to be transcribed later. Right now he writes notes on what is being discussed. The son laughs lightly when he reads "little Georgia boy."

"I don't believe you were ever little," he says, gesturing at the six-foot-seven frame of his father who is still standing.

Three years earlier Dr. Baxter received the NCAA Silver Anniversary Award, the only recipient from a small college. He was nominated by Mercer for his basketball days but part of the recognition was for his distinction around the world in sports medicine. Three thousand people, 1,600 of them college presidents, were in attendance at the presentation. Giving the main address was former President Ronald Reagan.

Dr. Baxter teaches at the Baylor and University of Texas Medical Schools. His awards number in the hundreds. But on this occasion his attention is fixed on his ailing son. And on a failed foreign missionary. He turns to his son and reminds him of when the Commandant of West Point sat beside them at the NCAA dinner. They talk briefly—the father frantically scribbling notes—of the father's subsequent visit to West Point as the honored guest of the general.

The doctor talks again about Mobley's sermon. And about his Atlanta pastor, Dr. Louie D. Newton, asking what the nineteen-year-old parishioner thought about it. "I told him I thought you hit the nail on the head but you didn't drive it in far enough."

Mobley relates that Dr. Newton wrote to him. "He didn't say, 'Dear Harris,' or 'Dear Brother Mobley.' Just scrawled on a piece of scrap paper: 'Send me a copy of your recent address at Mercer'."

Mobley said he didn't respond. Both men laugh at rebuffing the powerful Louie D. Newton.

Each one is, in a sense, a casualty to the rank of Southern Baptist ministers—yet who knows what "ministry" they have accomplished. The same is true of Sam Oni. He was marked early by the Southern Baptist missionaries to be a preacher. His experience at the Sadler Baptist Secondary School and in America shook his faith and changed his direction.

Dr. Baxter wants to know what Harris Mobley is doing now. Mobley tells him that he has retired after twenty-five years of teaching Anthropology at Georgia Southern University. "Now I have a little chain of Huddle House restaurants," he says.

"Still feeding the sheep," Dr. Baxter teases.

I sat enraptured by their camaraderie. But something seemed to be missing in that celebration. A pall seemed to envelop the room. At first I thought it was a moment of mourning for the brilliant young son, sitting there in his world of silence, awaiting some miraculous cure, else never to be a world-famous surgeon, retire from a professorship he might hold, or add volumes to the world of literature he knows and loves. Then out of the silence came a question from Harris Mobley. "Where is Sam Oni?"

"I was going to ask you. My God! I don't know where he is."

Baxter says he used to come by every few years. James's eyes light up when his father writes Oni's name and shows it to him. He looks toward the door, as if expecting Oni to join us. But Sam Oni is not there.

❑

All of that occurred on the first day of my research for this account of Mercer University in transition. It seemed appropriate to begin by gathering those who were pivotal to the telling of the tale. Every effort had been made to include Sam Oni, the one who left home and country to start it all. All my efforts had failed. A former classmate had visited him in California. But that was several years ago. He doesn't remember when and has no address for Oni. Congressional offices, the alumni association at Berkeley where he did graduate work after Mercer, Social Security records, the State Department, Immigration, legations in Ghana and Nigeria—no one seemed to know him. Missionaries and pastors in Ghana and Nigeria knew nothing of him. He had disappeared from the face of the earth.

The book would have to end, it seemed, without the hero. Yet it could not. Sam Oni had to be found.

Finally the ubiquitous Joseph Hendricks, with the help of a private detective, found Mr. Oni's adult son in California. After considerable hesitation Chris Oni agreed to tell the whereabouts of his father. "My father is in Lagos, Nigeria. I will give you his telephone number."

An international telephone operator reaches Mr. Oni in Nigeria. In the same crisp accent as when he first arrived at Mercer University he greets his caller. He talks freely of his life since Mercer. What was once bitterness over his American experience—the years of the American civil rights struggle and his involvement in it, the murder of Dr. King who had become his friend, his rejection at Tattnall Square Church—has evolved into a deep understanding of the human condition. The freedom from colonial rule in his own land did not exempt his countrymen from the frosty fetters of hubris any more than throwing off that same yoke made a utopia of America. His country is under police dominion, with an out-of-order economy.

He seems pleased that the Tattnall Square Baptist Church left the Mercer campus and moved away. The building was bought by the University. We talk of the Mercer of thirty years gone.

> Ah, yes. I remember Joe Hendricks and Johnny Mitchell, standing there in the rain at the depot to meet me. Yes, yes. You say it has been thirty years! I suppose I felt a little sorry for them. No one should be required to be that exuberantly friendly, I remember thinking.
>
> And who was the chap who with such dispatch took the beautiful young lady from the awkward scene? President of the nearby woman's college, I believe.
>
> It was the first time I realized the width of the chasm I had come to cross, grasped the intensity of America's fear of the color black. Maybe it was the first time I was alive to my blackness. It had always been with me. Here in my country it does not mean the same thing.

For a long time we talked of the Mercer he had come to. And of the one he left. I knew that soon a portrait of him would be unveiled in the Mercer W. G. Lee Alumni House, and that he was to be invited for the ceremony. It was not my place to tell him. That is for others. He will be pleased that the artist is Oliver Snow, the legendary Mercerian who took Don Baxter on a wild trip to Florida, and after failing in his attempt to get the ministerial student drunk, tried to scare him out of rooming with the black man already on his way from Ghana. Sam Oni will recall that Snow later befriended him and remains close to Dr. Baxter. Perhaps Oni will also be pleased that the portrait will be the first likeness of a black person on Mercer walls since Lee Battle, the beloved janitor, beloved because he was not dangerous. Then again, perhaps Mr. Oni will not be pleased with that at all.

"The story must be told," he says. "For the young. Whether they read it or not, it will be there for them."

He talks of the short memory of young African-Americans, and of whites.

"Doctor King is ancient history for them. Has nothing to do with them today. They don't know—don't seem to care—what we went through."

His words are reminiscent of an earlier comment from William Randall: "Nostalgia with them is what they had for breakfast."

For half an hour winged words flow from Mr. Oni, now fifty-three years old, like the flashes of Neptune. Our telephone voices are as clear as if we are sitting in the same room.

He talks of all that happened to that little bit of turf called Mercer while he was there, not then aware that he was soon to see it again. The little village of his birth became a global village during those four short years, he says:

> World problems are local problems.
> I am sitting here in Lagos watching CNN. I know what happened in your city two hours ago and you know what is happening right now in my country. The world is moving too fast for its people to keep up with it.

We talked for a long time. About many things. Then, "Good-bye, my dear friend. Please visit me soon. Lagos is so close now. And I will visit you. I will sign off now. So, good-bye . . . uh, may I call you Will?"

His question is not one of counterfeit subservience. It is mature civility, deference to longevity.

"Yes, it's Will. We met once before. When you were here. But only once. In the '60s."

"Yes, yes. I know. I know. But I do not wish to be immodest. Very well. Good-bye, Will."

"Good-bye, Sam."

Somehow it did not seem a fitting ending of a tale. I had thought earlier, when Baxter and Mobley were reminiscing and no one knew where Oni was that he was the missing component. Now that he had been found there was still something else. Something has not yet been said, done, written. I did not know what. I was sure, however, that my conversation with Mr. Oni was no ending at all. From the slaveholding ghosts of Penfield to the coming of an African to Mercer, soon to be followed by hundreds of the issue of slavery, is a long journey.

Still.

What?

Something.

Three months later I found it in the very building that had denied spiritual refuge to Sam Oni. And to the sons and daughters of slavery.

Ah, slavery! That haunting, still stalking scandal that will not turn loose of America's conscience.

"The child is father of the man."

Unless.

Yesterday is today and today will be tomorrow.

Unless. And until.

Unless and until what?

◻

Chapter 21

Where sound the cries . . .

. . . I'll kneel down,
And ask of thee forgiveness. So we'll live,
And pray, and sing, and tell old tales, and laugh
At gilded butterflies, . . . —Shakespeare, *King Lear* 5.3.10-13

Sam Oni has returned to Macon, Georgia. All the way from Lagos, Nigeria. It has been thirty years since Harris and Vivian Mobley sent him here as the first black student ever admitted to Mercer University.

Mr. Oni's tenure in America was a turbulent one, for it was the 1960s, the years of America's Civil Rights Movement and the Vietnam War. When he graduated he said he would never return to Georgia, such was his displeasure with the land he had struggled so hard to be a part of. When he came in 1963 he was a zealous convert, called by the press a "missionary in reverse." He had been the darling of Baptist missionaries in Africa until he challenged their teaching methods and was expelled as a troublemaker and ingrate. The missionaries had anointed him to receive a theological education, then serve as an evangelist to his people. That was not to be.

In 1967, when he graduated from Mercer, he departed a bitter and angry young man. He had tasted the galling fruit of America's racism and it had been a faith-shattering experience. Now he is back for a two-day celebration of the thirtieth year of desegregated education at Mercer University. All of it was organized and orchestrated by the Heritage Life Committee of the Student Government Association, with the full cooperation of the university administration. The students named it: "30 Years Later—Celebrating Our Rebirth."

Mr. Oni's wife Habeebat Olut "Toyin" Dabiri, a stunningly beautiful, urbane product of the University of London, is with him. Their son Chris and daughter Simone have flown in from California.

At six o'clock Tuesday evening, January 11, 1994, there is a gathering at Newton Hall. This is the same building that had once been the Tattnall Square Baptist Church, the church whose deacons had bodily turned Sam Oni away.

When the congregation fled the campus for suburbia, the university purchased the building and named it for the Reverend Dr. Louie D. Newton, revered pastor of the Druid Hills Baptist Church in Atlanta.

Newton's was the church that produced Don Baxter, the only student at Mercer University who would room with a black man in 1963. Dr. Newton was not enthused by his protege's act of charity. Nor with the coming of blacks to his alma mater.

Donald Baxter, M.D. will be here tomorrow. As will Harris and Vivian Mobley. As Mr. Oni moves about the campus his former teachers, most of them old men and women now, address him as "Sam Jerry," though that was never his name.

This is the beginning of an occasion that will, hopefully, heal some of the hurt of the past. After a brief ceremony remembering Dr. Martin Luther King, Jr., whose birthday is three days away, the students and guests will light candles and ceremoniously march to Connell Student Center for a reception. Thirty years ago lighting a candle publicly on this campus for Martin Luther King would have been as unthinkable as praying to Judas Iscariot.

I have been invited because I am writing a book about the things that happened to and at this school in the decade now famed as "The Sixties." It is almost as if time began then. The Sixties.

Tomorrow Sam Oni will speak in Willingham Hall, the massive auditorium that has heard many notable orations over the past hundred and four years, ranging in diversity from Senator Walter George, seen by most whites as a patriot for his ardent segregationist views, to Jane Fonda, seen by a similar number as a traitor for her fierce opposition to the Vietnam War. Oliver Snow's portrait of Mr. Oni will be unveiled and placed on a prominent wall of the W. G. Lee Alumni House in a room that will bear his name. A portrait of Rufus Carrollton Harris, president of the university while Oni was here, hangs nearby.

As Mr. Oni is speaking tomorrow, Shannon Faulkner will be in a courtroom in South Carolina, arguing for her right to be the first female of any color ever admitted to the Citadel. The lance of justice seems in every case a drowsy tool, seldom prevailing without a hefty thrust from the oppressed.

Many African-Americans have returned for the occasion, some with bruised memories: isolation, rejection, loneliness. I suspect many of them have ambivalent feeling about being back here at all, scant and uncertain loyalties to this place. Particularly the building we are about to enter. But that is not apparent in this scene. The atmosphere is almost carnival. Men and women, some with children attending Mercer now, greet one another with childlike fervor, hugging, throwing the high-fives of the young, extending the Movement grip of their youth, teasing, laughing, "Remember that time when. . . . "

As they gather I move from one small grouping to another, trying to be inconspicuous with my voice-activated microcassette recorder and notepad. I want to get as much information as possible while yesterday is gathered.

As I approach each merrymaking group I gain no audience. It is neither rejection nor acceptance. I am neither alien nor pal. I am invisible. I think of Ralph Ellison, and wish someone would at least insult me.

In my head I understand: they are with their own friends, sharing their own memories. I was not privy to what they are about. For a moment I feel as Joseph Hobbs, and others, must have felt as a new school year began and they were alone as returning whites exulted in similar camaraderie. I wonder if these black alumni who have returned can understand now that the rejections they felt during those dismal years were not always out of calculated hostility, but sometimes of callous affinity to what is.

The African and African-American students who are currently enrolled are gathering too. They look so young. I get no more notice from them than from those who were here thirty years ago. Also on campus is a thirty-six-year-old white man. He read of this event in the morning paper. He was the six-year-old-child who watched his father turn Sam Oni away from this door. Only now does he understand what it was about. The conflict between his love for his father and what he saw his father do that day has bothered him all these years. He has come for healing.

I drift away. From the lonely shadows I stand and watch the crowd. I feel a begrudging approbation of what I am watching. And a certain envy. The haunting lyrics of Dick Holler's song of the 1960s, "Abraham, Martin, and John," run through my head, further ruffling my spirits, a sharp contrast to the happy faces that surround me.

He freed a lot of people,
But it seems the good they do die young,
I just look around and he's gone.

Across the street stands the once rich and magnificent Tattnall Square, now offering no hint of its past glory. My mood is almost as one facing a sudden calamity.

Where are my people?

Here are your people, comes the answer, like an echo from across the years.

Then why won't they let me in?

Maybe because you didn't let them in.

But I tried. I thought I really did try.

Maybe the trying came too late.

Well, hey! Over here! Look at me! I marched before you were born. Look! I have scars! I may be white, I may be from Mississippi, but I was in the Movement. I was with Dr. King at the beginning. And two hours after he died I stood beside his congealing blood on the balcony of that accursed Memphis motel. Why are you there and I am here?

Because.

Because what?

Just because. The Movement, you say. Were you there because your mama was called "girl" when she was sixty, and had to ride the back of the bus on her way to wash the white folks' clothes?

Scars? Come now! Scars without wounds perchance? Were they because you fell mute when your children were called nigger? Or when you watched your daddy lynched? Come on. Fess up, whitey!

Can a clean thing be brought out of unclean?

Job asked that. And you're not Job.

No, I'm not Job. Just someone trying to put together a story. So I need to talk to every black student that ever went to this university.

"Fess up," the phantom voice had said. Like a morning wake-up call. Fess up? Is that what's missing from this momentous day?

Fess up? Was the summons directed at me? If so, it seemed neither fitting nor fair. I am not a Mercerian. It was not I who wouldn't let Sam Oni come inside this building. Nor was it I who yelled "Nigger!" at Ernestine Cole as she walked across the campus, who made Joseph Hobbs cry when he was all alone in his room that first night. At most I am a surrogate reporter, not a party to what I write, with no jurisdiction. My role is not a propitiate one. Still. . . .

For some reason, I had misgivings about this project from the beginning. Dr. G. McLeod Bryan, who taught here many years ago, had warned me against writing a "How bad things were then to how good things are now" melodrama. His voice was not one to be ignored. Harris Mobley had told me Mac Bryan invented him.

I knew things were bad in 1963 when Sam Oni, Bennie Stephens, and Cecil Dewberry were finally admitted to these grounds. Really bad. I suspected that motives for their admission were not of one pure cloth. I was ambiguous about being the one who should attempt to write the story. Nor was I sure why I was unsure. Something simply kept on gnawing. What right do I have to tell this story? Can one person express the hurt of another? Does not the wounded bird know more about the hunter than the hunter knows of himself? I had wondered when I began if it would be possible for me to write anything more than one more white version of the black saga. I did not know then. I do not know now. One can only write from where one stood. Or sat.

The venerable professor who admonished me had said something else. He cautioned that without genuine repentance on the part of the offending party there can be no real reconciliation.

Suddenly the air changes. An African-American student comes from among the celebrants and greets me. It is Cedric Soloman, a princely young man whose countenance befits his name. He is chairman of the Heritage Life Committee. He is cordial and warm, his voice as soft as the fifing of the wind. He addresses me by name as if I am an old friend. He says it is time to go inside.

Emboldened by his good manners I follow him, yet even that further bedims the vision of my mission. He leads me to the rostrum where I am to speak briefly to the congregation before the candlelight march. When I am finished the young Mr. Soloman will light a candle, pass the light to another who will pass it on until they all file into the rainy night in a ghostly procession, honoring a man slain five years before most of them were born. Mourning, too, the silent perseverance of those in every generation who chose prison and death over blind obedience to oppression.

Mercer University is now about as well racially integrated as any institution I know. Still its genes, its chronicles, are white. As are my own.

I remind myself again that I am not of this story. If I am to write it at all, I must stand on the outside looking in. The detached, dispassionate scribe.

Generally, Mercer assemblies such as this are predominantly white, with a predominantly white agenda, based on white culture. This one is three-fourths black. African and American. What exactly do I have to say to them? Certainly not the words I have prepared.

They are all quiet and in place now. Mr. Oni is seated on the front row of this edifice he was not allowed to enter almost thirty years earlier. What is he thinking? Feeling? I smile at him and he smiles back. A friendly smile.

Joseph Hendricks, the white man who carried the black man's trunk across Adams Street, through a hostile throng and into Sherwood Hall thirty years ago, is sitting beside Oni. Mary Wilder, the English professor who gave up her family evenings to tutor high school students as the 1960s began so that SAT scores could not be used to bar them from college, is three rows back. There is an aura of expectancy about her. I see Ray Brewster. He influenced many students in the 1950s, including Joe Hendricks. Al Bond demonstrated against McCarthyism at Dartmouth forty years ago. He is chairman of the sociology department now and remains the quintessential Mercer liberal. I see him also.

I begin to speak. I try to be funny. "I write rare books," I tell them. No one laughs. I feel silly. I look at Mr. Oni and he smiles again. An enabling smile.

Instead of the valedictory-like pabulum I have prepared I begin with the account of the ugly treatment Sam Oni received almost thirty years earlier when first he sought entry to this very space.

The deadly silence is disquieting as the story unfolds. The anger of the congregation, the deacons with their burlesque hip movements to bump Sam Oni down the steps, Sam sitting in the patrol car with the whirling red lights, the sounds of "Where cross the crowded ways of life, where sound the cries of race and clan" melding with the rage permeating the sanctuary as a stray dog wandered in and out of the edifice door.

I tell all of the story I can remember. The quickening silence is intimidating. Perhaps I should not be reminding young blacks of past whiteness. Why are they so quiet? Am I simply exacerbating their wrath?

I wonder if any of them have ever heard the name Josiah Tattnall, or know that he gunned down their rebelling slave ancestors at Abercorn Creek and shot the Chinese in the back on the Yangtze River in a war over opium, or know that the spot where they are sitting bore his name for many years when it was a house of prayer.

These walls, these floors, these pews, the stained glass figure of Jesus, standing barefoot and holding a snow-white lamb are all the same as before. Only the patrol car waiting outside, the stray dog, and the deacons on the steps are missing.

When the story is finished I see no appropriate ending. Like a cross-country runner who must keep on moving. Sam Oni sits at rigid attention, Joe Hendricks beside him, both, it seems, waiting.

When first I met Joseph Millard Hendricks thirty-five years ago he was a boy. Now he looks old. All day I have heard students, black and white, men and women, freshmen to seniors, greet him as "Papa Joe." "Hey, Papa Joe," they call. It is obvious they hold him in the highest esteem. For an awkward moment I stand looking at the two men, the rhythm gone, like a choirmaster who has lost his place on a musical score.

Professor Bryan's words about repentance of the offending party come back as spangles of light, branching out in jets and convolutions. By some strange, unexpected epiphany I ask Sam Oni to join me on the dais. Even before I finish the sentence he is beside me. I face him squarely and begin some unrehearsed, unplanned verbalizing of troubled feelings. Haltingly.

Mr. Oni. I am not a Mercerian. But I am white. I am Christian. I am American. A Southerner. So I was here that morning when we turned you away. I am sorry, sir, for what we did to you that day. I am sorry for what we did to ourselves. And to our God. Forgive us.

Then a black Nigerian in his middle years, and a white Mississippian who has reached the biblical three-score years and ten, held each other in a prolonged and passionate embrace.

For a long while continued applause, like a long meter psalm of thunder, swept rafters once a roost of fear-become-hatred. And this principally African-American assembly of young Mercerians took an exculpating stance. As one body.

In the long ago Jesse Mercer might have owned them.

Now, at last, they are Mercer's issue.

And Mercer is theirs.

For the first time I felt entitled, empowered, free, to tell their story.

□ ▢ □